The Revd Frances M. Young, FBA

LIBRARY OF NEW TESTAMENT STUDIES

295

Editor
Mark Goodacre

WILDERNESS

Essays in Honour of Frances Young

EDITED BY
R. S. SUGIRTHARAJAH

t&t clark

Published by T&T Clark International
An imprint of Continuum
The Tower Building, 11 York Road, London SE1 7NX
15 East 26th Street, Suite 1703, New York, NY 10010

www.tandtclark.com

British Library Cataloguing-in-Publication Data
A catalogue record for this book is available from the British Library

ISBN 0-567-04142-5 (hardback)

Typeset by CA Typesetting, www.sheffieldtypesetting.com
Printed on acid-free paper in England by Antony Rowe Ltd, Chippenham, Wiltshire

CONTENTS

PREFACE

Let me begin on a personal note. The sedate world of English theology has the habit of occasionally producing books which create a theological stir and have implications beyond the narrow confines both of the usual theology-reading public and of the British Isles. In the 1960s it was John Robinson's *Honest to God* and in the 1970s it was *The Myth of God Incarnate*, edited by John Hick. This was a time when, to rephrase the remark of a British prime minister, the liberals had never had it so good. The theological and hermeneutical issues that these volumes raised had all the hallmarks of the Enlightenment, although, sadly, they were in a way among the last books to reflect the legacies of the Enlightenment before it became clear that modernist models were no longer acceptable to articulate theology. However, the 1980s theological scene in South Asia, thanks to our expatriate educators, was still dominated by the Enlightenment values, and the issues raised in these volumes resonated with my own thinking. It was *The Myth of God Incarnate*, which had a number of essays by members of the Birmingham theology department, that attracted me to come to Birmingham to do my doctoral work under Frances.

I still remember well some of the things Frances told me on our first meeting, though I am sure she will have forgotten them by now. She advised me to write a sharp, short thesis in such way that any informed layperson would be able to read it. This seemed to be fair enough. I guess the experience of reading impenetrable doctoral dissertations must have led her to warn me against producing one more in that mould. But what was striking was what she said next: 'If you are a perfectionist don't bother embarking on this project. In our field there are no perfect conclusions but only tentative suggestions. The important thing is not to make silly mistakes which will annoy the examiner.' I try to pass on these remarks to my students, especially that about producing a perfect thesis, a noble ambition with which most doctoral candidates start their research.

Frances is one of those theologians who cross the boundaries both within and between disciplines. Her work is both academic and pastoral. She is one of those scholars involved in affirming and clarifying the faith. In this, she stands among the Victorian biblical interpreters who, unlike their German colleagues, saw their task as interpreting the faith to Christian congregations ravaged by the newly emerging historical criticism of the time. As a biblical interpreter, her foremost concern is not only to employ the best critical tools available but also to elucidate the message of the Bible to ordinary people. The four hermeneutical templates which inform and influence her articulations – Scripture, reason, primitive antiquity and experience – place her within the Methodist tradition, a tradition which nourished her and which now through her life and work she nourishes. Her articulations, however, are never a narrow Wesleyan understanding, but rather a genuine attempt to speak to and address the concerns of the ecumenical Church. What is critical to her work is the message of the whole Bible. While paying attention to particular parts of the Bible, she is seeking to understand the message of the entire book – God reconciling humanity to Godhead.

This volume centres upon the theme of 'wilderness', which acts as a symbolic motif to highlight the areas which have impacted on her work over the years, and reflects her interests in biblical studies, theology, liturgy and spirituality. Wilderness in the biblical narratives signifies many things. It is the place of both rejection and hope. It was in the wilderness that there emerged a radical programme outlined in the Law books of the Hebrew scriptures to safeguard the interests of the socially disadvantaged – the widow, the orphan and the stranger. In this programme the marginalized and the inferior are elevated and the socially disadvantaged become not only the source of blessing for all but also a particular blessing for those who care.

The volume opens with an essay by the Archbishop of Canterbury, highlighting Frances Young's work. The rest of the essays are grouped under two categories – 'hermeneutical connections' and 'theological explorations'. The division is artificial, and the essays grouped in one section are almost equally at home in the other.

The essays in the first section, 'Hermeneutical Connections', reinforce Frances' idea that the Bible and the literature of the early Church are very much intertwined and act as a single continuum, the latter elucidating and clarifying the former. The section begins with Simon Horne's article exploring two encounters between Jesus and people with impairments – the stooping woman and the man with paralysis – and the light shed by the early Church interpreters, and how these two examples were used to illustrate the central issues of faith and held up as examples of Christian discipleship. Christine Trevett's essay is an attempt to restore Miriam, a key figure in the history of Israel, but like most biblical women kept out of the hermeneutical limelight. Diane Treacy-Cole argues for an antecedent for the woman clothed with the sun in Revelation 12 within the Hebrew Bible, rather than the usual hermeneutical practice of placing her within non-Jewish traditions. David Parker invites us to reconsider the Gospel portrayals of mountains, especially the high ones where the significance is not the height but the increased isolation and desolation. Lynn Wall juxtaposes the wilderness experience of the biblical Jews and the Maori people, and shows how both grew in self-understanding and faith. Steve Moyise, in his article, attempts a rereading of the wilderness quotation in Mark using historical and narrative method and attempts to adjudicate between them. Judith Lieu engages with Jesus' temptation as it is reflected in theology, exegesis and narrative in the earliest and the most recent periods. Paul Joyce looks at biblical references to wisdom and shows how these are often related to a condition of weakness rather than strength, and that tears and joy go hand in hand. Alistair Stewart-Sykes's essay is a study of the narrative of institution found within an early anaphora and explains the developments that led to the appearance of such a narrative and explores the significance of this development in later eucharistic prayers. Susan Ashbrook Harvey investigates the fourth-century Syrian holy man Julian Saba and how he helped to redefine asceticism and the changing piety of early Syrian Christianity.

The second section, 'Theological Explorations', contains articles which underline Frances' other concern, that theology should be rooted in life and practice. Christopher Rowland's essay deals with the radical Christian writings of the seventeenth and eighteenth centuries and demonstrates how the wilderness functioned both as a place of exile and as a place of prophetic and political renewal. Angela Tilby revisits the problem of sin and looks at a model provided by Evagrius of Pontus as a way of meeting pastoral situations. Sparked off by a statement by Jean Vanier, David Ford argues for prophetic wisdom as a potential theological paradigm for the third millennium, one which takes into account Arthur, the severely handicapped son of Frances, and the L'Arche communities for the mentally handicapped. Jean Vanier in his essay talks about loneliness and being in the wilderness, and being at home. Emily Hunt looks at the wilderness motif in Tolkien's popular novel *The Lord of the Rings* and teases out christological elements hidden in the narrative. The section ends with Neal Robinson's piece on the quranic Jesus and its significance.

All that remains is to express my sincere thanks to those who helped me in the production of this volume. Special thanks, of course, are due to all the friends and colleagues of Frances who accepted the invitation to contribute, and proved so helpful throughout. Thanks also to Philip Davies of Sheffield Academic Press, who arranged the contract, and Philip Law of Continuum after the merger of the two presses. Both of them extended to me their unstinted support. Finally, to Helen Ingram who helped me in the demanding task of the editorial process. She not only prepared the manuscript for the press but also liaised with the various contributors, doing all these with enormous enthusiasm and expertise and with a sense of humour.

R. S. Sugirtharajah
November 2004

CONTRIBUTORS

David F. Ford taught for fifteen years with Frances Young in the University of Birmingham. Since 1991 he has been Regius Professor of Divinity in the University of Cambridge.

Susan Ashbrook Harvey is Professor of Religious Studies at Brown University, Rhode Island.

Simon Horne is a Team Vicar working in Hampshire and is married to Mel, who is a wheelchair user. With Frances Young's encouragement and supervision, he completed his Ph.D. on impairment and disability in the Bible and the ancient world.

Emily J. Hunt gained her Ph.D. in Theology from the University of Birmingham in 2000. She researches first- to third-century patristics and the impact of theology on literature.

Paul M. Joyce is a University Lecturer in Theology in the University of Oxford and Fellow of St Peter's College. From 1989 to 1994 he was a University Lecturer in the University of Birmingham.

Judith Lieu is Professor of New Testament Studies and Head of Department in the Department of Theology and Religious Studies, King's College London.

Steve Moyise is Principal Lecturer in New Testament at University College Chichester.

David Parker is Professor of New Testament Textual Criticism and Palaeography at the University of Birmingham and Editor of the International Greek New Testament Project.

Neal Robinson was Frances' first Ph.D. student. He is currently senior research fellow in the Catholic University of Leuven.

Christopher Rowland is Dean Ireland Professor of the Exegesis of Holy Scripture, University of Oxford.

Alistair Stewart-Sykes is vicar of Sturminster Marshall, Kingston Lacy and Shapwick in Dorset, England, and a scholar of Christian liturgical origins.

Angela Tilby is Vice-Principal of Westcott House Theological College, Cambridge.

Diane Treacy-Cole is currently a Research Fellow in the Department of Archaeology at the University of Bristol. Previously she was a Lecturer in New Testament and Early Christianity in the Department of Theology and Religious Studies, University of Bristol.

Christine Trevett is a professor in the School of Religious and Theological Studies at Cardiff University, teaching mostly biblical studies and researching in Christianity of the first three centuries.

Jean Vanier is founder of L'Arche, a network of communities for and with people with learning disabilities.

Lynne Wall is Ranston Lecturer in Biblical Studies at Trinity Methodist Theological College in Auckland, New Zealand.

The Most Revd Dr **Rowan Williams**, Archbishop of Canterbury.

ABBREVIATIONS

1–2 Clem.	*1–2 Clement*
ABD	David Noel Freedman (ed.), *The Anchor Bible Dictionary* (New York: Doubleday, 1992)
ANF	Anti-Nicene Fathers
BAGD	Walter Bauer, William F. Arndt, F. William Gingrich and Frederick W. Danker, *A Greek–English Lexicon of the New Testament and Other Early Christian Literature* (Chicago: University of Chicago Press, 2nd edn, 1958)
BDB	Francis Brown, S. R. Driver and Charles A. Briggs, *A Hebrew and English Lexicon of the Old Testament* (Oxford: Clarendon Press, 1907)
BETL	Bibliotheca ephemeridum theologicarum lovaniensium
Bib	*Biblica*
CBQ	*Catholic Biblical Quarterly*
CChr	Corpus Christianorum
CSCO	Corpus scriptorum christianorum orientalium
CSEL	Corpus scriptorum ecclesiasticorum latinorum
Did.	*Didache*
ETR	*Etudes théologiques et religieuses*
EvT	*Evangelische Theologie*
FC	Fathers of the Church
FemTh	*Feminist Theology*
HR	*History of Religions*
Ignatius, *Trall.*	Ignatius, *Letter to the Trallians*
Int	*Interpretation*
JBL	*Journal of Biblical Literature*
JEH	*Journal of Ecclesiastical History*
JJS	*Journal of Jewish Studies*
TU	Texte und Untersuchungen
Josephus	
Ant.	*Antiquities of the Jews*
War	*The Jewish War,* or *De Bello Judaico*
JQR	*Jewish Quarterly Review*
JSNT	*Journal for the Study of the New Testament*
JSNTSup	*Journal for the Study of the New Testament*, Supplement Series
JSOT	*Journal for the Study of the Old Testament*
JSOTSup	*Journal for the Study of the Old Testament*, Supplement Series
JSP	*Journal for the Study of the Pseudepigrapha*
JTS	*Journal of Theological Studies*
LCL	Loeb Classical Library
LPGL	G. W. H. Lampe, *A Patristic Greek Lexicon* (Oxford: Clarendon Press, 1961)

LSJ	H. G. Liddell, Robert Scott and H. Stuart Jones, *Greek–English Lexicon* (Oxford: Clarendon Press, 9th edn, 1968)
NovT	*Novum Testamentum*
NPNF	Nicene and Post-Nicene Fathers
NRSV	New Revised Standard Version
NTS	*New Testament Studies*
PG	J.-P. Migne (ed.), *Patrologia cursus completa…*
Philo	
Abr.	*De Abrahamo*
Det. Pot. Ins.	*Quod deterius potiori insidiari soleat*
Fug.	*De fuga et inventione*
Leg. Gai.	*Legatio ad Gaium*
Praem. Poen.	*De praemiis et poenis*
Rer. Div. Her.	*Quis rerum divinarum heres sit*
Virt.	*De virtutibus*
Vit. Mos.	*De vita Mosis Series graeca* (166 vols.; Paris: Petit-Montrouge, 1857–83)
Prot. Jas.	*Protevangelium of James*
SBLDS	Society of Biblical Literature Dissertation Series
SBLSS	Society of Biblical Literature Semeia Studies
SBT	Studies in Biblical Theology
SC	Sources chrétiennes
SJT	*Scottish Journal of Theology*
TDNT	Gerhard Kittel and Gerhard Friedrich (eds.), *Theological Dictionary of the New Testament* (trans. Geoffrey W. Bromiley; 10 vols.; Grand Rapids: Eerdmans, 1964–)
VT	*Vetus Testamentum*
WBC	Word Biblical Commentary
WUNT	Wissenschaftliche Untersuchungen zum Neuen Testament

The Most Revd Dr Rowan Williams, Archbishop of Canterbury

Faith is never hereditary; there are no second-generation Christians. We all know this, but we also know that family and environment contribute a lot to the accent with which we speak our Christian language. Both of Frances Young's grandfathers were Methodist ministers, both her parents local preachers. It is a background that makes perfect sense of the feeling many readers will have that Frances has a natural 'pitch' in her theological voice which owes a great deal to that fundamentally traditional but entirely unfussy and rather undogmatic ortho-doxy that typifies so much of Methodism; a 'feel' for essentials that does not get too worked up about tightly confessional matters or formulae but revels in the task of communicating in word and image a sensed abundance. Combine this with Cambridge (where Frances' parents met, she met her husband, and their son met his wife), the mixture of critical discipline and a strongly ethical undertow to the doing of theology, and you may see also why Frances might be claimed as one of the foremost modern representatives of a long tradition of Cambridge-formed writers in the classical Protestant mould (Oman, Farmer, Dodd, Rupp) who hold together some 'Enlightenment' virtues of scholarly and personal integrity with warmth of Christian sensibility in a way not all that common. And the mediation of all this, in Frances' case, through a long journey towards ordination and through the utterly life-altering experience of bringing up a son, Arthur, with severe mental and physical impairment, adds to the sense of hard-won and compassionate integrity in life, ministry and writing.

Some theologians have the gift of being able to articulate their most important insights in the briefest of essays even more than in their substantial treatises; Austin Farrer is a case in point, as is Donald MacKinnon. Frances Young, I'd argue, is another. This is in no way to disparage the value of the longer works – in Frances' case, especially the early scholarly research on the concept of sacri–fice and the more recent and very original work on patristic exegesis, above all her Speaker's Lectures of 1992–3, which ought to bear fruit in a rewriting of most textbook accounts of how the Fathers used the Bible; it is simply to under-line the fact that she has the gift of distilling an enormous amount in simple and economical words. This is why I have chosen to take my cue for discussing her theology from a very brief piece in a collection which she edited in the 1990s, *Encounter with Mystery: Reflections on L'Arche and Living with Disability*

(Darton, Longman & Todd 1997). A full – and intensely moving – account of her theological thinking about disability is of course to be found in her book about her son Arthur, *Face to Face: A Narrative Essay in the Theology of Suffering*, but these few pages on 'The Creative Purpose of God' (pp. 167–9) seem to go to the very heart of her vision of God and creation with a rare directness.

Briefly: we are not made for Utopia. She describes her vision as a 'theology of limit', limit in at least two senses. God's kingdom is not about the removal of all imaginable obstacles to the exercise of our individual will and the enjoyment of our individual welfare. Some of the language of the Gospels, particularly as medi-ated through the aspirations of a more conventional liberation theology, just might suggest that the Kingdom was primarily the removal of suffering. But what about the kind of suffering, above all, long-term disability, that doesn't lend itself to straightforward hopes for resolution? She encourages us to read the Beatitudes again, as a statement about limits, about coming to terms with something that already exists instead of projecting value and meaning into a post-revolutionary future. The Beatitudes tell us that God's meanings are already here, in the lives of those who don't make ambitious bids for safety and control. Only on such a basis can we recognize in what's before us what it is that God sees and loves; the worth of a person is always prior to what any of us may do to honour or establish it. Where we face what can't be changed, we are most sharply challenged to acknowledge this – though the proper response is not passive acceptance but active and *receptive* love.

This points to the second sense of 'limit' at work here. The human self is lim-ited in that it stands always in need of other selves; extreme and non-negotiable vulnerability in a human being puts this to us starkly; but at the same time puts to us our own need of those we think of as vulnerable. Our redemption is nothing at all to do with some fantasy of deliverance from vulnerability or from the unset-tling presence of the vulnerable, some equipping for a state of constant giving from our own secure height to those who, unlike us, are needy. Rather is it an opening of eyes and of selves to our mutual need, in such a way that the other's skill, the other's strangeness, the other's simple presence, becomes an occasion of receiving what God has to give. In the introduction to this same collection, Frances speaks briefly but effectively of how her son has 'made me competent, through years of practice, in non-verbal communication' (p. xiii); yet there is no sentimental desire here of the fact that she is writing of a person who suffers what are, by any imaginable standards, enormous impairments to his human func-tioning. The point is not that these impairments somehow don't matter or can all be dissolved in an intensified togetherness, but that they challenge and extend what communication might mean in ways that will take me (the 'normally' func-tioning agent or speaker) into places where I might not want to go, as they will take the other beyond some of the immediate limits of a disabled condition. So, if we are ever to speak of limits transcended, it is in a communication that is always *difficult* and always transforming. To see the entire work of grace, to see the cross and the resurrection, as issuing in an essentially difficult and mobile communion and communication takes us close, I think, to the central motif of Frances Young's theology.

Bible and Early Christianity

The sense of a difficult communication as the fruit of the events of redemption ties in with a good deal of what Frances has written about the theological language of early Christianity. Her contribution in the 1970s to *The Myth of God Incarnate* was far from typical of that curious collection, in its painful wrestling with the necessity for a 'Calvary-centred religious myth' (p. 34), its vivid awareness of the significance of (for example) Cappadocian trinitarian theology as a sort of warning to any theological idiom too taken up with clarity and problem-solving, and its refusal to treat metaphor as a regrettable and ultimately dispensable tool for communicating simpler truths. Difficult communication is one thing that established the kind of enterprise we are involved in, one thing that shows that we are being introduced into a new world, even, in patristic language, participation in divine life. More than once, Frances returns to this point, in early work and late: the mark of being involved directly with the active life of God is not more but less satisfaction and lucidity in what we say. This applies as much in getting to grips with Gregory of Nyssa as in the experience of being at a loss in a L'Arche foyer. When, in a public lecture given in Birmingham in 1994, Frances offers some cautiously critical remarks about 'non-realist' theology, it is in the context of speaking of the danger in trying to avoid both the sheer awkwardness, even embarrassment, of being bound to a conviction about a real and active God in a horribly painful and disappointing world, and the risk of that wild and unmanageable reality witnessed to by classical theology actually coming upon us unawares (not for the only time, she quotes R. S. Thomas to powerful effect; the lecture is 'A Time for Silence: Dare We Mention Prayer?', in F. Young (ed.), *Dare We Speak of God in Public?* Mowbray 1995: 133–50). We have no business in trying as theologians to avoid either embarrassment or risk.

Frances Young's willingness to venture continually into personal and (awful word) 'devotional' writing is witness to her own freedom from anxiety about such embarrassment and risk. In a way it takes us back to where we began, to the theme of 'limit'. Paradoxically, perhaps, the readiness to cross conventional academic boundaries, not only between different bits of theology (patristics, New Testament exegesis, systematics) but between what many would consider respectable and non-respectable genres for an academic, is not an ignoring of limits and boundaries but a recognition that certain styles of academic discourse need to be cured of their aspirations to self-sufficiency. What she has written on early Christian exegesis is related to just this insight. Most of us grew up with the general idea that, in the patristic period, theologians divided neatly between those who preferred to use allegory and those who clung to the 'literal' sense. In a series of specific studies, culminating in the 1993/4 Oxford lectures, Frances Young challenges this model, inviting us to look far more closely at what people actually thought they were doing in the ancient world when they interpreted a text. If the theologians of Antioch emphasized the 'historical' in their exegesis, this was not at all because of a concern with what a modern would call historical accuracy or plausibility in a text (though such issues were recognized and discussed): it is rather to do with knowing how to read a text in awareness of the idioms and conventions of a writer, having the right kind of information about context to make an informed judgment about what must be meant. This is an acknowledged aspect of what a rhetorical education in late antiquity involved. Understanding what an Antiochene exegete was doing, then, requires us to abandon any notion of a modern investigation into history for its own sake. The interpreter is trying to identify as fully as possible the context in which these words make sense, and that context is more than a set of distant events to be excavated. And in this respect, the so-called literalists in the early Church shared the bulk of their methodology with so-called allegorizers.

The central point for both schools in the early Church (if we can really call them schools any longer) is the need to take the text as an intelligible whole. But the way in which Scripture functions as an intelligible whole is prescribed by its use in a commentary that teaches certain things about God and the world. Doctrinal considerations, in other words, are always already at work in the reading of the Bible, and the considerations that determine what a good reading looks like are grounded in an entire vision of how God acts. To understand the Bible is to understand what God is doing now, pervading your life and persuading your mind and heart; what God can intelligibly be thought of as doing depends on a whole 'culture' of reflection and teaching, what Frances Young calls a 'narrative logic' informing and underlying the text as it is read. It's in this sense that I think her more general theological commitments relate to this perspective on patristic exegesis. There is no way around the difficulties of communication by appeal to a single 'literal' meaning, even for those who privilege the 'literal' sense and are suspicious of symbolic or spiritual readings. *All* readings are 'spiritual', to the extent that they require a commitment to become naturalized into the world revealed by Christian doctrine and – crucially – Christian prayer as shaped by and shaping that doctrine.

The sense of becoming native to a new and immeasurably enlarged imaginative world as reflected in the learning of a new and at first sight strange kind of speech allows Frances to make excellent use time and again of hymnody, poetry and musical analogy. Her extended reflection on reading the Bible today, *The Art of Performance*, makes luminous use of the basic image of Scripture as a 'score' for us to realize; and her earlier book, *Can These Bones Live?*, is distinguished particularly by its bold engagement with the metaphors of hymnody in the Bible and beyond. It is, I suppose, one reason why commentators seem unsure whether or not to call her a 'systematic' theologian. It's clear enough that she is a great deal more than a writer of impressionistic sketches; as the above should have made clear. She is in fact a writer with impressive inner consistencies, and a coherent attitude to the central words and images of doctrine. But they are deployed in a manner and a context that is always close to the pastoral edge. As much as any of the patristic theologians she discusses, she is always writing 'applied theology'; and the care, patience, reticence and subtlety of her work remind us that 'applied theology' is emphatically not less complex or demanding an exercise than systematic construction.

A Feminist?

One of the most intriguing features of Frances Young's work is the sense in which she is and is not a 'feminist' writer. From most of the internal debates of mainstream feminist work, in Europe or the USA, she has kept an austere distance; she is unlikely to feature in anthologies of women's theology. And yet her willingness to cross some dangerous boundaries, and above all to theologize out of a highly particular and painful experience of unfreedom and constraint, might be thought to typify what many feminist theologians look to as the distinctive theological liberty of the woman writer in a world of spurious and self-deceiving objectivities. I have never heard or read her at length on this issue. I suspect that some of what has been said earlier about 'limit' may be significant here. Frances is cautious, as we have seen, about any rhetoric of liberation that looks to a world in which tragedy has become out of date, a world where (to echo Lionel Trilling's fierce parody of a certain sort of radicalism) death is seen as unacceptably reactionary.

One of the conversations I'd most like to hear in contemporary theology is between Frances and Angela West, a far more explicitly feminist theologian in some ways, yet sharing very fully Frances' suspicion of what might be called the violence of utopias towards the insoluble tragedies and inescapable limits of being human. I wonder whether Frances' relative silence in this area implies a sense that here again salvation is being identified with a sort of boundary-less emancipation. In the 1994 lecture on prayer already quoted, she has some tantalizing remarks in passing on the relegation of religious practice to the private 'feminized' sphere in the modern world: 'In a post-Christian world, where atheism is, in practice, the privileged position, the lack of public religious discourse is not unlikely to consign religion to a private female ghetto, dismissed as irrelevant by men who think they know better' (p. 147). Yet the way beyond this, as she sketches it, is not in a simple denial that there is a 'private' sphere, or that women in some ways know how to operate in such a world where men do not; it is more of a plea that 'private' and 'public' find ways of reconnecting and educating each other, enlarging each other.

The connection of this with her own biography is obvious. She has worked for practically the whole of her career in one, generally secular, institution, and has functioned there as a public figure, a respected and seasoned administrator in the complicated world of modern academic politics. She has also (like her former colleague David Ford, with whom she wrote that exceptional essay on 2 Corinthians) kept deliberately close to the world of popular urban piety, that world which, on the very doorstep of so many academic religious institutions, baldly questions a vast percentage of the generalizations made by the inhabitants of those institutions about what is and isn't, or what can and can't be, believed. As a Methodist local preacher and latterly an ordained minister, Frances has consciously allowed herself to be nourished by the spirituality of those who make no claim to high theological literacy in the conventional sense, but who may yet be exemplary readers of the Bible and speakers of the odd and difficult language of faith. She is a person in whom spheres intersect; and evidently believes that this is a good place for a theologian to be.

It certainly entails no sentimental or uncritical avoidance of hard questions, no attempt to soften the reality of conflict in the Church. Those who heard her Bible studies at the 1993 Faith and Order conference in Compostela will recall the profound honesty of her treatment of these matters as she read Galatians with us – and will also recall some of the unease with which this honesty was met among those Christians who found it virtually impossible to believe that apostles *really* disagreed about basic matters. Once again, we are pointed back to 'difficult communication': the Church witnesses to the givenness of its foundation not by a smooth and polished discourse but by the very fact of its quarrelsome labouring to speak in a new way. 2 Corinthians really is determinative for this understanding, and might be read as the text which all Frances Young's theology is seeking to 'read'.

Equally, there is a biographical equation to be made here in the nature of Frances' commitment to the two spheres of her work as disciple and theologian. It is not all that usual to spend an entire academic lifetime in the service of one institution; the climate of academic life these days encourages migrations, the search for a more satisfying, less stress-laden environment. Frances Young has accepted the limit of inescapable constraint, in her faithfulness to a single and imperfect setting; her commitment to the University of Birmingham has been parallel in character to her commitment to the Church – without illusion and with patience. There are no academic utopias any more than there are ecclesial ones, or human utopias overall.

The strength and importance of the witness in life as in theology is in this resolute acceptance of difficulty. The fact that it is wholly impossible to categorize Frances Young as liberal or conservative in theology is important: despite her contribution to *The Myth of God Incarnate*, she has refused to be classified as a straightforward sceptic about classical doctrinal formulation: despite her eloquent deployment of the classical images of Wesleyan hymnody, she has refused to be classified as a pietist or traditionalist. Her reflections on the formative period of biblical exegesis put the most serious questions to modern fundamentalism and its false simplicities, yet insist upon the indispensability of reading Scripture in a context of doctrine and prayer. Her theological reflection on her own experience is quintessentially contemporary in method, yet it produces a result that is deeply uncomfortable for any kind of conventional liberal optimism. The sheer human particularity of her son's life and her engagement with it allows little room for comforting generalities. We return constantly to the governing theme of a communion that transfigures because it isn't obvious or easy or simply reducible to fluent verbal communication, a perspective in which suffering is not a problem to be solved but a breach in any and every self-sufficiency in the thinker or speaker, a perspective 'where crying is not the end of the world but the beginning of new life' (from the introduction to *Encounter With Mystery*, p. xiii).

Frances has seldom engaged directly with anything that could be called philosophical theology (except, rather tangentially, in thinking about language in patristic thought). Her writing about the early Church might be read as indicating a bit more sympathy with the 'rhetorical' concerns of the school of Antioch rather than the speculative enthusiasms of Alexandria, and this is reflected in her priorities as a teacher of the faith now. What matters isn't system, if that implies a completed vision viewable at arm's length, but persuasion and invitation into the normally fractured and stumbling speech of believers transformed by the awareness of God alongside in pain and unclarity. The biblical writers tell stories in order to induct you into an experience of your humanity as it is in God's eyes. The biblical interpreter seeks to uncover the 'narrative logic' of those stories more and more deeply so as to lead towards the same experience. The contemporary theologian tells stories in the same way and for the same purpose. Frances Young is unusual in being so painfully candid and moving a storyteller in this vein. Those of us who consider her a benchmark of honesty and wisdom in the wordy, self-dramatizing climate of a good deal of modern theology, left and right, are grateful for this gift of vulnerable narration more than anything else. If theology ought to help us to live as creatures, that is as minds and bodies negotiating limits and finding joy and salvation in this process and not in a fantasy Elsewhere, Frances is an exemplary theologian. I think that it ought, and that she is.

This article first appeared in the *Epworth Review* 28/1 (2001): 10–20. Reprinted with permission of Epworth Press.

Part I

HERMENEUTICAL CONNECTIONS

'THESE THEN LET US EMULATE'[1]
THE EARLY CHURCH ILLUMINATES TWO
GOSPEL IMPAIRMENT ENCOUNTERS

Simon Horne

How the Bible is seen to portray people with impairments is often met with hostility or embarrassment: 'The churches … are themselves handicapped by their theological legacy. Nowhere is this more potently visible than in the Bible's view of those who are other than physically whole' (Fontaine 1994: 112). But such views do not always take into account the wider context of how impairment was seen in the ancient world: it was a common experience, widespread in every level of society. Impairment was an inevitable fact of life – like death, in 'the common nature of humankind' and from which no one was exempt.[2] Conditions of birth, disease, occupation, injury, wars, and (for those who reached it) old age, produced populations who knew only too well what could and could not be done by people with impairments and what the experience of impairment entailed. It has only been in the modern era that people with impairments have been removed from mainstream society, and, correspondingly, it has been in the modern age that misunderstandings and ignorance about impairment have flourished. In contrast, people of the ancient world, including biblical and early Church writers, were both more realistic and more imaginative in their use of impairment in narrative and imagery – not denying the negative, but also aware of and making full use of the positive. This breadth of vision is almost always overlooked by modern commentary.[3] In this essay, two encounters from the Gospels between Jesus and people with impairments are looked at in the light shed by early Church interpreters of the encounters. We will see specifically how the early Church identified with these Gospel characters with impairments: they were viewed as illustrating key issues of faith and as modelling discipleship qualities.

---

1. John Chrysostom, *Hom. Matt.* 66.1; *PG* 58: 625–6; NPNF 1st series 10: 404. For further references from the early Church of people with impairments in the Gospels modelling discipleship qualities and issues of faith, see Horne (1999: 349–95).

2. Impairment in the common nature of humankind: John Chrysostom, *Hom. Jo.* 12.2; *PG* 59: 83; NPNF 1st series 14: 41; cf. John Chrysostom, *Hom. Jo.* 56.2; *PG* 59: 307; NPNF 1st series 14: 201. No one exempt from impairment: Augustine, *De civitate Dei* 19.4; CChr 48.666f; NPNF 1st series 2: 401f.

3. See Horne (1999).

A Stooping and Burdened Woman Set Free (Luke 13.11–16)

The woman who encounters Jesus in Lk. 13.11–16 is often described in modern Bible translations and commentary as 'bent double'. This translation is misleading. Modern commentary understands the word applied to her – συγκύπτουσα – simply as a recognized medical condition.[4] But συγκύπτουσα is not a medical term at all: the word does not occur in the entire surviving corpus of Greek ancient medical texts. The word that medical texts do use for spinal curvature or for limbs that are distorted is συγκάμπτω.[5] This medical word appears in the Septuagint and so was known to Luke – but when Luke describes the woman who encountered Jesus he chooses not to use that medical term (despite his supposed medical background!).[6] Instead, Luke chose this rare and unusual image συγκύπτουσα. Why this image? What sense did it carry? To help us grasp the sense associated with συγκύπτουσα we look at how the image was used by other ancient writers.

We see from ancient texts that συγκύπτουσα does not convey, as a medical term would, distortion or twisting, but either a curved shape or the shape caused by a heavy weight. It was used to describe the shape made by the bowing of a person's body as they made an appeal to someone in authority.[7] When a column of soldiers approaches a confined space, the word was used of the shape that the column makes as the soldiers alter their dress in order to pass through, specifically the curving of the column's corners.[8] It was also used for the effect of a great weight, such as a statue of Atlas with the world on his shoulders: 'Atlas was bowed over and crushed by the weight.'[9] Words associated with συγκύπτουσα carry the same two senses, describing for instance the curve of a person's body in uncontrollable laughter[10] or in extreme fury,[11] and also the effect on a tree's branches of the weight of ripe fruit.[12] The meanings were sometimes combined, such as in the shape of an older person's body, 'bowed with age and wisdom untold' and weighed down by a lifetime of troubles.[13]

Luke may have chosen an unusual image to describe the woman who encountered Jesus, but for early Church writers his image had become very familiar – with the same sense either of a curved shape or of the shape of something being weighed down. Chrysostom for instance used it to describe the body shape of a person who begs, the people of Antioch loaded with anguish, or Jacob burdened by grief.[14] But early Church writers did not always describe this shape of the

---

4.   e.g. Wilkinson (1998: 131–41); *ABD* VI: 14; *Oxford Bible Commentary* 2001: 945.

5.   e.g. LSJ, 1662; Moulton and Milligan (1949: 609).

6.   e.g. Psalm 68.24 LXX, 4 Kingdoms LXX 4.35.

7.   Aristophanes, *Vespae* 570f; LCL 1: 462f.

8.   Xenophon, *Anabasis* 3.4.19, 21; LCL 3: 472f.

9.   Philostratus, *Imagines* 2.20.372K.25; LCL, 218–21.

10.   Phrynicus Comicus, 3.6 – quoted in LSJ, 1668.

11.   *Greek Anthology* 2.6; LCL 1: 58f.

12.   Theophrastus, *De causis plantarum* 3.22.1; LCL 2: 164f; 4.14.1; LCL 2: 344f.

13.   Aegyptius in Homer, *Odyssey* 2.16; LCL 1: 36f. Older people bowed by troubles: Aristophanes, *Acharnenses* 703; LCL 1: 68f; *Greek Anthology* 16.265; LCL 5: 316f; cf. 6: 37; LCL 1: 316f.

14.   A person who begs: John Chrysostom, *Hom. 1 Cor.* 11.10; *PG* 61: 94; NPNF 1st series

human form curved forward in the same way. The shape of a person engaged in idol-worship, for instance, was conveyed by προσκυνέω. In contrast, συγκύπτω – Luke's Gospel word – was used of a heartfelt penitent, asking for 'mercy and crumbs, the food of a dog that is very hungry'.[15] Luke's image was even used of Jesus himself to demonstrate his humility: both generally in his stooping to take human form, and also specifically as he bends over to wash the feet of the disciples:

> Wilt thou deem Him little on this account, that He humbled Himself for thee? ... Because for the soul that was bent to the ground [συγκύπτουσαν] He humbles Himself, that He may raise up with Himself the soul that was tottering to a fall under a weight of sin? ... If so, we must blame the physician for stooping [συγκύπτει] over sufferings ... that he might heal the sick.[16]

When early Church writers drew on Luke's image of stooping forward and being weighed down not simply in isolation as in these examples, but when interpreting the story in Luke 13 as a whole, they applied συγκύπτουσα in a remarkably consistent way. They used the word of a person bending forward under the weight of a great burden, specifically the burden of sin, with the weight of this burden forcing the person to look only at the ground, that is, only at worldly matters. This way of living, the theme continued, is brought about through the activity of Satan. However, when Jesus encounters this person, their burden is lifted and they are set free: their sins are forgiven. Freed of their sins, they are now able to raise their head and to look up upwards, that is, towards the things of God:

> How many others are still bowed down and bound by Satan, who hinders them from looking up at all, and who would have us look down also! And no-one can raise them up, except the Word, that came by Jesus Christ... Jesus came to release those who were under the dominion of the devil.[17]

Each detail in the Luke 13 impairment story was used to build this picture: burdened and stooping (Lk. 13.11), unable to look up (Lk. 13.11), this way of living caused by Satan (Lk. 13.16), the person set free by Christ (Lk. 13.12), now seeing the things of God (Lk. 13.13).

In developing this theme, the early Church writers drew on another word also associated with impairment, namely the word that Luke used when the woman is

12: 63. Cf. John Chrysostom, *Hom Matt.* 88; *PG* 58: 778; NPNF 1st series 10: 522. The people of Antioch: John Chrysostom, *Ad populum Antiochenum* 2.6; *PG* 49: 36; NPNF 1st series 9: 345. Jacob weighed down by sorrow: John Chrysostom, *Hom. in Genesim* 65.3; *PG* 54: 559; FC 87: 244.

15. Gregory of Nazianzus, *In sancta lumina* 16; *PG* 36: 356; NPNF 2nd series 7: 358. Cf. the curved back in worship of the hesychasts in Greek Orthodox tradition – following the position of Elijah at 1 Kgs 18.42, who 'put his face between his knees' (Ware 1997: 106f). For early Church use of προσκυνέω and associated words, see *LPGL*, 1174–8. προσκυνέω was used of both idol-worship and true worship, but Luke's image was not used of idol-worship.

16. Gregory of Nazianzus, *In theophania* 14; *PG* 36: 328; NPNF 2nd series 7: 349f; cf. Gregory of Nazianzus, *In sancta Pascha* 2.26; *PG* 36: 660; NPNF 2nd series 7: 432f; Basil of Caesarea, *Epist.* 8.5; Courtonne, 1: 29; NPNF 2nd series 8: 118; Jerome, *Tractatus in psalmos* Hom. 41 / Psalm 119.130–3; CChr 78.250; FC 48: 304f.

17. Origen, *Contra Celsum* 8.54; SC 150: 294f; ANF 4: 660.

finally able to look up – ἀναβλέπω. As well as meaning 'look up', this word is directly linked to blindness as the word regularly used for regaining sight. This ambiguity in ἀναβλέπω, both 'looking up' and 'regaining sight', was commonplace in ancient texts, a famous example being Plato's cave – πρὸς τὸ φῶς ἀναβλέπειν.[18] Combining this ἀναβλέπω ambiguity with the image of bending forward was not confined to early Church writers, as we see from these lines in Philo:

> Look up then, so as to convict the blind human race, which, though it appears to see, is blind. For how can it be otherwise than blind, when it sees evil instead of good… Even if they ever do open their eyes [ἀνάβλεψον], [they] still bend them down towards the earth, pursuing only earthly things.[19]

As with the other biblical impairment encounters, the early Church interpreted this impairment encounter at Luke 13 as describing the experience of current disciples. Gregory of Nazianzus applied the image directly to Christians recently baptized:

> Yesterday you were a … soul bowed over [συγκύπτουσα] by sin; today you have been made straight by the Word. Do not be bent [συγκύψῃς] again, and condemned to the earth, as if weighed down by the Devil with a wooden collar, nor get an incurable curvature.[20]

And Augustine associated the looking up of the woman after Jesus had touched her to the *sursum corda* of the Eucharist: hearing those words, he says, Christians can recall the woman of Luke 13 and, like her, look up to their own hope 'laid up in heaven'.[21]

Luke's image – συγκύπτουσα – was a rare and unusual word describing the woman as stooping forward under a great burden. Luke deliberately chose a word for this woman that was not a medical term, alerting his readers and listeners that the bodily element of the story was carrying a figurative sense. The earliest interpreters of Luke 13 (in contrast to modern interpreters) had no thought whatsoever that the story shows what can happen if only a person with an impairment has enough faith. To the early Church the story was not about impairment or faith at all – it was a universal story about what happens when Jesus encounters a human person. The stooping, burdened woman who encounters Jesus represents every person, loaded down by the weight of human living, and bowed so far over that no way out can be seen and the promises of God are lost sight of. Here, at this lowest ebb, Jesus meets her. Through this encounter, she is set free, released, seeing again or catching sight of for the first time the things of God, the light of God. The συγκύπτουσα woman of Luke 13 was not suffering from a specific medical condition that Jesus was able to heal. Hers was a universal human condition from which Jesus was able to set her free. The striking image that Luke

---

18. Plato, *Respublica* 7.1, 515c; LCL 6: 122f.
19. Philo, *Rer. Div. Her.* 15.76–8; LCL 4: 318, 320 (Yonge 1993: 282). Cf. LSJ, 210.
20. Gregory of Nazianzus, *In sanctum baptisma* 33–4; *PG* 36: 405, 408; NPNF 2nd series 7: 372f.
21. Augustine, *Enarrationes in Psalmos* 68.2.8; CChr 39: 923; NPNF 1st series 3: 383f; cf. Augustine, *Enarrationes in Psalmos* 73.23; CChr 39:1020; NPNF 1st series 3: 512f.

chose to describe this woman alerted the early Church that in her encounter with Jesus she is representing all people – in this figurative sense, what happens to her can happen to others.

A Paralysed Man Braced, Released and Raised Up:
Matthew 9.1–8 and John 5.2–18

In two respects, the early Church found that the impairment encounters between Jesus and the man with paralysis had great significance and usefulness to them: in the verbal imagery of the word for paralysis, and in the visual aspect of the person moving from a horizontal position to a vertical one. These encounters were seen to illustrate both how Jesus responds to someone's impairment of soul, and how that person responds with trust and obedience – for the early Church, a response that was a model for current disciples.

The central image in the word παράλυσις is the 'loosening' or 'undoing' of whatever holds the given condition in place. For someone who had bodily paralysis, the tensions holding their body in balance were said to have been undone: 'all the veins are relaxed and dissolved; this state is followed by a complete prostration of the harmony and due arrangement of the limbs'.[22]

Figuratively, the image was applied to someone exhausted from great effort. The people of Sodom, for instance, 'were wearied [παρελύθησαν] with their exertions to find the door'.[23] This loosening image could be used with a positive sense of historical events. High praise is given to the Emperor Augustus,

> who calmed the storms which were raging in every direction, who healed the common diseases which were afflicting both Greeks and barbarians … This is he who did not only loosen but utterly abolish [παρελύσας] the bonds in which the whole of the habitable world was previously bound and weighed down.[24]

However, the undoing of what is established had its negative side too: παραλύω was used of violating ancient customs,[25] breaking peace treaties,[26] and the catastrophic effect on a city of being occupied by an enemy.[27]

Two responses to παράλυσις were identified by ancient writers that drew on this central image of loosening. One response was to reverse the loosening by 'bracing' or 'tightening'. A medical text states: 'Paralysis is a slackening and

---

22. Philo, *Praem. Poen.* 25.145; LCL 8: 402, 404 (Yonge 1993: 678); cf. Philo, *Det. Pot. Ins.* 46.167; LCL 2: 312, 314 (Yonge 1993: 130). Cf. Celsus, *De medicina* 2.1.12; LCL 1: 92f – 'resolutio nervorum (paralysin Graeci nominant)'; cf. Celsus, *De medicina* 3.27.1a; LCL 1: 344f. Cf. with a dry humour: 'The daughter of limb-relaxing Bacchus and limb-relaxing Aphrodite is limb-relaxing Gout' – λυσιμελοῦς. *Greek Anthology* 11.414; LCL 4: 270f.

23. Philo, *Fug.* 26.144; LCL 5: 86 (Yonge 1993: 334). Cf. of exhaustion in sleep: Euripides, *Bacchae* 683; LCL 3: 58f; Philostratus, *Imagines* 1.2.297K.13; LCL, 10f.

24. Philo, *Leg. Gai.* 21.145–6; LCL 10: 72, 74 (Yonge 1993: 770).

25. Philo, *Leg. Gai.* 30.200; LCL 10: 104 (Yonge 1993: 775); 36.293; LCL 10: 146 (Yonge 1993: 783); 37.298; LCL 10: 150 (Yonge 1993: 784).

26. Philo, *Abr.* 39.226; LCL 6: 110; (Yonge 1993: 430).

27. Lysias, *Against Agoratus* 46–7; LCL, 304f.

looseness of the nerves, and it is necessary to tighten them.'[28] The other response drew on the experience of someone who had bodily paralysis – of being bound fast: 'shackles and fetters on my flesh' (Lambert 1960: 45). Through λύω as the root word in παράλυσις, this second response was identified as 'loosening' or 'releasing' the person. So for instance Hippocrates was said to use λύω for the treatment of a mild case of apoplexy, 'because he knew that in cases of apoplexy the cause is like a fetter [ὥσπερ ὑπὸ τινων δεσμῶν] that impedes the brain; so he used the opposite term to describe recovery'.[29]

The early Church used both these responses – bracing and releasing – as they interpreted Gospel impairment encounters involving people with paralysis. First, the word they commonly used of Jesus' healing of paralysis (though it was not a New Testament word) was σφίγγω– a bracing or tightening of the body. However, Jesus' healing of physical impairment was not the focus of interest for early Church interpreters other than as a way of revealing his divine nature. So σφίγγω was often used of the soul, for example when the soul is strengthened or encouraged during times of endurance or when temptations threaten: 'Let us entreat Him, that He would brace our paralysed soul.'[30] In this very respect, the paralysed man of John 5 was said to be an encouragement to all people: 'his paralysis is sufficient to brace up our souls' on the grounds that how he lived his life 'has encouraged you to patience and urged you to match his zeal … [and] has exhibited to you the lovingkindness of God'.[31] Chrysostom's wordplay here is lost in translation: this Gospel character whose body is loosened and who braces our souls. The paradox in this imagery is the equivalent with paralysis of the blind person who gives sight.[32]

Secondly, the root image of λύω in παράλυσις was also used for striking wordplay, in ways that radically undermine the modern preoccupation with sin when interpreting these Gospel impairment texts. On occasions, λύω was used of the taking away of different kinds of impairment, sometimes with a technical sense relating to demons.[33] But given a context of forgiveness, the early Church

28. *Book of Medicines* (Wallis Budge 1913: II, 144; II, 124).

29. Hippocrates' use of λύω for treating apoplexy: Hippocrates, *Aph.* 2.42; LCL 4: 118f. The analysis of why he used λύω in Stephanus, *Commentary on the Aphorisms of Hippocrates* (Westerink 1995: II, 41). Cf. paralysis as a state of being bound and/or loose in early Jewish texts in Preuss (1993: 230).

30. ἵνα σφίγξῃ τὴν ψυχὴν ἡμῶν παραλελυμένην – John Chrysostom, *Hom. Matt.* 14.5; *PG* 59: 221; NPNF 1st series 10: 89; cf. John Chrysostom, *Hom. Jo.* 37.1; *PG* 59: 208; NPNF 1st series 14: 129.

31. John Chrysostom, *In paralyticum demissum per tectum* 1; *PG* 51: 50; NPNF 1st series 9: 212 – τὰς ἡμετέρας ἐπισφίγξαι ψυχάς. Cf. a similar image used with Peter – 'Ananias he bound with the bond of death, and the weak in his feet he absolved from his defect of health': Tertullian, *De pudicitia* 21.12; CChr 2.1327; ANF 4: 99.

32. As we find, for instance, in John 9. For discussion and further examples of impairment paradox in ancient texts, including biblical texts, see Horne (1997: 125, 168, 241–3, 253, 260–8, 282–3, 290–1, 294–6, 345–9, 353, 363, 380, 387).

33. Use of λύω in the New Testament for release from impairment, e.g. Mk 7.35; Lk. 13.16. Examples of λύω in early Church texts for release from impairment – John Chrysostom, *Hom. Eph.* 8; *PG* 62: 60; NPNF 1st series 13: 88. Cf. John Chrysostom, *Hom. Act.* 38; *PG* 60: 274; NPNF 1st

could combine λύω with παράλυσις and have a field day with paradoxical statements. With the paralysed man of Matthew 9 for instance, Jesus was said to have 'loosed' his paralysis of soul, that is, released the man's sins, and 'fastened' the man's bodily paralysis: ἔλυσα τὰς ἁμαρτίας τοῦ παραλυτικοῦ, τὸ σῶμα ἔσφιγχα.[34] The contrast was put even more epigrammatically: among Christ's works witnessed by the disciples were 'a paralytic new-strung, and sins remitted' – παραλυτικὸν σφιγέντα καὶ ἁμαρτήματα λυθέντα.[35] Even Jesus' own words in the Gospel were adapted to make the wordplay and bring out the contrast:

> Now what He said is like this, 'Which seems to you easier, to bind up a disorganized body, or to undo the sins of a soul?'– σῶμα σφίγξαι διῳκισμένον, ἢ ψυχῆς ἁμαρτήματα λῦσαι;[36]

Latin writers too used the same imagery to make the same contrast. Augustine points out how Christ 'made the inner man whole of his palsy, by loosing his sins, by binding fast his faith' – 'fecit interiorem hominem salvum a paralysi, remittendo peccata et constringendo fidem'.[37] Similar imagery is put to the same use in the New Testament itself: at Rom. 3.25, Paul uses a word that has the double meaning of 'paralysis' and 'forgiveness' – τὴν πάρεσιν – and the early Church made much of the deliberate ambiguity.[38]

Early interpreters were making the most of the wordplay certainly, but also, according to the earliest interpreters of the Gospel impairment texts, the link in the Gospels between sin and paralysis was not one of cause and effect, that a person's impairment was somehow caused by their sin – a connection that Jesus explicitly denies at Jn 9.3. Rather, sin and paralysis were linked in terms of the rich resonance of the imagery – bracing, fastening and encouraging on the one hand; releasing, undoing and forgiving on the other. By focusing exclusively on an assumed cast-iron bond between sin and impairment in terms of cause and effect, modern interpreters are missing the point completely.

Early Church writers made quite another use of the παράλυσις image, namely the visual aspect of a person with paralysis when healed by Jesus moving from a

---

series 11: 238; *Hom. Jo.* 12.2; *PG* 59: 83; NPNF 1st series 14: 41. For λύω as a term of release in magical texts, and in relation to impairment in particular, see Horne (1999: 389; cf. 312–15).

34. John Chrysostom, *Hom. Matt.* 30.3; *PG* 57: 365; NPNF 1st series 10: 200; cf. John Chrysostom, *Hom. Jo.* 37.1; *PG* 59: 208; NPNF 1st series 14: 129. Cf. John Chrysostom, *Hom. Matt.* 29.2; *PG* 57: 360; NPNF 1st series 10: 197; 26.6; *PG* 57: 339; NPNF 1st series 10: 180.

35. John Chrysostom, *Hom. Matt.* 32.4; *PG* 57: 380; NPNF 1st series 10: 213; cf. 29.2; *PG* 57: 360; NPNF 1st series 10: 197.

36. John Chrysostom, *Hom. Matt.* 29. 2; *PG* 57: 360; NPNF 1st series 10: 197.

37. Augustine, *Enarrationes in Psalmos* 37.1–3; CChr 38: 382–4 (Tweed *et al.* 1847–57: II, 48–51).

38. John Chrysostom especially develops this double meaning, e.g. John Chrysostom, *Hom. Rom.* 7; *PG* 60: 444–5; NPNF 1st series 11: 378. In a similar way, Chrysostom explains the bodily paralysis image of Heb. 12.12f as referring to a soul 'relaxed' and 'paralysed' and collapsing into sin: John Chrysostom, *Hom. Heb.* 31.3; *PG* 63: 214–15; NPNF 1st series 14: 507. See also, in the context of Lk. 4.18f, discussion in Sloan (1977: 36–8). In the Gospels, sins forgiven combined with paralysis: Mt. 9.2–6 and parallels; Jn 5.14.

horizontal position to a vertical position.[39] Several times in the Gospels Jesus addresses the person with paralysis in the same way: 'Arise!'[40] Crucially, the person responds: there is no sense here that the biblical character with an impairment is simply passive or helpless.[41] Again, this command of Jesus was interpreted in terms of paralysis of the soul, in the sense both of urging oneself to rise up from a bed of wrongdoing, and also of stirring oneself not to fall back to one's former ways, for instance once baptismal enthusiasm has passed:

> Wherefore even though you stand, yet take heed lest you fall ... All of us, so to speak, having fallen, and lying prostrate on the ground ... Our exhortation is concerning the ability of them that are fallen to arise. Let us rise again then, and let us stand nobly. How long do we lie prostrate? ... Let us stretch out a hand to each other and thoroughly raise ourselves up.[42]

This same visual dimension was used to illustrate not only baptism but also the resurrection itself. So striking was the parallel that John Chrysostom said that the paralysis healing of John 5 was a type of baptism[43] and an image of the resurrection: 'He had given no trifling proof of the Resurrection by bracing the paralytic...[which] fell little short of resurrection.'[44] Here too the command that Jesus speaks is crucial, highlighting the parallel between the man with paralysis commanded to arise and the dead commanded to arise. This same command featured in early baptismal liturgy with the implication that the rising up of the

39. Perhaps this revolutionary movement from horizontal to vertical that was so striking for ancient cultures has become lost in modern times in those societies where people with paralysis use wheelchairs.

40. Jesus' command to those with paralysis – ἔγειρε; : Mt. 9.6; Mk 3.3; ἀνάστηθι; : Mk 9.27; Lk. 5.25. Cf. the Apostles' command: Acts 9.18, 34; 14.10. We can compare Jas. 5.15 on the sick person: 'The Lord will raise them up.'

41. For this theme that people with impairments were not passive or helpless in the context of the healings of Asclepius and in the Gospels, see Horne (1999: 324f, 350–64).

42. John Chrysostom, *Hom. 1 Cor.* 23.6; *PG* 61: 194; NPNF 1st series 12: 135. Cf. John Chrysostom, *Hom. Phil.* 11; *PG* 62: 268; NPNF 1st series 13: 237. Cf. 'Arise! The way itself has come to thee, and roused thee from thy sleep; if, however, it has roused thee, up and walk...the word of God has healed even the lame': Augustine, *Tract. Ev. Jo.* 34.9; CChr 36: 316; NPNF 1st series 7: 203; cf. John Chrysostom, *Hom. Acta.* 35; *PG* 60: 256; NPNF 1st series 11: 222; 8; *PG* 60: 72–3; NPNF 1st series 11: 52. See also John Chrysostom, *Hom. Matt.* 26.10; *PG* 57: 344; NPNF 1st series 10: 184. The paralysed man of John 5 is frequently used to illustrate the rousing and not falling back: John Chrysostom, *Hom. Matt.* 67.4; *PG* 58: 638; NPNF 1st series 10: 413; John Chrysostom, *Hom. Jo.* 37.1; *PG* 59: 207; NPNF 1st series 14: 128. Compare also Psalm 20.8 – 'They will collapse and fall, but we shall rise and stand upright.' Philo puts the image to similar use: 'There is no small number of things in human life which are confessed to be very difficult to endure ... by which weak spirited men are broken down, not being able to raise themselves at all through their want of courage; but those men who are full of high thoughts and noble spirits, rise up to struggle against these things, and contend against them with fortitude and exceeding vigour': Philo, *Virt.* 2.5; LCL 8: 164, 166 (Yonge 1993: 640).

43. John Chrysostom, *Hom. Jo.* 36.1; *PG* 59: 203–4; NPNF 1st series 14: 126 – ὡς ἐν εἰκόνι καὶ τύπῳ ; cf. John Chrysostom, *De incomprehensibili Dei natura* 12.8f; *PG* 48: 803f; FC 72: 288f.

44. John Chrysostom, *Hom. Jo.* 39.3; *PG* 59: 224; NPNF 1st series 14: 140. On the command spoken by Jesus to the paralysed man – ἔγειρε; – as a resurrection term in the early Church: *TDNT* 2: 333–9; BAGD, 214f; *LPGL*, 398f.

baptized person immediately after their encounter with the Holy Spirit in the act of baptism prefigures their own resurrection.[45] At Rom. 6.3–11 Paul links baptism, the resurrection and walking 'in newness of life'. The early Church associated the same three in visual terms, and incorporated in addition the healing of the man with paralysis. The rising of the dead, the rising of those who have just been baptized, and the rising (also in obedience to Jesus' command) of the biblical character healed of paralysis, were linked together through a weaving of allusion to illustrate the utterly radical nature of walking 'in newness of life… and alive to God in Christ Jesus' (Rom. 6.4, 11).[46]

We find supporting evidence for this direct identification with biblical characters with impairments in the contexts of baptism and resurrection from a data resource largely overlooked by modern biblical interpreters: early Christian art. In view of early interpreters' use of the visual in the biblical impairment texts, it is not surprising that these impairment encounters were used extensively in early Christian artistic representation. As recent scholarship has shown,

> There is a high degree of resonance between [early] Christian literature and art… written documents and art objects emerge from the same or similar communities and have common purposes or outlooks. (Jensen 2000: 30)[47]

What is surprising, however, is the fact that the early Church made such extensive use of impairment in their art at all. Culturally, this was a highly unusual development, if not unique to the early Church. Several studies have shown that impairment was a very rare subject for artistic representation in the ancient world, especially in Graeco-Roman traditions.[48] The art of the early Church is totally in contrast to this. In early Christian art, impairment has a very high profile: impairment encounters, especially relating to the blind men and the paralysed man, are identified as 'ubiquitous… the core, the mainstay of Early Christian imagery'

---

45. Whitaker 1970: 6, 7, 14, 15, 16, 19, 29, 30, 31, 34f, 41, 49.

46. 'This act made manifest the Resurrection, for it was an image of the Resurrection': John Chrysostom, *Hom. Act.* 8; *PG* 60: 70; NPNF 1st series 11: 50; cf. John Chrysostom, *Hom. Act.* 9; *PG* 60: 79; NPNF 1st series 11: 58. Cf. John Chrysostom, *Hom. 1 Cor.* 23.6; *PG* 61: 194; NPNF 1st series 12: 135. Rising of those healed of impairment (body and soul), of the dead, of those baptized – linked together: John Chrysostom, *Hom. 1 Cor.* 40.2; *PG* 61: 348–9; NPNF 1st series 12: 245; Gregory of Nazianzus, *De baptisma* 40.9; *PG* 36: 369; NPNF 2nd series 7: 362; cf. Tertullian, *De baptisma* 2; CChr 1: 277f; ANF 3: 669. The same association made in the context of Paul's impairment encounter: John Chrysostom, *Ad populum Antiochenum* 16.7; *PG* 49: 166; NPNF 1st series 9: 448; cf. Tertullian, *De baptisma* 13; CChr 1: 288f; ANF 3: 676. Cf. the command to arise spoken by Christ to the deceased son of the widow at Nain and the daughter of Jairus: Lk. 7.14; 8.54. We can compare a similar use of the image of the returning from death to life for the return of the lost son: Lk. 15.24, 32. In the context of Isa. 53.4, Tertullian states that the freedom of this newness of life in Christ is as powerful as a healing: 'liberare curatio est' – *Adv. Marcionem* 4.8; CSEL 47: 438; ANF 3: 354.

47. This is discussed and illustrated further by Jensen (2000: 1, 15, 19, 26f, 29, 30f, 35f, 77–9, 102, 182).

48. Little interest in artistic representation of people with impairments, especially in Graeco-Roman traditions (Garland 1995: 105–7, 111–14, 121f; Dasen 1993: 164–75, 247; Dasen 1988: 268f). People of restricted growth, however, were popular subjects of artistic representation (Dasen 1988: 267, 273).

(Mathews 1993: 59f). Art historians suggest that this prominence results from associations with Christ's power (especially in the light of the rivalry with other healing cults and with magic), and because the healings are symbolic of deliverance, of forgiveness of sins, of trust and hope.[49] However, the insights given to us from the early Church's interpretation of the Gospel impairment texts lead us to a further explanation for this prominence of impairment in early Christian art. Written interpretation shows that characters with impairments who encounter Jesus in the Gospels held considerable significance for the early Church as models, types and exemplars for the whole Christian community – and the same can be seen in their art. In several of the representations of the paralysed man, for instance, there is no other figure present: viewers were clearly being led to identify with him. Similarly, the Christ figure in other representations is looking directly at or touching the characters with impairments, leading the viewer to the same focus. These representations often occur in the context of baptism or death and resurrection, such as in baptisteries or on tombs.[50] In contemporary written sources links were being made between biblical characters with impairments and universal facets of discipleship such as coming to faith and baptism, and rising up at the resurrection. In early Christian art too, biblical characters with impairments were being used in very similar ways: as models for the processes and experiences of discipleship. In exegesis and liturgy, interpreters were leading those they were engaging with to identify with the people with impairments in the Gospel stories: such interpretation was 'mimetic of scripture, and intended to inspire *mimesis*' (Young 1997: 240).[51] Early Christian art was widely used as a resource to describe and explain 'the faith and daily life of Christians' (Jensen 2000: 64), and biblical characters with impairments played a very significant role in this process.

We have seen that the impairment encounter between Jesus and the oppressed woman was used by early Church writers to illustrate and interpret the experience of the people they were addressing. The impairment encounters between Jesus and people with paralysis were used in a similar way. Those who heard or read these early interpreters were being led to identify with the characters with impairments so that central Christian processes could be articulated. With the woman weighed down, it was the liberation that comes from the lifting of over-

49. Very high profile of representation of people with impairments in early Church art, and suggested explanations (Di Berardino 1992: II, 650; I, 108f; Mathews 1993: 59–65; Simon 1938: 206f, 212f; Cabrol and Leclercq 1907–53: I, 2.3230–3234; XIII, 2.1616–1626; Kraeling 1967: 208f; du Bourget 1965: 16, 31; Lowrie 1965: 58; Gough 1973: 41; Milburn 1989: 12; Volbach and Hirmer 1962: 12f; Jensen 2000: 48, 65, 69, 75f, 90, 97; Beckwith 1970: 1–12).

50. A particular link with baptism identified (Di Berardino 1992: II, 650; I, 108f; Lowrie 1965: 58; Milburn 1989: 12, 203; Cabrol and Leclercq 1907–1953: XIII, 2.1617; Kraeling 1967: 208f; Smith 1938: 102–8; Beckwith 1970: 38, 101; Jensen 2000: 43, 51, 48, 84–8, 175–8). Images of the paralysed man associated with the resurrection (Di Berardino 1992: II, 650; Cabrol and Leclercq 1907–53: XIII, 2.1622f; Mathews 1993: 59, 61f; Kraeling 1967: 208f; Jensen 2000: 71f, 168, 169, 171, 179).

51. On early Church use in biblical exegesis of exemplars as models for discipleship, see Young (1997).

whelming burdens. With the characters with paralysis, it was the liberating release of being forgiven, the bracing of encouragement, and the radical newness of life that results when Jesus is encountered and baptism embraced, even a foretaste (or rather forevision) of the resurrection. Through verbal and visual allusion, people taking part in contemporary liturgical practice were linked to scriptural impairment texts and were led to identify with biblical characters with impairments.

Impairment was a familiar experience in the ancient world, part of life at every level of society. With this basis of familiarity, the early Church used impairment imaginatively. Whether in exegesis, liturgy or visual art, impairment was a valuable tool: the experience of impairment was used to illustrate the experience of Christian discipleship. For modern cultures, however, people who live impairment have largely been marginalized, not least in the Church itself. But for the early Church, what it's like to live impairment was the key that unlocked the rich Gospel encounters between Jesus and people with impairments. The early Church demonstrates how the experience of people who live with impairment in our own day is the proper focus for how we interpret the biblical impairment texts.

Texts and Sources

1. *Biblical*
1 Kgs 18.42
Ps. 20.8
Isa. 53.4
Mt. 9.1–8
Mt. 9.2–6
Mt. 9.6
Mk 3.3
Mk 7.35
Mk 9.27
Lk. 4.18f.
Lk. 5.25
Lk. 7.14
Lk. 8.54
Lk. 13.11–16
Lk. 13.16
Lk. 15.24
Lk. 15.32
Jn 5.2–18
Jn 5.14
Jn 9
Jn 9.3
Acts 9.18
Acts 9.34
Acts 14.10
Rom. 3.25
Rom. 6.3–11
Heb. 12.12f.
Jas. 5.15

LXX Psalm 68
LXX 4 Kingdoms
Alfred Rahlfs (ed.)
    1935   *Septuaginta* (Stuttgart: Wurttembergische Bibelanstalt/Deutsche Bibelgesell-
              schaft).

2. *Non-biblical Jewish*

Philo
Abr.
Det. Pot. Ins.
Fug.
Leg. Gai.
Praem. Poen.
Rer. Div. Her.
Virt.
Colson, F. H., *et al.* (ed. and tr.)
    1929–53   *Philo* (LCL, 12 vols.; London: Heinemann/Cambridge, Mass.: Harvard Univer-
              sity Press).
Yonge, C. D. (tr.)
    1993   *The Works of Philo* (Peabody, Mass.: Hendrickson Publishers, revised edn).

3. *Patristic*

Augustine
De civitate Dei
Enarrationes in Psalmos
Tractatus in Evangelium Joannis
Dekkers, D. E. and I. Fraipont (ed.)
    1956   *Enarrationes in Psalmos* (*Aurelii Augustini opera* CChr, vols. 38, 39, 40).
Verheijen, L. (ed.)
    1981   *De civitate Dei* (*Aurelii Augustini opera* CChr, vol. 48).
Willems, D. R. (ed.)
    1954   *Tractatus in evangelium Joannis* (*Aurelii Augustini opera* CChr, vol. 36). ET in
              NPNF, 1st series, vols. 1–8.
Tweed, J., *et al.* (tr.)
    1847–57   *Exposition on the Book of Psalms by Saint Augustine* (6 vols.; Oxford: J. H.
              Parker).

Basil of Caesarea
Epistulae
Courtonne, Y. (ed.)
    1957–66   *Saint Basile: Lettres* (Paris: Bude, vols.1–3). ET in NPNF, 2nd series, vol. 8.

Gregory of Nazianzus
De baptisma
In sancta lumina
In sancta Pascha
In sanctum baptisma
In theophania
Migne, *PG*, vols. 35–6.
ET in NPNF, 2nd series, vol. 7.

Jerome
Tractatus in lix psalmos
Morin, D. G. (ed.)
    1958   *Opera homiletica* (*Sancti Hieronymi presbyteri opera* CChr, vol. 78).
Ewald, Marie Ligouri (tr.)
    1964   *Saint Jerome: The Homilies of Saint Jerome*, vol. 1: *(1–59 On The Psalms)*
             (FC, vol. 48; Washington, DC: Catholic University of America Press).

John Chrysostom
Ad populum Antiochenum
De incomprehensibili Dei natura
Homiliae in 1 epistulam ad Corinthianos
Homiliae in Acta apostolorum
Homiliae in epistulam ad Ephesios
Homiliae in Genesim
Homiliae in epistulam ad Hebraeos
Homiliae in Joannem
Homiliae in Matthaeum
Homiliae in epistulam ad Philomenum
Homiliae in epistulam ad Romanos
Homilia in paralyticum demissum per tectum
Migne, *PG*, vols. 47–64.
ET in NPNF, 1st series, vols. 9–14.
Hill, Robert C. (tr.)
    1992   *Saint John Chrysostom: Homilies on Genesis 46–67* (FC, vol. 87; Washington,
             DC: Catholic University of America Press).

Origen
Contra Celsum
Borret, M. (ed. and tr.)
    1969   *Origene: Contre Celse* (SC, vol. 150). ET in ANF, vols. 4, 10.

Tertullian
Adversus Marcionem
De baptisma
De pudicitia
Dekkers *et al.* (eds.)
    1954   *Opera Catholica: Adversum Marcionem* (*Quinti Septimi Florentis Tertulliani*
             opera CChr, vol. 1).
    1954   *Opera Montanistica* (*Quinti Septimi Florentis Tertulliani opera* CChr, vol. 2).
Kroymann, A. (ed.)
    1906   *De patientia*, etc. (*Quinti Septimi Florentis Tertulliani opera* CSEL, vol. 47).
             ET in ANF, vols. 3, 4.

4. *Classical*

Aristophanes
Acharnenses
Vespae
Rogers, B. B. (ed. and tr.)
    1924   *Aristophanes* (LCL, 3 vols.; London: Heinemann/Cambridge, Mass.: Harvard
             University Press).

Celsus, *De medicina*
Spencer, W. G. (ed. and tr.)
    1935–38   *Celsus: On Medicine* (LCL, 3 vols.; London: Heinemann/Cambridge, Mass.:
                Harvard University Press).

Euripides, *Bacchae*
Way, A. S., *et al.* (eds. and tr.)
    1912–64   *Euripides* (LCL, 4 vols.; London: Heinemann/Cambridge, Mass.: Harvard Uni-
                versity Press).

Greek Anthology
Paton, W. R. (ed. and tr.)
    1916–18   *Greek Anthology* (LCL, 5 vols.; London: Heinemann/Cambridge, Mass.: Har-
                vard University Press).

Hippocrates, *Aphorisms*
Jones, W. H. S., *et al.* (eds. and trs.)
    1923–95   *Hippocrates* (LCL, 8 vols.; London: Heinemann/Cambridge, Mass.: Harvard
                University Press).

Homer, *Odyssey*
Murray, A. T. (ed. and tr.)
    1919   *The Odyssey* (LCL, 2 vols.; London: Heinemann/Cambridge, Mass.: Harvard
                University Press).

Lysias, *Against Agoratus*
Lamb, W. R. M. (ed. and tr.)
    1930   *Lysias* (LCL; London: Heinemann/Cambridge, Mass.: Harvard University
                Press).

Philostratus, *Imagines*
Fairbanks, A. (ed. and tr.)
    1931   *Philostratus the Elder: Imagines,* etc. (LCL; London: Heinemann/Cambridge,
                Mass.: Harvard University Press).

Plato, *Respublica*
Fowler, H. N. *et al.* (eds. and tr.)
    1914–26   *Plato* (LCL, 12 vols.; London: Heinemann/Cambridge, Mass.: Harvard Univer-
                sity Press).

Stephanus, *Commentary on the Aphorisms of Hippocrates*
Westerink, L. G. (ed. and tr.)
    1995   *Stephanus of Athens: Commentary on Hippocrates' Aphorisms* (CMG, XI.1, 3,
                3, 4 vols.; Berlin: Akademie Verlag).

Theophrastus, *De causis plantarum*
Hort, A. F. (ed. and tr.)
    1916   *Theophrastus: Enquiry into Plants* (LCL, 2 vols.; London: Heinemann/Cam-
                bridge, Mass.: Harvard University Press).

Xenophon, *Anabasis*
Brownson, C. L. (ed. and tr.)
    1922   *Xenophon*, vol. 3: *Anabasis* (LCL; London: Heinemann/Cambridge, Mass.:
               Harvard University Press).

Bibliography

Beckwith, J.
    1970   *Early Christian and Byzantine Art* (Harmondsworth: Penguin).
Cabrol, Fernand, and Henri Leclercq (eds.)
    1907–53   *Dictionnaire d'archéologie chrétienne et de liturgie* (15 vols. in 30; Paris:
               Letouzey et Ane).
Dasen, Veronique
    1988   'Dwarfism in Egypt and Classical Antiquity: Iconography and Medical His-
               tory', *Medical History* 32: 253–76.
    1993   *Dwarfs in Ancient Egypt and Greece* (Oxford: Clarendon Press).
Di Berardino, Angelo (ed.)
    1992   *Encyclopedia of the Early Church* (ET by Adrian Walford; 2 vols.; Cambridge:
               James Clarke).
du Bourget, Pierre
    1965   *Early Christian Painting* (ET by Simon Watson Taylor; London: Weidenfeld
               & Nicolson).
Fontaine, Carole R.
    1994   Untitled contribution in 'Roundtable Discussion: Women with Disabilities – A
               Challenge to Feminist Theology', *Journal of Feminist Studies in Religion* 10/2:
               108–14.
Garland, Robert
    1995   *The Eye of the Beholder: Deformity and Disability in the Graeco-Roman
               World* (London: Duckworth).
Gough, Michael
    1973   *The Origins of Christian Art* (London: Thames & Hudson).
Horne, Simon
    1999   *Injury and Blessing: A Challenge to Current Readings of Biblical Discourse
               Concerning Impairment* (Ph.D. thesis; University of Birmingham).
Jensen, Robin Margaret
    2000   *Understanding Early Christian Art* (London and New York: Routledge).
Kraeling, C. H.
    1967   'The Decorations of the Dura Baptistry and Early Christian Art', in C. Bradford
               (ed.), *The Excavations at Dura Europos* (Final Report 8/Part 2; New Haven:
               Dura Europos Publications / New York: J. J. Augustin), 204–20.
Lambert, W. G.
    1960   *Babylonian Wisdom Literature* (Oxford: Clarendon Press).
Lowrie, Walter
    1965   *Art in the Early Church* (New York: Harper & Row, 2nd edn).
Mathews, Thomas F.
    1993   *The Clash of Gods: A Reinterpretation of Early Christian Art* (Princeton, NJ:
               Princeton University Press).
Milburn, Robert
  1989 [1988] *Early Christian Art and Architecture* (Aldershot: Wildwood House, Reprint
               from Scolar Press).

Moulton, James Hope, and George Milligan
    1949   *The Vocabulary of the Greek Testament Illustrated from the Papyri and Other Non-Literary Sources* (London: Hodder & Stoughton).
Preuss, Julius
    1993   *Biblical and Talmudic Medicine* (ed. and tr. by Fred Rosner; Northvale, NJ: Aronson, revised edn).
Simon, M.
    1938   'Sur l'origine des sarcophages chrétiens du type Bethesda', *Mélanges d'Archéologie et d'Histoire de l'Ecole Française de Rome, Antiquité* 55: 201–23.
Sloan, R. B., Jr
    1977   *'The Favourable Year of the Lord': A Study of Jubilee Theology in the Gospel of Luke* (Austin, Tex.: Schola Press).
Smith, E. B.
    1938   *Early Christian Iconography* (Princeton, NJ: Princeton University Press).
Volbach, A., and M. Hirmer
    1962   *Early Christian Art* (New York: Abrams).
Wallis Budge, E. A. (ed. and tr.)
    1913   *Syrian Anatomy, Pathology and Therapeutics or 'The Book of Medicines'* (2 vols.; London: Oxford University Press).
Ware, Kallistos
    1997   '"My Helper and My Enemy": The Body in Greek Christianity', in Sarah Coakley (ed.), *Religion and the Body* (Cambridge: Cambridge University Press): 90–110.
Whitaker, E. C.
    1970   *Documents of the Baptismal Liturgy* (London: SPCK, 2nd edn).
Wilkinson, John
    1998   *The Bible and Healing: A Medical and Theological Commentary* (Edinburgh: Handsel).
Young, Frances
    1997   *Biblical Exegesis and the Formation of Christian Culture* (Cambridge: Cambridge University Press).

WILDERNESS WOMAN
THE TAMING OF MIRIAM

Christine Trevett

The prophet Micah articulated what scholars suspect had once been the truth: Miriam, now a minor supporting player in the drama of an exodus from Egypt and Israel's wilderness wanderings, had at an earlier stage been a central character in accounts of its history:

> I brought you up from the land of Egypt
> and redeemed you from the house of bondage
> and before you I sent Moses, Aaron and Miriam...
> (Mic. 6.4)

Without describing her prophesying, the Bible made Miriam the first female *prophet*[1] (Exod. 15.20).[2] Unnamed, in Egypt she helped to save the saviour, i.e. the threatened infant Moses (Exod. 2.1–10), initiating the discourse with Pharaoh's daughter, who made him her own (Exod. 2.7). Sister of Moses and of Aaron,[3] she was leader in the triumph at the Sea of Reeds (Exod. 15.20–1: Burns 1987: 11–40; Meyers 1991, 1994; Bird 1997: 95–6). Nevertheless, as the questioner of Moses' unparalleled authority (Num. 12.1–7) Miriam emerged subsequently as one who was punished, polluted, paradigmatic (Num. 13.9–15; cf. Deut. 24.8–9), thereafter silent in the Bible texts (Graetz 1994). She died and was buried in Kadesh (Num. 20.1)[4] with no mourning at her death (contrast that for Aaron and Moses, Num. 20.24–9; Deut. 34.8),[5] no acknowledged successor (contrast Num. 20.25–8; Deut. 34.9; Josh. 1.2–3).[6] Hers was a 'bit-part' in the biblical account of the exodus–wilderness story.

1. Thereafter Deborah (Judg. 4.4), Huldah (2 Kgs 22.14–20), Noadiah (Neh. 6.14). See Ackerman (2002: 48–55) and the literature there.
2. Cf. Num. 12.2, 6. Post-biblical Jewish traditions expanded on her prophesying, e.g. *b. Sotah* 12a–13a; *b. Baba Bathra* 120a; Pseudo-Philo *Liber Antiquitatum Biblicarum* (hereafter *Ant. Bib.*) 9.9–10; 9.15; *Mekilta* Tractate *Shirata* 10.59.
3. The 'sister of Aaron' in Exod. 15.20; 1 Chron. 6.3, and sister to Aaron and Moses in Num. 26.59, cf. Exod. 6.20 (LXX). She appears also in Num. 12.1–15; 20.1; 26.59; Deut. 24.8–9; Mic. 6.4. Rarely do the three appear together in the Torah.
4. Miriam died by the kiss of God (*b. Baba Bathra* 17a). Soon afterwards Aaron and Moses died.
5. Jewish tradition notes the 'mourning' of nature, as lack of water followed in the text (Num. 20.2).
6. It is this lack of succession etc. which Carol Ochs addresses in her modern *midrash* on 'Miriam's Way' (1995/6).

Given well-documented problems in determining the historical reliability of
exodus and wilderness accounts it is as well for my purposes that the end of the
story was not, and is not, the end of the story. Miriamic traditions continued to
resonate through the centuries[7] and were used for a variety of rhetorical, religious
and ecclesiological ends.[8] It would be possible to examine as a 'theme' the person of, and incidents relating to, Miriam – traced through a variety of genres of
interpretative discourse – from pulpits ancient (including that of John Chrysostom and Peter Abelard), early modern and modern, through patristic writings
and ecclesiastical documents (Young 1995). Yet much of it would turn over the
same ground. Description and comparison are fundamental for discerning the
history of exegesis, and 'to track the unoriginality of commentators' is part of the
task, as Thompson observed (2001: 8). However my intention is more modest.

It was born of noticing references to Miriam in early Christian and seventeenth-
century discourse about women and public ministry (Trevett 2000).[9] Also the
texts about her touched on such matters as where God stands in relation to the
maimed and the excluded; sustenance (spiritual and physical); where public
religion, priesthood and a woman's ministry meet. Such things, along with the
use of Scripture, have been the stuff of Frances Young's life and many writings,
so Miriam seemed a resonant subject to choose. Yet it will become clear that in
fact I am not expounding on these things in what follows and that it does not
illustrate well that inseparability of theology, exegesis of Scripture and spirituality which Frances Young has discovered through patristic study (2002: 265).

This piece can not show the Fathers' fusion of great themes nor relate to
panegyrics – there is no eulogy to study, no *Life* of Miriam. In the figure of
Miriam we are dealing with one example (and exemplar) plucked from the
deposit of Scripture to which Christian writers looked, and from which patterns
in moral casuistry were derived. Jewish exegesis made more of her. I shall con-
centrate mostly on material of the first to fourth centuries, acknowledging also
the midrashic treatments of Miriam's story which take us past those centuries.[10] I
will point to one aspect of an anti-heretical Christian hermeneutic which involved
Miriam, who was a 'wilderness woman'. Much of what was said of her related to
accounts of post-exodus wilderness wanderings. Moreover, like politicians in

7. Though in the case of the Moses nativity story it was referred to nowhere else in the Hebrew
Bible. Cohen (1993: 5–8) describes its *genre* as a legendary tale, different from, and perhaps later
than, accounts of exile in Egypt and time in the wilderness. A figure assumed to be Miriam appears
in the fresco of the discovery of Moses, taken from the third-century Dura-Europos synagogue.

8. 'A narrative once set in motion is no longer entirely in the control of its author. It takes on
its own life' (Rosen 1996: 423–4).

9. Examples include Margaret Fell (1666), *Women's Speaking Justified, Proved and Allowed
from the Scriptures* (London: no printer); Elizabeth Bathurst (1695), *The Sayings of Women Which
Were Spoken on Sundry Occasions* (London: Tace Sowle) and several in George Fox (1998), *A
Collection of Many Select Epistles and Testimonies* (London: Tace Sowle).

10. Neusner's reminder is apposite (1993: 13): 'For no document in the canon of Judaism as
produced in late antiquity is there a named author, let alone a clear-cut date of composition, a
defined place or circumstance in which a book is written.' Aggadic midrashim such as *Exod.
Rabbah* and *Num. Rabbah* make use of Tannaitic and other material but are later in date (Herr
1997).

their biographies, Miriam has also had 'wilderness years' – consigned, one sus-
pects, to the margins of what once was a fuller and now irrecoverable story in
which she had had a greater role.[11] The biblical Miriam, not one of the matriarchs, neither an anti-heroine (such as Potiphar's wife or Jezebel[12]) nor a heroine
of the people (as was Esther, Rahab or Deborah), has not attracted much attention
from modern writers. Phyllis Trible (1989) determined on 'Bringing Miriam out
of the Shadows' by employing 'the play of many methods but the dogmatism of
none', but in relation only to the Hebrew Bible. So far as I know Miriam as
treated in early Christian writings has received no comment.[13]

Miriam and the Bible Text

Canonical sources must be my first concern, and it is hard to escape the impression that in the Bible there is 'something missing' where Miriam is concerned.
On three occasions she figured in narratives whose form and textual difficulties
have suggested to scholars the conflation of sources, radical editing and the
demotion of this woman in the tradition, to the advantage of Moses[14] (Coats
1982: 97–8; Halpern-Amaru 1988: 168).[15] *First*, Moses' unnamed 'sister' (Exod.
2.4) stood close by and spoke for an infant who was (so the text also anoma-
lously implied) the *firstborn* to his parents (Exod. 2.1–2).[16]

Secondly, in the so-called *Song of Moses* (Exod. 15.1–18) which recorded
poetically the demise of the Egyptians in their pursuit of the Hebrews, 'Moses
and the Israelites' sang (15.1). But then (15.20) in a short repetition based on
15.1, so did 'Miriam the prophetess, Aaron's sister', timbrel in hand, with all the
women going forth after her. This sudden intrusion of Miriam's victory song[17] ('a
jarring way to organize the text', Trible 1995: 16) has long aroused suspicions
that she, and not Moses, had at an earlier stage in the tradition been singer of the
longer poem. Moreover, in the statement that 'she sang *to them*' the referent is
unclear. The responsive singing involved women, but the Hebrew for 'them' is a
masculine pronoun.

Thirdly, Numbers 12 offered an opaque account of Miriam and Aaron who
'spoke against' Moses (cf. *1 Clem.* 30.1, 3; 35.5). This narrative is important for

---

11. The idea of wilderness as romantic, utopian, the place of testing and lack of compromise is
not my concern. See e.g. Louth (1991) and Oelschlaeger (1991).

12. Cf. too the Midianite women in Josephus, *Ant.* IV.129–30 (Num. 25.1–9); Halpern-Amaru
(1988: 144–5, 153–6).

13. Thompson (2001: 6) notes that few have 'looked at the careers of … women's stories in the
history of interpretation', but Miriam was not one of his concerns.

14. There are interesting insights on Moses in and beyond the biblical tradition in Britt (2003).

15. Scholars have detected redactional oddities (Margoliot 1983; Sakenfield 1985) even in the
narrative which begins with Miriam's death (Num. 20.1) and which had death as a recurring theme
(Num. 20.1–4; 24–8). See too Culley and Ben-Amos (1990).

16. 'Her presence introduces a heroine whom the narrative cannot assimilate. Her appearance
comes as a surprise' (Cohen 1993: 21 n. 34). See too Leach (1983: 42–3). Certainly many of the
later traditions serve to explain the existence of older children.

17. See Burns (1987: 11–40).

my purposes and it included *Miriam*'s (but not Aaron's) punishment with a skin disease – an anomaly or injustice which has exercised commentators ever since.[18] Their criticism of Moses was said to have been on account of 'the Cushite woman' (Moses' foreign wife) and Miriam was named first of the two critics.[19] The verb describing their challenge (12.1), however, was feminine and singular (Noth 1962: 93; Burns 1987: 68, 92; Phillips 1998: 78–9).[20] Consequently commentators have assumed the subject order and verbal form to be pointers to Miriam as instigator of the challenge.[21] This challenge to Moses was also linked, in a less-than-clear manner, with the matter of oracular authority, whether prophetic or priestly:

> Has the Lord indeed spoken only through Moses? Has he not also spoken through us?
> (Num. 12.2)

As Eryl Davies has written recently, 'There are some indications in the Hebrew Bible to suggest that Miriam occupied a position of prominence and prestige in Israel' (2003: 86), yet 'the very texts that hint at Miriam's significance at the same time manage to undercut it'.[22] More than forty years ago Martin Noth was surely correct:

> Aaron and Miriam belong in the tradition to a group of those figures surrounding Moses about whom only remnants of an originally much richer tradition remain and whose originally independent role we can no longer detect. (Noth 1962: 122–3)

Still the tenacity of Miriamic traditions overcame the editorial tendency to bury them in entirety. Some writers have surmised that the 'richer tradition' and 'independent role' of Miriam had concerned (among other things) her priestly status. This will be considered next.

Aaron was both priest and prophet (Exod. 7.1; 29.30). The isolated reference to Aaron's sister as prophet (Exod. 15.20) neatly distanced her from priesthood. The seemingly fanciful surmise, that Miriam too might originally have been a priestly figure, seems less improbable given the hotly debated opaque passage (Exod. 4.24–6) in which Moses was rescued again. Zipporah, Moses' wife and

---

18. *Sifre Num.* 105 hinted briefly that Aaron had become leprous.

19. Only in Num. 12.1 is a 'Cushite' referred to. Usually the region concerned (Cush) is Ethiopia (as Isa. 18.1; 20.3 *et passim*; Jer. 13.23 and elsewhere in the prophets), and the LXX unambiguously used the word 'Ethiopian' in Num. 12.1 (so too the Vulgate: see Barton 2001). 'Cush', however, might also signify the area of Midian (e.g. Hab. 3.7) and Zipporah, who is identified with 'the Cushite' in a number of Jewish traditions, was a Midianite (Exod. 2.15–22). The text's explanatory 'for he had married a Cushite woman' (omitted in the Vulgate) speaks of editorial recognition that this tradition was late and not well known. In Judg. 1.16 and 4.11 Moses was said to have had a Kenite father-in-law. Evidently there were traditions about a foreign wife or wives, though the details are not now recoverable.

20. In Hebrew, however, where a verb has more than one subject the subject standing closest may sometimes determine the verbal form.

21. Any suggestion of impurity befalling Aaron, the paradigmatic priest, would surely not have been tolerated by the priestly circles to which we owe much in the text. In *Sifre Num.* 105, R. Judah ben Baterah challenged a claim about Aaron's own leprosy.

22. Cf. too Plaskow (1990: 38–9).

daughter of the Midianite priest Jethro (Exod. 2.16; 3.1; 18.1),[23] circumcised
Gershom their son (Exod. 4.24) and perhaps Moses ('the bloody bridegroom')
too.[24] If she and the Cushite woman were one and the same, commentators
surmise, Miriam's complaint[25] may have related to the exercise of priestly power
('has not the Lord spoken through us ...?') and concerns about cultic purity now
threatened by Moses' marriage to a foreign woman. 'The text implicated Miriam
in cultic affairs', as Trible observed (1989: 21).[26]

The matter was considered more fully (and with reference to earlier literature)
by Burns (1987: 48–76), noting theories that underlying the present text (edited
in priestly circles) lay either conflict between Aaronic and Levitical priesthoods
or a prophet–priest conflict. Miriam stood either for the prophetic type and was
indeed associated with 'cultic affairs' or (as Burns maintained, 1987: 78–9), she
functioned in Num. 12.2–9 (a controversy about oracular authority) not as a *prophetic* oracular figure[27] but rather, with Aaron, as one representing the (Aaronic)
priestly group in dispute with the Levites (Moses).[28] The outcome was God's
assertion of a unique 'mouth-to-mouth' relationship with Moses, while Miriam's
punishment put her beyond the pale of ritual purity.

For seven days Miriam was 'outside the camp'. In this exclusion in Num. 12
there was, O'Donnell Setel has suggested (1992: 32), 'a legendary condensation'
of Miriam's exclusion from priesthood, with her seven-day separation reversing
the priest's seven days of consecration (Exod. 29.35).[29] In the earlier work Burns
had acknowledged, however, that the case for this woman originally having been
a priestly figure had to remain unproven (1987: 98–100, 122).

The sparse biblical traditions about Miriam were the products of revision and
editing. Only timbrels and song (Burns 1987: 11–40), being 'sister' to Aaron (the
later figurehead of priesthood), the title 'prophet' and an interest in matters of
authority and marital arrangements survived to hint at what earlier traditions may
have said of a more diverse and significant role in the cult. To look at matters
another way, in the Bible's Exodus and Numbers narratives the liminal state of
Miriam's people, caught ambiguously and without certainty between the *already*
and the *not yet*, and in the 'betwixt and between' liminal region of wilderness
(Leach 1983: 37, 41; Ackerman 2002: 64–71), matched the state of Miriam

---

23. Exod. 2.16–22 and perhaps Num. 10.20–32 identifies him as Reuel.

24. 'Feet' (as in Exod. 4.25) is a common euphemism for genitalia. The word for *bridegroom*
may also indicate father-in-law and the referent is not clear. The literature on Exod. 4.24–6 is
extensive. See for introduction Ackerman (2002: 72–4).

25. As Davies (2003: 65) notes, the form of the Hebrew, with *only* and *also* in close proximity,
indicates that the complaint was 'most emphatic'. See too Davies (1995: 113–26).

26. Some years later Trible was stating more categorically that 'Most probably, the attack impli-
cates Miriam in a struggle over the priestly leadership of Moses' (2000: 128).

27. Burns (1987: 70) sees the single biblical reference to Miriam as prophet (Exod. 15.20) as 'a
loosely-applied anachronistic term which stemmed from a need to define Miriam's role'.

28. 'The writer, then, appears to cast Miriam as belonging to Israel's priestly personnel' (Burns
1987: 99). Burns and others have posited an association with a sanctuary at Kadesh (Num. 20.1),
where Miriam was buried (1987: 99).

29. Thereafter a 'disempowered' Miriam reappears only in her dying (Ackerman 2002: 80).

herself. This Bible character moved from the distanced and unnamed person of Exodus 2 to one who was temporarily 'outside the camp' because of her claim (Num. 12.14).[30] Nevertheless there remained Mic. 6.4 and Miriam's inclusion in the genealogies of Num. 26.60 and 1 Chron. 5.29 (MT and LXX). These listed her among the children of Amram,[31] suggestive, perhaps, of there once having existed a further pool of Miriamic traditions in which she was 'parallel with Moses and Aaron' (Burns 1987: 97).

Miriam and Post-biblical Jewish Traditions

In some respects subsequent Jewish writings retrieved for her a little of that respected place which the ambiguities of the Bible suggest she may once have enjoyed. The prophesying of Miriam (*Mariam*, LXX), the elder sister (Cohen 1993: 117–19) was now evident. She had foreseen the greatness of Moses (*Mekilta* Tractate *Shirata* 10.59; Pseudo-Philo, *Ant. Bib.* 9.10; *b. Meg.* 14a; *b. Sotah* 13a (Cohen 1993: 102–4, 117) and the rabbis contrived/derived moral lessons, as exegetes questioned the text.[32] They told of her intervention, encouraging marriage and procreation among her fearful people in Egypt,[33] without which Moses would not have been born at all.

Cultural assumptions and an interest in moral types had fed first-century treatment of Miriam. Philo of Alexandria in the *Vita* (his *Life of Moses*) made of the pure Miriam 'not a typical female' (Wegner 1991: 56–7).[34] Josephus (*Ant.* II.212–16) in some respects marginalized Miriam in favour of Amram, as part of 'the general trend of later sources to give the father greater weight' (Cohen 1993: 32).[35] Thus it had been Amram who (like Joseph the father of Jesus) learned of the child's future role as saviour, and through a dream. Josephus nevertheless enhanced the account of Miriam's death and burial (*Ant.* IV.78). The former was relocated to mountain from wilderness (with no reference to Kadesh, cf. Num. 20.1) and her burial was a formal public affair, followed by thirty days of mourning.[36]

---

30. Ackerman (2002) suggests that the narrative located Miriam's identity as a prophet in 'a liminal period of anti-structure' when gender conventions might be suspended. The same might be said of a priestly role also.

31. 'The only woman named in post-exilic genealogies of the Aaronic priesthood who is not someone's wife or mother…the memory of Miriam was alive during the latest periods of composition of the canonical books' (Burns 1987: 97 and n. 43).

32. It is beyond the scope of this piece to consider parallels between Hellenistic and rabbinic treatments of texts and exegesis. See for introduction Neusner (1990); Young (2002: 91–4).

33. A number of the *midrashim* speak of ways in which procreation was hindered in the days of the Hebrews' enslavement in Egypt (Cohen 1993: 87–91).

34. Wegner's distinction (1991: 65) between the 'Hellenistic culture' (which mediated those 'Greek ideas' so in evidence in Philo's work) and the inherited Jewish scriptures should not be emphasized, given that Judaism, its scriptures (already widely read in Greek) and other religious writings were not un-'Hellenic'.

35. See too Halpern-Amaru (1988: 157). Pseudo-Philo (*Bib. Ant.*) is notable in terms of this tendency. See Cohen (1993: 39, 43–4, 48).

36. Josephus also relocated the ritual of the red heifer for corpse-contact uncleanness. It had

Josephus' incorporation of *midrash* in his *Antiquities* bore witness to its antiquity, but in Hellenistic fashion biblical women were also made personifications
of virtues and 'idealized abstractions'.[37] Thus as one writer has observed:

> The context (historical narrative) and form (idealized typologies) of Josephus' portray-
> als reflect his hellenistic world; the exegetical method reflects his peculiarly Jewish
> one. In his midrashic treatment of biblical women the two worlds are substantively and
> structurally interwoven. (Halpern-Amaru 1988: 170)

In retelling such tales at the end of the first century, Josephus was looking to
the tastes of his prospective readers and the standards of contemporary Hellenistic histories (Cohen 1993: 52).[38] Questions of power were minimized, in
that by omission of elements which the Bible account had contained, Moses'
position was not in jeopardy.[39] Thus while Miriam made reasoned conversation
with Pharaoh's daughter (*Ant.* II.226), Josephus omitted reference to her song
as leader at the Sea of Reeds and her challenge (with Aaron) to Moses.[40]

Other concerns emerged in Pseudo-Philo's pre-100 CE *Bib. Ant.* (9.9).[41] Notably its polemic against both idolatry and intermarriage spoke of a readership
among which there was close contact between Jews and Gentiles. The author[42]
recorded that Miriam received God's spirit and prophesied: the one to be cast
into the water would also be the leader who would cause waters to dry up (*Bib.
Ant.* 9.10).[43] Yet again portions of Miriam's story were omitted, e.g. her watch
over the infant Moses[44] and there was no mention of Moses' marriage to the
daughter of a Midianite priest in this source.[45]

Two themes (a) of encouraging procreation (which has no place in the Bible
text) and (b) of challenge, recur in the Miriamic traditions. According to a
Tannaitic tradition Miriam it was who had brought together again the divorced

---

preceded reference to her death (its ashes were kept 'outside the camp' for use in future purification: Num. 19.9). In *Ant.* III.79–81, however, the rite was introduced after mourning for Miriam.

37. Albeit 'not at the Philonic level' as Halpern-Amaru was eager to stress (1988: 143). See too
'Women in Precritical Exegesis: Figurative Readings', in Thompson (2001), 236–41.

38. Thus for example verisimilitude required that Miriam would have kept the infant's floating
basket in view *by walking along the river bank*, as he recorded.

39. See for example Cohn (1993: 52). Rabbinic traditions similarly assured Moses' prominence.
Cohen (1993: 132–5) discusses *Exod. Rabbah* 26.1, which 'skilfully transforms the [baby] Moses'
late appearance into an expression of his greater importance' (p. 135).

40. There was no confrontation with Zipporah over circumcision (Exod. 4.24).

41. Murphy (1993); DesCamp (1997). The extant Latin translation of this work has come via the
Greek from a probably Hebrew original.

42. DesCamp's 1997 treatment of the text is interesting but I am unconvinced by it that the
author of *Bib. Ant.* was a woman, though the suggestion was not original to DesCamp.

43. *Bib. Ant.* has been described as an aggadic midrash (Genesis to 2 Samuel), a description
other writers contest strongly.

44. By contrast that aspect of her story was expanded in the book of *Jubilees* so that Miriam
guarded him by day while his mother suckled him by night (*Jub.* 47.4). See Cohen (1993: 24–5,
39).

45. Pseudo-Philo's 'abiding worries over Jewish intermarriage' appears in relation to other
biblical women also. See Thompson (2001: 186).

Jocheved and Amram (*b. Sotah* 12a–13a; *b. Baba Bathra* 120a; see DesCamp 1997: 64–5). Amram and men who copied him had divorced their wives in the light of the decree about putting to death the male children (Exod. 1.22).[46] Pseudo-Philo, 'preoccupied with fecundity' though he was (DesCamp 1997: 79), never-theless made her father Amram the one who had challenged the decision to refrain from intercourse. Fear of slavery and idolatry for future offspring and of the use of Hebrew women (untouched by the decree to kill infants) in the breeding of slaves had fuelled the Hebrews' decision (*Bib. Ant.* 9.1–8; DesCamp 1997: 64–5).

Other writings preserved the picture of Miriam as one who challenged and rebuked. *Exod. Rabbah* 1.13 made the girl child one who rebuked even Pharaoh and the rabbis interpreted Miriam's rebuke of Moses as being *on behalf of* 'the Cushite'[47] and (taking clues from Exodus) in defence of fecundity and husbandly duty. The neglected Zipporah, it was said (*Sifre Num.* 99), had ceased to expect her gifted husband's interest in her (Neusner 1993: 65–76; Phillips 1998: 80–2; DesCamp 1997: 64–5).[48]

For Jews aggadic *midrashim* continued to fill the gaps in the biblical accounts (Cohen 1993: 46–59), variously including consideration of characters' motiva-tion, making more central the marginal, posing questions and answering them, accounting too for discrepancies in the material, while in dialogue with it (Phillips 1998: 78–88; Steinmetz 1988). In various ways the rabbis enhanced Miriam's role as described in the Bible and ensured that she manifested those virtues and concerns which befitted the Jewish woman (Neusner 1993: 65–7; Bronner 1994: 169–70). The rabbis identified Miriam with Puah, one of the midwives who had tried to foil Pharaoh's destructiveness (Exod. 1.15; *Exod. Rabbah* 1.13; Rashi, *b. Sotah* 11b).[49] The Miriam of post-biblical literature was indisputably married, whether to Hur (Josephus, *Ant.* III.54;[50] cf. Exod. 17.10–12), or to Caleb (1 Chron. 2.19: and so was identified with Azubah).[51]

Physically marred as punishment and excluded as she had been, the people nevertheless had waited for Miriam before moving on through the wilderness (Num. 12.15–16). The midrash-makers saw significance in this. Liberated from slavery, healed and purified from sickness Miriam retained a place in Jewish imagination as one who nurtured and guided.[52] Notably she lived on in the hopes,

46. The refusal of procreation thus sentenced potential *female* as well as male children, Miriam observed. She sang and danced at her parents' remarriage. On this remarriage see Cohen (1993: 117–21).

47. Rabbinical writing generally was favourably disposed towards Miriam (Graetz 1994: 235).

48. *Sifre Num.* 103 on Num. 12 reads 'mouth to mouth I instructed him to give up procreation' (Neusner 1993: 75). The command to keep apart from women in Exod. 19.2 was his and not God's. In Exod. 18.2 Zipporah and their sons had been sent away.

49. See Cohen (1993: 16 n. 26). The dominant tendency in interpretation was to make the midwives Hebrews and not Egyptians (Cohen 1993: 92–5, and the literature there).

50. Moses' upraised arms in the battle against the Amalekites were supported by Aaron and (H)ur, according to Josephus. The rabbis made him her son and not her husband, however.

51. She was mother to Hur (*Exod. Rabbah* 1.17; cf. too Josephus *Ant.* III.105). Neusner (1993: 13–15, 75–86).

52. The announcement of her death appeared between (a) prescriptions suggesting cleansing

spirituality and self-definition of Jewish women (Ochs 1995; Frankel 1996: 226–7).[53] Motifs of Wisdom, salvation and nurturing combined in traditions about the Well of Miriam.[54] This had been among the phenomena created on the eve of the first Sabbath (*M. Avot* 5.6; *b. Ta'an* 9a) and it appeared miraculously because of her: 'the well was in the merit of Miriam…when Miriam died the well subsided' (cf. Num. 20.1–2).

Miriam and Christian Writers

Moses was significant as type and exemplar in Christian exegesis, and Miriam played little role. The other Miriam/Maryam (Mary) in the Christian tradition was the prophetic singer of the *Magnificat*. Given the Evangelist's presentation of a Moses-like infancy for Jesus (Mt. 1.18–2.18)[55] that same Mary was a woman who had been present (like Miriam) through the danger to a threatened infant and an exile in Egypt. Luke's Mary, according to some MSS of Lk. 2.4, was also a descendant of David (cf. Lk. 1.27; Mt. 1.16).[56] Miriam had been his ancestress (according to *Sifre Num.* 78; *Exod. Rabbah* 48.3–4).[57] If Christian tradition built no substantial association (Le Deaut 1964) in the Qur'an there was conflation of the figures of Miriam and of Maryam, the latter being both 'Aaron's sister' and the virgin mother of Jesus (Sura 19.29).[58]

Aspects of the Miriam traditions continue to interest modern Christian commentators nevertheless, who may be drawn into the text in seeking truth from it. Numbers 12 (Miriam and 'the Cushite woman') speaks again in *Womanist* biblical commentary. From the (assumed) blackness of the Cushite and the white-as-snow-ness of the punished Miriam there may be derived God's word on oppression and vulnerability,[59] and Zipporah ('the Cushite'[60]) becomes one who

from leprosy (cedar wood, hyssop, scarlet thread, cf. Lev. 14.1–9) and corpse-contact (cf. Num. 12.12, 'let her not be as one dead') and (b) the statement that there was then a lack of water (Num. 20.1–2). Subsequently the people complained against Moses. This portion, Trible ventured (1995: 20), 'counters the vendetta against her'.

53. Cf. Rosen (1996: 423–4): 'I want midrash … to be an advocate for biblical figures over whom the ages have kicked considerable dust … Miriam …honored yet by-passed …'

54. Frankel (1996: Prologue xv–xviii, 226–7). Ginzberg's 7-volume *Legends of the Jews* (see index) cites such traditions.

55. Embellished accounts of the birth and infancy of Moses are found in Josephus, the Babylonian Talmud and midrashim. Moses is prototype of the Messiah. Similarities and differences in relation to the Matthaean nativity story are considered in Cohen (1993: 157–71) and see Allison (1993).

56. *Mary*'s Davidic ancestry is significant in e.g. the *Protoevangelion of James* 10.1 (Cohen 1993: 171–6), for Tertullian in *Adv. Jud.* 9.26 (Dunn 2001) and elsewhere.

57. By identifying Miriam with Azubah, wife of Caleb (*b. Sotah* 11b–12a) the rabbis were drawing her into the Davidic line. This and her concern about procreation (continuity) and perhaps intermarriage is considered by Steinmetz (1988). Cf. Phillips (1998).

58. This is variously accounted for by scholars of Islam. Cf. Suras 3.31; 23.52; 66.11–12 (where Mary/Maryam is juxtaposed with the wife of Pharaoh). The sister who watched over the infant Moses was unnamed in Suras 20.41–2; 28.10–12.

59. 'Many of us see a connection between Miriam harassing her sister-in-law because of the

makes liberation possible (Barton 2001: 77–8). It is the early Christian centuries which concern me, however.

The accounts of the wilderness generation were used to provide instructional examples (e.g. 1 Cor. 10.1–11).[61] The events of Exodus, Reed Sea crossing and wilderness wanderings prefigured events in the life of Christ and of the Church (Exod. 17.6 // 1 Cor. 10.1–4; Num. 21.9; and Exod. 12.3–10 // Jn 3.14 and 19.36).[62] And while echoes of Miriam's association with liturgy and celebration (cf. Pss. 81.2; 149.3–4; 150.4; Anderson 1987) were not to the fore, matters of authority, ecclesiology and a woman's place were. Miriam's association with Moses and her clear demotion in favour of his enhancement moulded exegetical assumptions.[63]

By citing Miriam's ambition and punishment both Clement of Rome in his late-first-century letter to Corinth (*1 Clement*) and the later *Apostolic Constitutions* warned against schism, and threat to rightful church leadership (*1 Clem.* 4.11; *Ap. Const.* 6.1–2).[64] The exhortatory use of the Bible permeated *1 Clement*.[65] There we find the 'collage' (as Frances Young termed it) of allusive phrases, mixed quotations and echoes, as also mimetic use of exemplars male and female, exemplifying tendencies worthy of imitation 'rather as the classics did in Hellenistic literature' (Young 2002: 227). The Roman church was deploring the friction-creating, faction-mongering jealousy/rivalry which had led (so its deliberative rhetoric affirmed)[66] to the deposing of properly constituted leaders in Corinth.

Biblical figures were cited, examples of righteousness and meekness, hospitality[67] and courage, among them Abraham and Lot, Noah and Enoch and the women Rahab, Judith and Esther. Suffering had come of factious rivalry, both under the Christian dispensation (Peter and Paul, *1 Clem.* 5.2–7) and in the exodus and wilderness period (Moses, Dathan and Abiram: *1 Clem.* 4.10–12 // Exod. 2.14; Num. 16). Briefly alluded to, the one female *perpetrator* of such rivalry had been Miriam:

---

colour of her black skin and herself becoming as white as snow with leprosy' (Barton 2001: 74; cf. Ben-Culley and Amos 1990: 40). The text 'played significantly in religious debates over interracial marriage' (Sakenfeld 1992: 47–9).

60. See Neusner (1993: 66–7) on the rabbinic treatment of 'Cushite', which relates to 'difference' of a superior kind, and not skin colour.

61. There without reference to Miriam. On Paul's deliberative rhetoric and 'proof by cumulative example' Mitchell (1992: 40) and the literature there.

62. Simonetti (1994: 10–13), commenting on Pauline *type* and allegory.

63. Phillips (1998) reflected on the exaltation of Moses *and of Torah* in the Jewish traditions.

64. Also titled *Ordinances of the Holy Apostles through Clement*, a composite, probably Syrian, fourth-century document of ecclesiastical laws.

65. 'Packed with scriptural allusion, or, if not allusion, language that can be paralleled in scriptural material' (Young 2002: 222). On this, Miriam, etc. in *1 Clement*, see Trevett (2005: pt. 1) and the literature there.

66. On Clement's deliberative rhetoric and for examples, Mitchell (1992: 40–1), noting analogies with Paul in 1 Corinthians. Bowe (1988) and Lampe (2003: ch. 1) consider rhetorical genre.

67. Refusal to 'receive' some Christians seems to have figured in the action in Corinth. For full discussion and literature see Trevett (2005: pt. 1).

> Through jealousy Aaron and Miriam were lodged outside the camp. (*1 Clem.* 4.11)

According to the Bible text, of course, Aaron had not been so lodged, but the story had indeed been about complaint (that power was improperly monopolized). Clement used the 'insider/outsider' language in which *the camp* (of Israel) was the boundary. By implication he was warning the Corinthians that rivalry and challenge to legitimate leadership, such as might fracture a community, were punishable by separation from the elect[68] (LXX Num. 12.8[69]). This was the crux of the matter. Aaron and Miriam had unjustly criticized Moses,[70] who, according to the carefully created biblical text, had possessed in abundance the leader's virtue of meekness which (Christian and other) writers praised.[71] In Corinth (as the Roman church's rhetoric insisted) the deposed presbyters had had God-given appointments and (like Moses) had never been overbearing or blameworthy in their service.

In women meekness went with a silent tongue (*1 Clem.* 21.6–7):

> Let us lead our wives to that which is good. Let them exhibit the lovely habit of purity, let them show forth the innocent will of meekness, let them make the gentleness of their tongue manifest by their silence. (tr. K. Lake)

Miriam was the paradigm of *female* non-compliant rivalry, her expulsion a warning to all.

In the *Apostolic Constitutions* (Bradshaw 1992: 80–110; Young 2002: 224–6[72]) the 'collage' approach to paraenesis incorporated Miriam among its spiritually gifted women. She stood first in a list of female prophets, as she would have done in terms of canonical order of biblical texts. Yet in the portion of *Ap. Const.* given to the lifestyle of women the Christian unease emerges. She also had to be of the moral type of *humble* women of Spirit. They did not try to elevate themselves above their husbands (*Ap. Const.* 8.2).[73]

It is the Alexandrian tradition which is most fruitful for my purposes. Clement (*Strom.* 4.19), when praising both sexes, declared that 'Moses' sister… the prophet's associate in commanding the host', exceeded all the Hebrew women reputed for wisdom (contrast *Strom.* 1.23, echoing a point made by Philo).[74]

---

68. On being 'outside the camp' contrast the (probably also Roman) letter *To the Hebrews*, turning upside-down Jewish insider–outsider analogies in response to dominical precedent.

69. Cf. *1 Clem.* 30.1; 30.3; 35.5.

70. In *Num. Rabbah* 16.6–7 Miriam serves as a warning to all who would slander.

71. Num. 12.3, cf. for example 2 Tim. 2.25; Tit. 3.2; *Did.* 15.1; Ignatius, *Trall.* 3.2. Clement drives the message home in 13.4, quoting Isaiah: 'On whom shall I look, but on the meek and gentle and him who trembles at my oracles' (tr. Lake). Cf. John Chrysostom's treatment of Moses and meekness in *Hom. 1 Cor.* 1.

72. 'this literature seems to become increasingly packed with scriptural language, allusion and quotation…the *Apostolic Constitutions* saturated' (Young 2002: 226).

73. In the prayer for the consecration of deaconesses she was one whom God had 'replenished with the Spirit' (*Ap. Const.* 20).

74. In *Strom.* 1.23 the cause of the female Hebrew children being spared was that women were unfit for war. Cf. Philo *De Vita Mosis* 1.8–9.

Philo's version of Moses' nativity had impacted on his treatment of the story,[75] but Miriam's part in it matched its minimality in Exodus.[76] Yet Miriam does recur in texts of a certain kind. Alexandrian sources of the third and fourth centuries preserved evidence of debate about Montanism's[77] championing of women in leadership. Miriam figured in this.

From the 160s onwards Montanism had swept swiftly from Phrygia through Rome, North Africa and elsewhere. Anti-Montanist writings (Heine 1989; Trevett 1996) and some surviving epigraphy (Tabbernee 1997) indicate that they defended a prophetic 'succession' (Trevett 1996: 32–6, 185–96),[78] that women were public prophets, then associated with offices of a number of kinds within the subgroups of fragmented later Montanism (Cataphrygians, Pepuzians, Quintillianists and so on). Montanists appealed to the scriptures in support of their practice: Cataphrygians defended women deacons by appeal to 1 Timothy (3.8–11), according to 'Ambrosiaster' in his (probably Roman, polemical and non-allegorical) Latin commentary on Paul's letters. The Quintillianists had women presbyters and bishops (Epiphanius of Salamis, *Pan.* 49.2.2–3) and were probably taking issue with prevailing exegesis of the Eden story and the denigration of Eve, pointing instead to her primacy in access to knowledge. In response Epiphanius mustered both Gen. 3.16 and 1 Tim. 2.14.[79] It is from him, too, that we learn of a class of female virgin prophets who ministered publicly in congregational settings, in gatherings full of enthusiasm, emotion and the language of repentance (*Pan.* 49.2).[80] This much is by way of introduction to Montanism.

The evidence about Miriam and Montanism occurs mostly in Egyptian sources of the third and fourth centuries, Origen (c. 185–251), Didymus the Blind (c. 313–98) *De Trin.* 3.41[81] and the anonymous author of the *Dialexis*, which was a contrived dialogue between an Orthodox and a Montanist Christian (Heine 1989: 98–9, 124–6, 144–5).[82]

First, however, I must return to Epiphanius' *Panarion* (48), which included the witness of an earlier anti-Montanist source. Probably originating in early-

---

75. On Philo's legacy in Clement and Origen see Young (2002: 68). See too Cohen (1993: 45–6).

76. In this portion of *Strom.* is also a long quotation from Ezekiel the Tragedian's drama *The Exodus*, which mentioned Miriam (cf. too Eusebius, *Praep. Ev.* 9.28.1–3; Cohen [1993: 32–40]).

77. The term *Montanism* is retained for convenience. Its earliest supporters probably knew it as *The New Prophecy*, in which Montanus and the women Priscilla and Maximilla were leading figures (Trevett 1996).

78. This should not be taken necessarily to imply hostility to the idea of apostolic succession.

79. Both Augustine and John of Damascus wrote of women of clergy class among Pepuzians/Quintillians (Augustine, *De Haer.* 27; 76; John of Damascus, *Haer.* 87).

80. Pointing to the shadow of socially disruptive Bacchic frenzy was a common counter to evidence of enthusiasm (*Pan.* 49.3). See Trevett (1996: 185–6).

81. The attribution of this work to Didymus is disputed. Much of his writing was lost after his condemnation as an Origenist, though in 1941 some biblical commentaries in sixth- or seventh-century codex form were discovered in Egypt, at Toura.

82. It was rich in appeal and counter-appeal to Paul (who in some respects was to be interpreted allegorically, the Orthodox affirmed) and to other biblical writers. On 'Scripture in the Alexandrian Milieu', see Simonetti (1994: 34–52).

third-century Asia Minor it had been directed at 'the heresy of the Phrygians' (Heine 1989: 26–51).[83] Its key concerns were spiritual gifts and authority, notably that of prophecy and prophets. It challenged the Montanists in rhetorical politicized fashion:

> O Phrygians … you have again risen up against us like enemies even though you have modelled yourselves on the name Christian, but you have entered upon a battle of barbarians and are imitating the hostility of the Trojans and Phrygians, how can we believe you, when you say you have separated from the Church because of spiritual gifts? (Epiphanius, *Pan.* 48.12.1, tr. Heine 1989: 47)

Two elements in this source hinted at Numbers 12 as part of the ammunition in the war of words between Montanists and catholics. These were (a) that in its case for reason and control in prophecy (against the *ekstasis* which allegedly characterized the Montanist kind) it had included Moses in a litany of examples of such control, God's servant who was faithful in his house (Num. 12.7; *Pan.* 48.3.4).[84] Also (b) in a passage castigating Maximilla's prediction about prophecy itself (*Pan.* 48.2.4–9; Trevett 1997), those who succumbed to the Montanists' teaching were described as 'outside the fold' (48.2.8 cf. 'camp' of Num. 12.14).[85] Montanists of Quintillian type, Epiphanius recorded, did cite the case of Miriam when defending the existence of female clergy (*Pan.* 49.2).

This source, then, especially when taken with others, suggests to me that the biblical Miriam, female prophet, public figure, challenger of authority, was one whose significance was disputed between catholics and Montanists. Origen, Didymus and the author of the *Dialexis* clarify matters further.

In the commentary on 1 Cor. 14.34–5 (preserved in *catenae*, Heine 1989: 99; Jenkins 1908) Origen made his case for the subordination and silence of women in churches. It included 'reasoned' reply to 'the disciples of the women who were instructed by Priscilla and Maximilla'. His language suggested appeal to exemplary types on the Montanists' part, in a paraenetic reading of biblical texts. We should not assume, however, that Origen was familiar with such arguments from real debates. Certainly he may never have met a Montanist.[86] And neither he nor those considered below tell us how a Montanist dissenting reception and appropriation of scriptures might have determined their stance, if what is described is more than just a rhetorical construction.

As Origen described matters the Montanists' case rested, in part at least, on female exemplars whose public roles came of being prophets. The daughters of Philip were mentioned (Acts 21.9[87]), 'Maryam the sister of Aaron', Deborah and Huldah, Anna the prophetess of Lk. 2.36. Origen responded negatively to this

---

83. Epiphanius, *Pan.* 48.1(or 2)–13 is the extent of the unidentified source, see Trevett (1996: 48 and 242 n. 6).

84. For Philo and Pseudo-Philo, including the inspired state/ecstasy and the rewriting of Moses in the wilderness, see Aune (1983: 147–51).

85. The passage contains a collage of allusions to fold/wolf/shipwreck.

86. On Origen's exegesis and 'enquiry at the lexical level', see Young (2002: 82–96).

87. The daughters of Philip figured in the 'succession list' of prophets to which the Montanists appealed. It is clear from second-century sources that these women had been revered in Asia Minor.

mimetic use of scriptural heroines, moving from the letter to the application in treatment of 'problem' texts,[88] explaining case by case in terms of correct reading and without recourse to 'symbolic' reading (Young 2002: 202–12). It was not female prophesying that he challenged but its exercise in certain contexts.

Undercutting the plausibility of the Montanists' claims he separated prophesying from 'speaking in churches' (Philip's daughters and Anna had not done the latter), and from public address generally. Deborah did not address the people as did Isaiah or Jeremiah, he maintained, discounting both address *to an individual* (private rather than public: Huldah, 2 Kgs 22.14)[89] and address *to women only* (i.e. Miriam's case, mentioned twice and based on a reading of Exod. 15.20). Her action was thus not relevant for a debate which really concerned authority over men (1 Tim. 2.12).[90]

Didymus the Blind, heir to the allegorical tradition (Young 1983: 83–91), presented a critique of several points of Montanist doctrine and practice, including its view of ongoing prophecy. Scripture, he declared, recognized as female prophets the four daughters of Philip (Acts 21.9), Deborah (Judg. 4.4), 'Maryam Aaron's sister' and Mary the mother of God (Heine 1989: 144–5; *De Trin.* 3.41.3). Such women had not been *writers* in their own names, however[91] – and he cited 1 Cor. 11.5, implying that the unacceptably unveiled head was a metaphor applicable to publicity-seeking, by writing and disseminating Montanist books. As in the *Dialexis* the use of Scripture was coloured by Trinitarian controversy (Trevett 1996: 218–19).

The *Dialexis*, which came of the same school (a) laid out more fully those Montanist arguments which Didymus' rhetoric had presupposed and addressed. Also (b) it made rhetorical play of the allegorical versus the 'plain sense' approach to Scripture (Young 2002: 292–6). While appealing to 1 Cor. 11.5, to Philip's daughters and Deborah, the Montanist accused the catholic side of denying the validity of female prophesying (Heine 1989: 124–5). The Orthodox denied such denial, citing respect for 'holy Maria' (Lk. 1.48) and 'Maria the sister of Aaron'. Nevertheless he did refuse to women the right to speak in churches, to have authority over men and to write books. In the ensuing debate about writing and public utterance (= the unveiled head) the Montanist eschewed appeal to allegory.[92]

In proclaiming 'all generations shall call me blessed' was Mary behaving in 'unveiled' fashion? The Orthodox responded in the negative, for when being

---

88. On Origen and Montanism elsewhere in his writings see Trevett (1996: 175). In Origen's *Homilies on Numbers* 6 and 8, Miriam represents the Synagogue.

89. In the English early-modern treatment of such biblical texts the various nuances of 'speaking' are explored (Trevett 2000). Miriam sometimes figures.

90. The private versus public dimension of Miriam's actions appears also in a *Qal wahomer* example in *Sifre Num.* 99.

91. *Writing* women may have been in Origen's mind, too, when he contrasted Deborah and Jeremiah/Isaiah.

92. The *Dialexis*, like Epiphanius, *Pan.* 49.2.1–5, indicates that the Montanist side appealed to Gal. 3.28 in defence of its women's roles.

quoted in a Gospel written by the (male) Evangelist Mary was 'veiled', this, declared the Montanist, was taking allegories as if they were doctrines![93]

The foregoing examples suggest that Miriam was looked to as a foremother for Montanist female prophesying, and for an authoritative female public ministry.[94] In passing, the examples also shed a modest light on some tendencies in exegesis. What principles lay at the root of Montanist treatment of Scripture? ('I believe in the Gospels' declared the Montanist in the *Dialexis*, and some anti-Montanist writers acknowledged their loyalty to the same scriptures as catholic Christians used.) In what forum did Montanists determine their exegetical strategies? Sometimes described as a 'Jewish Christian' movement, was Montanism in closer touch with certain kinds of Jewish tradition than were its catholic opponents? Such questions must wait for another time.

Bibliography

Ackerman, J. S.
  1974   'The Literary Context for Moses' Birth Story (Exodus 1–2)', in K. R. T. Gros Louis, *et al.* (eds.), *Literary Interpretation of Biblical Narratives* (Nashville, Tenn. and London: Abingdon Press and SPCK), 74–119.
  2002   'Why is Miriam Also Among the Prophets? (And is Zipporah Among the Priests?)', *JBL* 121, 47–80.
Allison, D. C.
  1993   *The New Moses: A Matthaean Typology* (Edinburgh: T&T Clark).
Anderson, B. W.
  1987   'The Song of Miriam Poetically and Theologically Considered', in E. R. Follis (ed.), *Directions in Biblical Hebrew Poetry* (JSOTSup, 40; Sheffield: JSOT Press), 284–96.
Aune, D. E.
  2002   *Prophecy in Early Christianity and the Ancient Mediterranean World* (Grand Rapids, Mich.: Eerdmans).
Barton, M.
  2001   'The Skin of Miriam Became as White as Snow: The Bible, Western Feminism and Colour Politics', *JSNT* 25, 68–80.
Bird, P. A.
  1997   *Missing Persons and Mistaken Identities: Women and Gender in Ancient Israel* (Minneapolis, Minn.: Fortress Press).
Bowe, B. E.
  1988   *A Church in Crisis: Corinth* (Cambridge, Mass.: Harvard Dissertations in Religion).
Bradshaw, P.
  1992   *The Search for the Origins of Christian Worship* (London: SPCK).

93. The Orthodox half-defended the practice, with reference to Gal. 4.22–4, before demanding response to a concrete, if hypothetical case of a woman too poor to own a head-covering. Frances Young has considered 'The Fourth-Century Reaction Against Allegory', in *Studia Patristica* 30 (1997): 120–5.

94. No example survives of gainsaying the absence of canonical female *writing* prophets. I have argued, however, that Firmilian of Caesarea's third-century picture of a prophesying, teaching, baptizing woman is modelled on a female Montanist (Trevett 1999).

Brenner, A.
   1985   *The Israelite Woman: Social Role and Literary Type in Biblical Narrative*
               (Sheffield: JSOT Press).

Brenner, A. (ed.)
   1994   *A Feminist Companion to Exodus–Deuteronomy* (Sheffield: Sheffield Aca-
               demic Press).

Britt, B.
   2003   *Rewriting Moses: The Narrative Eclipse of the Bible* (JSOTSup, 402; Sheffield:
               Continuum).

Bronner, L. L.
   1994   *From Eve to Esther: Rabbinic Reconstructions of Biblical Women* (Louisville,
               Ky.: Westminster/John Knox Press).

Brown, C.
   1992   *No Longer be Silent: First Century Jewish Portraits of Biblical Women:
               Studies in Pseudo–Philo's Biblical Antiquities and Josephus's Jewish Antiq-
               uities* (Louisville, Ky.: Westminster/John Knox Press).

Burns, R. J.
   1987   *Has the Lord Spoken Only Through Moses? A Study of the Biblical Portrait of
               Miriam* (SBLDS, 84; Atlanta, Ga: Scolars Press).

Coats, G. W.
   1968   *Rebellion in the Wilderness* (Nashville, Tenn.: Abingdon Press).
   1982   'Humility and Honor: A Moses Legend in Numbers 12', in D. J. A, Clines,
               D. M. Gunn and A. J. Hauser (eds.), *Art and Meaning: Rhetoric in Biblical
               Literature* (Sheffield: JSOT Press), 97–107.

Cohen, J.
   1993   *The Origins and Evolution of the Moses Nativity Story* (Suppl. to *Numen*, 58;
               Leiden: Brill).

Culley, R. C., and D. Ben-Amos
   1990   Culley, 'Five Tales of Punishment in the Book of Numbers', and response by
               Ben-Amos, in S. Niditch (ed.), 25–34, 35–46.

Davies, E. W.
   1995   *Numbers* (New Century Bible Commentary; London: Marshall & Pickering).
   2003   *The Dissenting Reader: Feminist Approaches to the Hebrew Bible* (Aldershot:
               Ashgate).

DesCamp, M. T.
   1997   'Why Are These Women Here? An Examination of the Sociological Setting of
               Pseudo-Philo Through Comparative Reading', *JSP* 16, 53–80.

Douglas, M.
   1993   *In the Wilderness: The Doctrine of Defilement in the Book of Numbers* (Shef-
               field: JSOT Press).

Dunn, J. D. G.
   2001   'The Ancestry of Jesus according to Tertullian: *ex David per Mariam*', *StudPat*
               36, 349–55.

Exum, J. C.
   1993   '"You Shall Let Every Daughter Live": A Study of Exodus 1:8–2:10', *Semeia*
               82, 63–82.
   1994   'Second Thoughts about Secondary Characters: Women in Exodus 1:8–2:10',
               in A. Brenner (ed.), 75–87.

Frankel, E.
   1996   *The Five Books of Miriam: A Woman's Commentary on the Torah* (New York:
               Grosset-Putnam).

Ginzberg, L.
1909–38   *The Legends of the Jews*, tr. H. Szold (7 vols.; Philadelphia: Jewish Publication Society of America).

Graetz, N.
1994   'Did Miriam Talk too Much?', in A. Brenner (ed.), 231–42.

Halpern-Amaru, B.
1988   'Portraits of Biblical Women in Josephus' *Antiquities*', *JJS* 39, 143–70.
1991   'Portraits of Women in Pseudo-Philo's *Antiquities*', in A. J. Levine (ed.), 83–106.

Heine, R. E,
1989   *The Montanist Oracles and Testimonia* (Macon, Ga.: Mercer University Press; Leuven: Peeters).

Herr, M. D.
1997   'Numbers Rabbah', 'Midrash', etc., in *Encyclopaedia Judaica* CD-ROM edn (Jerusalem: Keter).

Jantzen, J. G.
1992   'Song of Moses, Song of Miriam: Who is Seconding Whom?', *CBQ* 54, 211–21.

Jenkins, C.
1908   'Origen on 1 Corinthians', *JTS* 9, 231–47, 353–72, 500–14.

Kessler, R.
2001   ' Miriam and the Prophecy of the Persian Period', in A. Brenner (ed.), *Prophets and Daniel* (A Feminist Companion to the Bible, Second Series; London: Sheffield Academic Press), 77–86.

Laffey, A. I.
1990   *Wives, Harlots and Concubines: The Old Testament in Feminist Perspective* (London: SPCK).

Lake, K.
1930   *The Apostolic Fathers* (LCL; London: Heinemann).

Lampe, P.
2003   *From Paul to Valentinus: Christians at Rome in the First Two Centuries*, tr. M. Steinhauser from *Die Stadtrömischen Christen* (Augsburg: Fortress).

Leach, A.
1983   'Why did Moses have a Sister?', in A. Leach and D. A. Aycock (eds.), *Structuralist Interpretations of Biblical Myth* (Cambridge: Cambridge University Press), 33–66.

Le Deaut, R.
1964   'Miriam, sœur de Moïse, et Marie mère du Messie', *Biblica* 45, 198–219.

Levine, A. J. (ed.)
1991   *'Women Like This': New Perspectives on Jewish Women in the Greco-Roman World* (Atlanta, Ga.: Scholars Press).

Louth, A.
1991   *The Wilderness of God* (London: Darton, Longman & Todd).

Margoliot, M.
1983   'The Transgression of Moses and Aaron: Num. 20.1–3', *JQR* 74, 196–228.

Méhat, A.
1951   *Origen: Homélies sur les Nombres* (SC, 29; Paris: Editions du Cerf).

Meyers, C.
1991   'Of Drums and Damsels: Women's Performance in Ancient Israel', *Bib. Arch.* 54, 16–27.
1994   'Miriam the Musician', in A. Brenner (ed.), 207–30.

Mitchell, M. M.
  1992   *Paul and the Rhetoric of Reconciliation: An Exegetical Investigation of the Language and Composition of 1 Corinthians* (Louisville, Ky.: Westminster/John Knox Press).
Murphy, F. J.
  1993   *Pseudo-Philo: Rewriting the Bible* (New York and Oxford: Oxford University Press).
Neusner, J.
  1986   *Sifré to Numbers: An American Translation* (Brown Judaic Studies, 118/119; Atlanta, Ga.: Scholars Press).
  1990   *A Midrash Reader* (Minneapolis, Minn.: Fortress Press).
  1993   *How Judaism Reads the Torah*, vol. 3: *Wayward Women in the Wilderness: An Anthology of Sifré to Numbers* (Frankfurt am Main and New York: Peter Lang).
Newsom, C. A., and S. H. Ringe (eds.)
  1992   *The Women's Bible Commentary* (London and Louisville, Ky.: SPCK and Westminster/John Knox Press).
Niditch, S. (ed.)
  1990   *Text and Tradition: The Hebrew Bible and Folklore* (SBL Semeia Studies; Atlanta, Ga.: Scholars Press).
Noth, M.
  1962   *Exodus* (tr. J. S. Bowden; London: SCM Press).
Ochs, C.
  1995/6   'Miriam's Way', *Cross Currents* 45/4, 493–509.
O'Donnell Setel, D.
  1992   'Exodus', in C.A. Newsom and S.H. Ringe (eds.), 28–35.
Oelschlaeger, M.
  1991   *The Idea of Wilderness from Prehistory to the Age of Ecology* (New Haven and London: Yale University Press).
Phillips, E. A.
  1998   'The Singular Prophet and Ideals of Torah: Miriam, Aaron and Moses in Early Rabbinic Texts', in C. A. Evans and J. A. Sanders, (eds.), *The Function of Scripture in Early Jewish and Christian Tradition* (JSNTSup, 154; Sheffield: Continuum), 78–88.
Pinero, A.
  1991   'A Mediterranean View of Prophetic Inspiration in the *Liber Antiquitatum* by Pseudo-Philo', *Mediterranean Historical Review* 6, 5–34.
Plaskow, J.
  1990   *Standing Again at Sinai: Judaism from a Feminist Perspective* (San Francisco: Harper & Row).
Propp, W. H.
  1993   'That Bloody Bridegroom (Exodus iv.24–6)', *VT* 43, 495–518.
Robinson, B. P.
  1986   'Zipporah to the Rescue: A Contextual Study of Exodus 4:24–6', *VT* 36, 447–61.
Rosen, N.
  1996   'Midrash, Bible and Women's Voices', *Judaism* 45, 422–45.
Sakenfield, K. D.
  1985   'Theological and Redactional Problems in Numbers 20:2–13', in J. T. Butler *et al.* (eds.), *Understandng the Word* (JSOTSup, 37; Sheffield: Sheffield Academic Press), 133–54.
  1992   'Numbers', in Newsom and Ringe (eds.), 45–51.

Siebert Hommes, J.
    1994   '"But If She Be a Daughter...She May Live": "Daughters" and "Sons" in
                Exodus 1–2', in A. Brenner (ed.), 62–74.
Simonetti, M.
    1994   *Biblical Interpretation in the Early Church: An Historical Introduction to
                Patristic Exegesis* ET A. J. Hughes (Edinburgh: T&T Clark).
Steinmetz, D.
    1988   'A Portrait of Miriam in Rabbinic Midrash', *Prooftexts* 8, 35–65.
Tabbernee, W.
    1997   *Montanist Inscriptions and Testimonia: Epigraphic Sources Illustrating the
                History of Montanism* (Patristic Monograph Series, 16; Macon, Ga.: Mercer
                University Press).
Thackery, J. StJ.
    1930   *Josephus* (LCL; London: Heinemann).
Thompson, J. L.
    2001   *Writing the Wrongs: Women of the Old Testament Among Biblical Commen-
                tators from Philo Through the Reformation* (Oxford: Oxford University Press).
Trevett, C.
    1996   *Montanism: Gender, Authority and the New Prophecy* (Cambridge: Cambridge
                University Press).
    1997   'Eschatological Timetabling and the Montanist Prophet Maximilla', *Studia
                Patristica* 31, 218–24.
    1999   'Spiritual Authority and the "Heretical" Woman: Firmilian's Word to the
                Church in Carthage', in J. W. Watt and J. W. Drijvers (eds.), *Portraits of
                Spiritual Authority: Religious Power in Early Christianity, Byzantium and the
                Christian Orient* (Leiden: Brill), 45–62.
    2000   '"Holy tremblers": Quaker Prophet Preachers', and 'Like Apostles and Proph-
                ets of Old: Quaker Women and their Early Christian Foremothers', in *Quaker
                Women Prophets in England and Wales 1650–1700* (Lewiston and Lampeter:
                Edwin Mellen Press), 23–61, 63–104.
Forthcoming
    2005   *Christian Women and the Time of the Apostolic Fathers (pre 160 CE): Corinth,
                Rome and Asia Minor* (Cardiff: University of Wales Press).
Trible, P.
    1989   'Bringing Miriam Out of the Shadows', *Bible Review* 5/1, 14–25, 34.
    1995   'Eve and Miriam: From the Margins to the Center', in P. Trible, T. Frymer-
                Kensky, *et al.*, *Feminist Approaches to the Bible* (Washington, DC: Biblical
                Archaeological Society), 5–26.
    2000   'Miriam I', in C. Meyers (ed.), *Women in Scripture: A Dictionary of Named and
                Unnamed Women in the Hebrew Bible, the Apocryphal/Deuterocanonical Books
                and the New Testament* (Grand Rapids and Cambridge: Eerdmans), 127–9.
Wegner, J. R.
    1991   'Philo's Portrayal of Women: Hebraic or Hellenic?', in A.-J. Levine (ed.), 41–
                66.
Wright, J. H.
    1997   'Patristic Testimony on Women's Ordination in *Inter insigniores*', *Theological
                Studies* 58, 516–26.
Young, F. M.
    1983   *From Nicaea to Chalcedon* (London: SCM Press).
    1995   'Interpretative Genres and the Inevitability of Pluralism', *JSNT* 59, 93–110.
    2002   *Biblical Exegesis and the Formation of Christian Culture* (Peabody, Mass.:
                Hendrickson; repr. from Cambridge University Press edn, 1997).

WOMEN IN THE WILDERNESS
REREADING REVELATION 12

Diane Treacy-Cole

In the nineteenth century scholars of the history of religions school identified the symbol of the Woman Clothed with the Sun in Revelation 12 as a composite image with antecedents in the Hellenistic Isis legends or the Greek Leto myth. Commentators in the twentieth century generally accepted the identification.[1] While I would not disagree that the descriptions of the goddesses share similarities with the Woman in Revelation 12, I want to argue that the reader does not need to look beyond the Hebrew Bible to identify a precedent for this Apocalyptic Woman.

Revelation owes much to a mythopoetic restyling of Hebrew Bible motifs. The author/redactor of the Apocalypse draws on idealized themes or moments from Israelite history to remind the readers of God's saving acts in history and to exhort them in their present tribulation. Commentators cite numerous allusions to Isaiah and Daniel throughout the Apocalypse. Other scholars note the author's familiarity with Genesis and the use of Exodus typologies.[2] Motifs appearing in Revelation 12 with parallels in Genesis or the Exodus cycle include Joseph's dream of the sun, moon and stars (Gen. 37.9–11); the serpent (Gen. 3); the earth swallowing the flood (Exod. 15.12; cf. Num. 16.32–4); the great eagle (Exod. 19.4); the stars thrown down to earth (Dan. 8.10); and the miraculous feeding (Exod. 16.4–17.7).

It is curious then that the model for the Woman Clothed with the Sun is drawn from non-Jewish traditions. A pagan antecedent becomes less convincing as the source for this intriguing figure when the woman in Revelation 12 is described not as the Woman Clothed with the Sun, but as the Woman in the Wilderness.

---

1. Many commentaries refer to these two myths as the most likely models for the Woman Clothed with the Sun. See for example Charles (1920), Farrer (1964) and Yarbro Collins (1976). David Aune (1986) and Bruce Malina (1995) thoroughly investigate the astral imagery in their more recent commentaries. W. K.Hedrick's unpublished Berkeley Th.D. dissertation (1970) 'The Sources and Use of the Imagery in Apocalypse 12' contains a list of other examples. The Leto myth as a parallel to the Woman of Revelation 12 was first argued by A. Dieterich, *Abraxas: Studien zur Religionsgeschichte des spätern Altertums* (Leipzig, 1891), 217; and *Nekya: Beiträge zur Erklärung der Petrusapokalypse* (Leipzig, 1913), 217. See also Beasley-Murray (1974).

2. See commentaries in the bibliography.

In the annals of Israel's history there is another biblical woman who flees to the desert.[3] Hagar's wilderness experiences in Genesis 16 and 21 present striking similarities to the desert flights of the unnamed Woman in the Apocalypse. Like Hagar, the Woman in Revelation 12 flees to the wilderness in the first instance and remains there in the second. As the only two biblical women in the wilderness, the narrative of the Woman in the last book of the Bible invites comparison with the story of Hagar in the first.

Hagar in the Wilderness

The reader is introduced to Hagar in Genesis 16. She is identified as an Egyptian, a maid (*šipḥâ*) to Sarai, Abram's wife. In the second episode of this story in chapter 21 Hagar is no longer described as a handmaid, but as servant or slave (*'amâ*) to Sarah. This change in status is reflected in the character of the corresponding flight to the wilderness.[4] In the first instance Hagar seizes the initiative, while in the second her fate is determined by another's action.

In chapter 16 Hagar offends her mistress as a consequence of the very act that Sarai has advocated. Hagar becomes Abram's wife (v. 3) and conceives a child. Despite her pregnancy, she is not recognized as a wife of equal status. Frymer-Kensky (2000: 86) points out that according to law 146 of the Hammurabi Code there is a possibility that a pregnant slave might claim equality with her mistress. The law also permits the mistress to treat the pregnant woman as a slave. Hagar may have been 'given' to Abram *as* a wife (v. 3), but subsequent events result in a confirmation of Hagar's precarious status in the household.

Whether the verb *qll* (v. 4) should be read as 'looked on her with contempt' or as the equally possible but less offensive translation 'lowered in her esteem' (*Tanakh*), Hagar's attitude toward Sarai is clear. Sarai pleads with Abram to intervene and right what she perceives as a wrong done to her. Thus far in the narrative Abram has acted as instructed by Sarai. Now he tells her to deal with Hagar as she will. Even though Hagar is carrying Abram's child, he remains aloof. Hagar is Sarai's maid. The narrator portrays the dispute as a female affair. Sarai retaliates against Hagar by treating her harshly (*'nh*), an intense verb (v. 6). In reaction to the treatment meted to her the pregnant woman flees.

Up to this point in chapter 16 Hagar is depicted as an object. She is given to Abram and she is treated badly by Sarai. She has no voice nor has she taken any action except to look with contempt upon Sarai's childless condition. Now, however, in response to Sarai's harsh treatment, Hagar acts. She escapes to the wilderness (*midbār*). She takes the initiative in confronting her circumstances. As a

---

3.   The terms 'wilderness' and 'desert' are used interchangeably in English translations and commentaries.

4.   A full exegesis of the two chapters would require a more detailed study than the scope of this piece allows. See Trible (1984); Bellis (1994); Frymer-Kensky (2000); Savina J. Teubal, *Hagar the Egyptian: The Lost Tradition of the Matriarchs* (San Francisco: Harper & Row, 1990); M. Tsevat, 'Hagar and the Birth of Ishmael', in *The Meaning of the Book of Job and Other Biblical Studies: Essays on the Literature and Religion of the Hebrew Bible* (New York: Ktav, 1980), 69–70.

result of her flight, she encounters God's angel and she engages in a dialogue with the divine messenger. The angel surprisingly instructs her to return to what was an abusive situation. Bellis thinks this is an example of the cruel manner in which Hagar is treated in the Genesis narrative (Bellis 1994: 78). Elsa Tamez, however, points out that as the child has not yet been born, returning to Sarai and Abram is in Hagar's interest (quoted in Bellis 1994: 76). With them her child would be provided for during its infancy. Sarai and Abram thus serve to protect Hagar and the child, even as there is continuing enmity between the mistress and the maid.

Astoundingly, the angelic conversation continues with an annunciation to Hagar that her offspring will multiply (v. 11). This promise is made to no other woman in the Hebrew Bible. The angel even provides a name for the expected child and pronounces a prophecy as to his future. Hagar is not a silent recipient of this amazing news. She replies, the only biblical character to do so in this way, by speaking directly and giving a name to God in return. This name El-roi, 'the one who sees me', plays on the motif of sight that has been present in the exchanges between the women in the previous verses. Although not explicitly stated in this chapter, Hagar apparently returns to Abram's dwelling and there her child is born.

In chapter 16 Hagar is proactive in fleeing an abusive mistress. Only after taking initiative does she encounter the divine. In this encounter she becomes the first biblical character to meet an angel and the first person to receive God's promise of descendants. She is also the only person in the Bible to name God. For Hagar the wilderness is a refuge, not a place of abandonment. It signifies escape from oppression, the nourishment of life and a revelation of the divine.

Hagar's story continues in chapter 21. The maid is now a slave. In the intervening chapters Sarai has become Sarah and Abram has become Abraham. The promise of descendants made to Hagar in the earlier account has been extended to Abraham and fulfilled from the author's point of view in the birth of Isaac. Previously Sarah, the wife, was depicted as jealous of the fecundity of Hagar, the maid. In this chapter Sarah, the mother, is jealous of the son Hagar has borne. The details of what occasioned Sarah's attitude toward Ishmael are not spelled out, only that Sarah sees the 'son of Hagar' playing with Isaac 'her son'. It may be, as some scholars have remarked, that the text is corrupt (Hackett 1989: 20). Hackett, however, suggests another possibility, that of wordplay on the theme of laughter, noting that the word for 'to laugh' also means 'to play'. She comments that Ishmael's play may in fact indicate that he is behaving like Isaac, whom both Sarah and the author of Genesis regard as Abraham's only legitimate heir (Hackett 1989: 20–21; Gen. 22.2). In this reading Sarah's demand that Abraham send Hagar away is to be understood as a mother securing her son's inheritance.

Distressed, but compliant, Abraham accedes to Sarah's demand to 'cast out' the 'slave woman and her son' (v. 10). Abraham is assured that because Ishmael is 'his son' as well, God will make a nation of Ishmael's offspring. Abraham provides bread and water for the travellers and sends 'her' away (v. 14). God does not intervene on Hagar's behalf. There is no consolation for her, no promise or reassurance. The woman at the centre of the story is without a voice. She has become an object, acted upon by others and banished.

Hagar wanders in this second outing coming eventually to the wilderness of Beersheba. In distress at the empty water skin she raises her voice for the first time to cry out in weeping. Many commentators point out that the angel seems to ignore Hagar's cry in favour of the boy's. However, the messenger addresses Hagar and the question that is asked, 'What troubles you?' seems to be a response to Hagar's cry. The voice of the child is also heard, but not in place of Hagar's. The messenger, now recognized as God, repeats the promise made to her in chapter 16. God will make a great nation of the child (v. 18). There is no dialogue between Hagar and the divine messenger in chapter 21. She is instructed what to do, but makes no audible response. God opens her eyes (v. 19), recalling her naming of God as the 'one who sees'. This time it is Hagar who sees by divine revelation. Hagar, the mother, gives the child drink from the well of water. The reader is told that God is with the boy (v. 20) and that he lived in the desert. The lad has now become the focal point.

At the conclusion of the chapter the reader is told that Hagar and Ishmael make their home in the wilderness, which becomes a place of refuge and provides sustenance for them. The episode closes with Hagar finding an Egyptian wife for her son, completing her maternal duties and by implication providing for the perpetuation of her lineage. The promise made to Hagar is kept. Her line will continue through Ishmael, but that is not the story the Genesis writer chooses to relate.

While commentators often describe this second wilderness journey as one of exile and deprivation, Trible among others, notes that for Hagar this second journey is her own exodus from the land of bondage, prefiguring the exodus of the Israelites from slavery in Egypt (Trible 1984: 21). Thus the provision of water and bread and the discovery of the well foreshadow the life-sustaining properties of water and manna divinely provided for the Israelites during the Exodus years. Thomas Dozeman argues that the inclusion of the wilderness setting presents Hagar's story as modelling the life of Moses even more than she prefigures the slavery of Israel (Dozeman 1998: 29). In this construction Hagar's story parallels that of Moses, and the wilderness journeys are recognized as transformations which enable each character to found a nation. In these two chapters Hagar emerges as a heroine. She is not only promised heirs, but once in the wilderness receives the assurance that she need not be afraid (v. 17). Her banishment is in fact release from enslavement and the divine word is a promise of salvation. The wilderness takes on the character of a location where God is encountered, personal transformation ensues and community is formed.[5]

The Woman in the Wilderness

Commentators almost universally describe the Woman in Revelation 12 as the 'Woman Clothed with the Sun'.[6] Although this designation accords with the open-

---

5.   The parallels between Hagar and Moses are explored further in Dozeman (1998).
6.   See for example Aune (1998); Malina (1995); Yarbro Collins (1976); Ford (1975).

ing verse and suggests parallels with astrological symbols, mythic goddesses or the Queen of Heaven, it is unfortunate in that the Woman's significance is reduced to what she wears instead of what she does in subsequent verses. Describing her by her appearance she can easily be stereotyped, marginalized and dismissed as a minor character, rather than the protagonist she is in this chapter.

The reader is told that the magnificent Woman is a sign, although the meaning of the portent is not immediately disclosed. Her identity has occasioned much speculation among exegetes. She has been interpreted as Eve, Mary, the true Israel, New Jerusalem or the Church.[7] However, commentators have not been able to agree her characterization. The red dragon is also introduced as a portent, although his identity is not in doubt. He is a monster. The Woman cries out in the process of giving birth and in the knowledge that the monster is attending in order to devour the child, having already removed one-third of the stars from heaven (v. 4; cf. Dan. 8.10). The only other voice in chapter 12 proclaims victory following the heavenly battle (vv. 10–12), presumably a coded reference to an event which the readership would recognize. There is no discourse in this chapter nor does the dragon ever speak.

As soon as the child is born, he is snatched away to God's throne. The verb ἡρπασθην from ἁρπάω 'snatched away' has the double sense of being carried off by force or of being rescued from danger of destruction (Thayer 1889: 74–5). There is no explanation offered for the child's conception or parentage. Nor does the child appear again in the chapter. Despite his frightening appearance and his threatening stance, the dragon fails to devour the child, increasing the chapter's dramatic tension and creating anticipation for what is to follow. Nothing is said about the infant being hidden, although it is certainly implied that the child is kept safe until the time when he is to rule all nations with a rod of iron (v. 5; cf. Ps. 2.9). The monster, clearly the villain of the story, is unsuccessful while the heroine and her child are protected.

After the child's removal the Woman is left on her own. There is no explicit threat made to her, but she takes pre-emptive action, escaping not to family or friends, but to the wilderness (ἔρημος). She flees at her own initiative. No named wilderness is specified, but the reader is told that the place is prepared for her by God (v. 6). The description of the wilderness as 'her place' is repeated subsequently in v. 14. Some commentators question whether 'her place' and the wilderness are to be understood as the same location (Ford 1975: 193). However, there seems no substantive reason to doubt the association.

The desert provides the Woman with a place of refuge. In this place she becomes the 'Woman in the Wilderness'. Here she is nourished by God, remaining for a specified time during which the war in heaven becomes the focus of the story. There is dramatic irony in the contrast between the dragon's intention to devour the child and the divine nourishment provided for the Woman. The dragon's destructive intent is restated, while the Woman's safety is secured. The irony is furthered by the wilderness being depicted as a refuge, running counter to notions of the desert as a place of chaos and danger. Pippin thinks the Woman's

---

7. See commentaries listed in the bibliography.

flight marginalizes her and leaves her abandoned. (Pippin 1992: 72), but that view is not justified. The Woman is not banished or abandoned. Nor does she remain in the wilderness indefinitely. Whatever implicit threat there is, she takes action. She is not sent away. Nor is she left without provision in the desert. On the contrary she is divinely nourished. She finds safety in the wilderness from the contest between the dragon and Michael. This is a powerful extension of the portrayal of the Woman and the dragon as portents.

The battle moves the narrative forward and prepares for the second episode between the Woman and the dragon. The author/redactor of Revelation 12 does not inform the reader as to the motive for the war in heaven which follows the Woman's flight. Writing that 'The discourse of war is inscribed in the text' (Pippin 1992: 97), Pippin claims the Woman is a victim of war. However, I am not convinced the Woman is a victim. It appears that the Woman removes herself from combat and so stands aloof from the battle. Michael fights on behalf of heaven and also on behalf of the Woman. She is not a combatant, nor a victim. Just as she did not strive with the dragon standing before her in anticipation of the birth of her child, so here she sits out the war in her wilderness place.

Scholars of the apocalyptic genre cite numerous mythic parallels for the cosmic battle in this chapter.[8] It is usually suggested that the events mirror some persecution faced by the readership, although the nature and cause of the trouble vary from commentator to commentator. The climax of the battle scene occurs with the dragon's expulsion from heaven. In a change from third to first person, the author, and by extension the reader, hears a heavenly voice announcing that salvation, power and the kingdom of our God and the authority of his Messiah are victorious (v. 10). The heavenly voice cannot be either the author or God, as the context does not allow it. The accuser before *our* God could indicate that the heavenly war is an internal dispute, rather than external persecution.[9] No foreign adversary, Rome or anyone else, is likely to accuse the 'comrades' before God.[10] The proclamation only makes sense if the combat is an internecine affair.

Obviously the heavenly speaker could be left unidentified. In previous chapters the author has explicitly identified angels, elders or visionary creatures as speakers. It is possible that the author understands the heavenly voice to be that of one of the angels. There is, however, another possibility to consider. Could the hymn of praise be the voice of the Woman? Pippin observes the Woman is speechless except for her cries of pain (Pippin 1992: 75). Yet, it is legitimate to ask whether the proclamation of the dragon's defeat is the Woman's voice of victory and the vindication of the audience that sees in her their own ultimate triumph. She is after all the heroine and the figure whom the readership is supposed to identify as a portent. The dragon's subsequent attack against the Woman would be readily understood if the song of victory were hers.

---

8. See for example Yarbro Collins (1976).

9. The Greek manuscripts are consistent and uncorrupted with regard to the person of the possessive pronouns in v. 10.

10. In Job, Satan, the adversary or accuser, is depicted as a member of the heavenly court. Although I cannot explore the complexities of the combat myth here, it seems that the language used in Revelation 12 warrants further consideration of a dispute within the Christian community.

The identification of the Woman as speaker depends in part on whether the wilderness of v. 6 is understood to be a heavenly location and not an earthly site. As mentioned above, there is no particular wilderness specified in this chapter. The author, however, has shown that when a specific site is meant, it is named, as in the letters to the churches in chapters 2 and 3, and in the naming of Jerusalem in chapter 21. Even the coded references to Babylon are easily understood by the readership as referring to Rome. As the wilderness is a place of refuge and not danger, it is plausible to locate the first wilderness metaphorically in heaven with its corresponding connotations of deliverance and salvation. If the Woman is the speaker, that would explain why having lost the heavenly battle the frustrated dragon turns against her. The dragon pursues the Woman in revenge.

In verse 13 the dragon pursues the Woman, who is now, like the serpent, on earth. The verb ἐδίωξεν from διώκω 'pursue' can also be translated 'persecute'. The meaning is clear. The author offers no explanation as to how the Woman came to be on earth. Possibly the period stipulated for the first wilderness sojourn has been completed, although this does not account for her transfer from heaven to earth.

There is a lack of clarity in the sequence of events beginning in verse 13. The Woman appears in heaven in the opening verse of Revelation 12. She is still in heaven when she delivers her child who is snatched up to the heavenly throne. The author does not inform the reader whether the wilderness to which the Woman flees prior to the cosmic battle is in heaven or on earth. There is no necessity to assume her refuge is on earth, since the term ἔρημος is employed to denote a metaphorical as well as a geophysical environment. Commentators are divided on its location. It makes sense to assume that the Woman's relocation to earth occurs because the time stipulated for her first wilderness sojourn has been accomplished, although the writer does not state this. What is clear is that in verse 13 the Woman is on earth where the dragon, having been expelled from heaven, attempts to destroy her in a second encounter.

Verse 14 tells the reader the Woman will escape the dragon's attack in this second episode by means of a flight on eagle's wings (cf. Exod. 19.4). Once again, the author uses a motif that has a precedent in the Exodus traditions.[11] He does not say who provides the eagle's wings, although the readership could infer that the donor is divine, since God is the provider in the Exodus citation. The wilderness is now identified, again not as a named locale, but as 'her place'. As such, it could suggest the Woman's marginality, if the wilderness were understood as a wasteland and if the sojourn were for an indefinite period.[12] Neither of which is the case here. In the first flight the wilderness provides protection and provision. In the second, the Woman is again nourished, presumably by divine

11. Parallels for the eagle's wings have been cited from a vast array of ancient near-eastern literature. It is my contention, though, that the traditions of the Jews provide adequate typologies for the symbols in Revelation 12. The possibility exists that the Jewish traditions were in themselves coloured by the stories circulating among neighbouring peoples.

12. The length of time the Woman is to remain in the wilderness is the same for both flights. In the first instance the time is stated as one thousand two hundred and sixty days, while in the second it is given as a 'time and times and half a time'.

intervention, and her length of stay is again defined. She is not to remain indefinitely in the wilderness, although the author does not indicate that the second sojourn has ended before he finishes relating his vision. The implication is that the Woman is still in the wilderness when the chapter concludes. It seems, then, that Pippin overstates the Woman's marginalization, whereas the removal to 'her place' is an act of deliverance.

The difficulty with the events in verses 14–16 is the sequencing of the Woman's flight and the dragon's flood. While verse 14 says the Woman has been given wings to flee, the phrase ἵνα πέτηται implies that she has not yet made her escape. She must still be on earth and not in the wilderness in order for the dragon to loose the waters against her. There is nothing said about the dragon being in the wilderness. Nor is there any indication in the text that the dragon flies after the Woman or follows her into the wilderness, which would then not be a safe place. The flood is clearly an earthly event, as the ground opens and swallows the water. Commentators note echoes here of the salvation of the Israelites at the Red Sea. The dragon's flood is doomed to fail as God provides streams in the desert to sustain life, not to destroy it (Isa. 35.6). The reader must then conclude that the dragon is firmly on earth as distinct from both heaven and the wilderness, and therefore that the Woman is also on earth and has not yet made her escape.

The author assumes the reader understands that the motive for the dragon's pursuit is his failure to devour the child, his defeat in the heavenly battle and his expulsion from heaven. His renewed attack, this time directly against the Woman as the one who gave birth to the male child, suggests the dragon is targeting a substitute. The dragon's failure to catch the Woman in the pursuit of verse 13 is coupled with his unsuccessful attempt to destroy her in the flood. As the character with whom the audience is to identify, the Woman presents a powerful example of survival under terrifying conditions.

The dragon finally accepts defeat and takes out his anger by shifting his attack not against the earth who helped the Woman, but against the Woman's other children, identified as those who keep the commandments of God and hold the testimony of Jesus (v. 17). This is surprising news as no other children have been mentioned previously. Nor is there any indication where these other children are. Regardless, they are clearly to be understood as siblings of the male child, that is, those who accept Jesus' messiahship.

Pippin claims that in the book of Revelation, 'the female is subordinate in the text; once women are used or abused they are either denied a place in the future world or their future function is left undefined' (Pippin 1992: 69–70). Yet, in respect of chapter 12 the Woman is not subordinate, she is a victor, not a victim, a sign to a suffering community that it, too, can escape persecution and find safety.

Women in the Wilderness

In reading Hagar's story as presaging Israel's Exodus, commentators note numerous parallels. The Egyptian Hagar suffers affliction at the hand of Sarah.

Israel is oppressed in Egypt. In both cases the verb 'afflict' (*'nh*) is a strong one, signifying harsh treatment. Hagar under Sarah's authority becomes a suffering servant, the precursor of Israel's plight under Pharaoh (Trible 1984: 13). Hagar flees bondage, as do the Israelites. They both wander in the wilderness. Just as the story of Hagar prefigures the experiences of Israel in the Exodus era, her double flight into the wilderness anticipates that of the Woman in Revelation 12.

It is clear that the Apocalyptic author also draws on elements from the Exodus story in the imagery used in chapter 12. As with the first flight of Hagar in Genesis 16, the Apocalyptic Woman flees, taking the initiative in her escape in Rev. 12.6. Hagar's flight is occasioned by abuse. The Apocalyptic Woman flees from the ever-violent intent of the dragon. At the beginning of both accounts the protagonists are about to become mothers. Hagar's flight precedes her delivery, while the Apocalyptic Woman's follows the birth. Both take the initiative in response to a perceived threat.

In both biblical narratives the desert is hospitable, not a wasteland. Both women find safety there from persecution and are divinely nourished in the wilderness environment. Both women cry out, Hagar in sorrow, the Apocalyptic Woman in birth pangs. Hagar speaks to an angel and names God. The Apocalyptic Woman, as suggested above, may be the voice of victory. Both leave the wilderness after their first journey there. Hagar returns to Abraham's camp. The Apocalyptic Woman in the mythic language of Revelation moves from a heavenly wilderness to earth.

Hagar is helped by the angel in the first flight. The Apocalyptic Woman is aided by the divine provision of eagle's wings and the earth's timely intervention in her second escape. Hagar flees from the enmity of her mistress. The Apocalyptic Woman is persecuted by the dragon.

Water features prominently in both the Genesis and the Apocalypse stories. Hagar is sustained by a well of water in the wilderness of Beersheba. The Apocalyptic Woman evades the flood spewed out by the dragon and escapes to the wilderness. As mentioned above, some commentators recognize in the parting of the Red Sea an antecedent to the earth's swallowing of the water in Rev. 12.16. The parting enabled the children of Israel to escape from bondage in Egypt and to find refuge in the wilderness. Likewise, the earth swallows the water and enables the Woman to escape her pursuer and find refuge in the desert. Water is provided for the survival of the heroine and the defeat of the enemy.

Both women remain in the desert in the second flight to the wilderness. Hagar's stay is permanent. The Apocalyptic Woman's sojourn is for a specified time, which has not concluded before the chapter's ending. Hagar has escaped the jealousy of her mistress and received the promise of heirs. Her place is in the wilderness as matriarch of a new nation. The Apocalyptic Woman escapes the dragon's hostility. She remains in the wilderness, denominated 'her place', while the dragon pursues her other children (v. 17). Although the Apocalyptic Woman is not explicitly promised heirs, she is also a matriarch.

Rereading Revelation 12

In Genesis, Hagar and her son are marginalized because Sarah and her son are the ancestors of interest to the author. The tribulations Hagar suffers are the consequence of an internecine struggle – perceived, at least by Sarah, to be two heirs in competition for the same inheritance. Might this Genesis conflict illumine the struggle between the dragon and the offspring of the Woman? I have argued in this paper that Hagar's story provides an analogy to the story of the Woman, while both stories draw on Exodus typologies. The cosmic battle between the dragon and Michael is not the only struggle in Revelation 12. The dragon, having failed to devour the Woman's newborn child in verse 4 turns on her other children in verse 17. Could this be an indication of an internecine contest whose context is lost to the modern reader? The book of Acts (ch. 11) indicates that the post-Easter Church was divided over the acceptance of Gentile converts. The controversy persisted into the second century, by which time Christians were persecuting other Christians and were being persecuted by Jews and Romans. While the dragon may be a metaphor for a Roman ruler, there is no conclusive evidence in support of that identification. It seems plausible in light of the parallels between Hagar's story and that of Revelation 12 to consider whether the dragon represents an opponent from within the Christian or Jewish-Christian community. Regardless of agreement on the dragon's identity, in Revelation 12 he is portrayed as a persistent failure. The message to the readership is that the dragon's malevolent efforts will not succeed.

Hagar and the Apocalyptic Woman are anti-heroines. The stories initially portray them as objects, but subsequent events reveal them to be actors. Danger does not immobilize them. They are resilient, creative in turning adversity into triumph. Hagar seizes the initiative in her first flight. It is true she is sent away in the second, but when her eyes are opened by God, she acts. The Apocalyptic Woman seizes the initiative in her first flight. In the second God provides her with the means of escape. The chapter ends before the second flight has reached its conclusion. In the wilderness both women are divinely nourished, sustained for the challenges yet to come. The message is one of salvation; of divine disclosure; of deliverance from bondage; of escape from persecution, from enmity and even from jealousy. In the references to heirs, it is also one of reassurance. The open-ended Apocalyptic chapter is actually provided with a conclusion by analogy with Hagar's story. Hagar's survival and that of her child provides a model for what the children of the Woman in the Apocalypse can expect.

BIBLIOGRAPHY

Ackroyd, P. R., and C. R. Evans (eds.)
    1970   *Cambridge History of the Bible*, vol. 1: *From the Beginnings to Jerome* (Cambridge: Cambridge University Press).
Allenbach, J., A. Benoit, C. A. Bertrand, A. Hanriot-Coustet, P. Maraval, A. Pautler and P. Prigent

1975   *Biblia Patristica: Des origines à Clément d'Alexandrie et Tertullien* (Paris: Éditions du Centre National de la Recherche Scientifique).

1977   *Biblia Patristica: Le troisième siècle* (Paris: Éditions du Centre National de la Recherche Scientifique).

Aune, David E.

1986   'The Apocalypse of John and the Problem of Genre', *Semeia* 36: 65–96.

1998   *Revelation 6–16* (WBC, vol. 52b; Nashville: Thomas Nelson).

Bauckham, Richard

1993   *The Climax of Prophecy: Studies on the Book of Revelation* (Edinburgh: T&T Clark).

Bauer, Walter

1974   *A Greek–English Lexicon of the New Testament and Other Early Christian Literature* (tr. William F. Arndt and F. Wilbur Gingrich; Chicago: University of Chicago Press).

Beasley-Murray, G. R.

1974   *The Book of Revelation* (New Century Bible; London: Oliphants).

Bellis, Alice Ogden

1994   *Helpmates, Harlots, and Heroes: Women's Stories in the Hebrew Bible* (Louisville, Ky.: Westminster/John Knox Press).

Bertet, Adolphe

1861   *Apocalypse du Bienheureux Jean* (Paris: Arnaud de Vresse).

Boccaccini, Gabriele

1995   'History of Judaism: Its Periods in Antiquity', in Jacob Neusner (ed.), *Judaism in Late Antiquity*, pt. 2: *Historical Syntheses* (Leiden, New York, Cologne: Brill), 285–308.

Boring, M. Eugene

1989   *Revelation* (Interpretation: A Bible Commentary for Teaching and Preaching; (Louisville, Ky.: John Knox Press).

Brenner, Athalya

1986   'Female Social Behaviour: Two Descriptive Patterns within the "Birth of the Hero" Paradigm', *Vetus Testamentum* 36/3: 257–73.

Brown, Francis, S. R. Driver and Charles A. Briggs (eds.)

1972   *A Hebrew and English Lexicon of the Old Testament* (Oxford: Clarendon Press).

Caird, G. B.

1986   *A Commentary on the Revelation of St. John the Divine* (London: A. & C. Black).

Casey, J. S.

1982   *Exodus Typology in the Book of Revelation* (Louisville, Ky.: Southern Baptist Theological Seminary).

Charles, R. H.

1920   *The Revelation of St. John* (International Critical Commentary; Edinburgh: T&T Clark).

Collins, John J. (ed.)

1999   *The Encyclopedia of Apocalypticism: The Origins of Apocalypticism in Judaism and Christianity* (vol. 1.; New York: Continuum).

Court, John M.

1979   *Myth and History in the Book of Revelation* (London: SPCK).

Davies, G. I.

1992   'Wilderness Wanderings', *ABD* (vol. 6; New York and London: Doubleday), 912–14.

1979   *The Way of the Wilderness: A Geographical Study of the Wilderness Itineraries in the Old Testament* (Cambridge: Cambridge University Press).

Day, Peggy L. (ed.)
1989   *Gender and Difference in Ancient Israel* (Minneapolis: Fortress Press).

Dochhorn, Jan
1997   'Und die Erde tat ihren Mund auf: Ein Exodusmotiv in Apc 12,16', *Zeitschrift für die Kunde der Alteren Kirche* 88: 140–2.

Dozeman, Thomas B.
1998   'The Wilderness and Salvation History in the Hagar Story', *JBL* 117: 23–43.

Dunn, James D. G.
1996   'Judaism in the Land of Israel in the First Century', in Jacob Neusner (ed.), *Judaism in Late Antiquity*, pt. 2: *Historical Syntheses* (Leiden, New York, Cologne: E. J. Brill), 229–61.

Farrer, Austin
1964   *The Revelation of St. John the Divine* (Oxford: Clarendon Press).

Ford, J. Massynberde
1975   *Revelation* (Anchor Bible, vol. 38; New York: Doubleday).

Frymer-Kensky, Tikva
2000   'Hagar', in Carol Meyers (ed.), *Women in Scripture: A Dictionary of Named and Unnamed Women in the Hebrew Bible, the Apocryphal/Deuterocanonical Books, and the New Testament* (New York: Houghton Mifflin), 86–7.

Funk, Robert W.
1959   'The Wilderness', *JBL* 78: 205–14.

Garrett, Susan R.
1992   'Revelation', in Carol A. Newsom and Sharon H. Ringe (eds.), *Woman's Bible Commentary* (London: SPCK), 377–82.

Hackett, Jo Ann
1989   'Rehabilitating Hagar: Fragments of an Epic Pattern', in Peggy L. Day (ed.), *Gender and Difference in Ancient Israel* (Minneapolis: Fortress Press), 12–27.

Hedrick, William K.
1970   'The Sources and Use of the Imagery in Apocalypse 12' (Th.D. thesis; Berkeley: Graduate Theological Union).

van Henten, Jan Willem
1999   'The First Testing of Jesus: A Rereading of Mark 1.12–13', *NTS* 45: 349–66.

Hellholm, David
1986   'The Problem of Apocalyptic Genre and the Apocalypse of John', *Semeia* 36: 13–64.

Keller, Catherine
1990   'Die Frau in der Wüste: ein feministisch-theologisher Midrasch zu Off 12', *Evangelische Theologie* 50: 414–32.

Kittel, Gerhard
1964   'erēmos', in Gerhard Kittel (ed.), *Theological Dictionary of the New Testament* (vol. 2, tr. Geoffrey W. Bromiley; Grand Rapids: Eerdmans), 657–60.

Levine, Etan
2000   'The Land of Milk and Honey', *JSOT* 87: 43–57.

Malina, Bruce J.
1955   *On the Genre and Message of Revelation* (Peabody, Mass.: Henrickson).

Marshall, John W.
2001   *Parables of War: Reading John's Jewish Apocalypse* (Études sur le christianisme et le judaïsme; Waterloo, Ont.: Wilfrid Laurier University Press).

Mauser, Ulrich
    1963   *Christ in the Wilderness* (London: SCM Press).
Mazzaferri, Frederick David
    1989   *The Genre of the Book of Revelation from a Source-Critical Perspective* (Berlin and New York: W. de Gruyter).
Minear, Paul S.
    2000   'Far as the Curse is Found: The Point of Revelation 12:15–16', *NovT* 33/1: 70–7.
Mounce, Robert H.
    1977   *The Book of Revelation* (Grand Rapids and Cambridge: Eerdmans, rev. edn).
Pippin, Tina
    1992   *Death and Desire: The Rhetoric of Gender in the Apocalypse of John* (Louisville, Ky.: Westminster/ John Knox Press).
    1993   'Revelatory Discourses: The Revelation to John', in Elisabeth Schüssler Fiorenza (ed.), *Searching the Scriptures: A Feminist Introduction* (London: SCM Press; vol. 2): 109–30.
    2000   'Woman in Labor, Clothed with the Sun', in Carol Meyers (ed.), *Women in Scripture* (New York: Houghton Mifflin), 544.
Prigent, Pierre
    1981   *L'Apocalypse de Saint Jean* (Commentaire du Nouveau Testament; Paris: DeLachaux et Nestlé).
Raphael, Melissa
    1996   'Thealogy, Redemption and the Call of the Wild', *Feminist Theology* 15: 55–72.
Schüssler Fiorenza, Elisabeth
    1989   *The Book of Revelation: Justice and Judgment* (Philadelphia: Fortress Press).
Sweet, John
    1997   *Revelation* (London: SCM Press).
Swete, Henry Barclay
    1911   *The Apocalypse of St. John* (London: Macmillan).
Talmon, Shemaryahu
    1966   'The "Desert Motif" in the Bible and Qumran Literature', in A. Altmann (ed.), *Biblical Motifs* (Cambridge, Mass.: Harvard University Press).
Teubal, Savina J.
    1990   *Hagar the Egyptian: The Lost Tradition of the Matriarchs* (San Francisco: Harper & Row).
Thayer, Joseph Henry (ed.)
    1889   *A Greek–English Lexicon of the New Testament* (New York, Cincinnati, Chicago: American Book Company).
Thompson, Leonard L.
    2001   *The Book of Revelation: Apocalypse and Empire* (New York and Oxford: Oxford University Press).
Tresmontant, Claude
    1983   *Apocalypse de Jean* (Paris: O.E.I.L).
Trible, Phyllis
    1984   *Texts of Terror: Literary-Feminist Readings of Biblical Narratives* (London: SCM Press).
Tsevat, M.
    1980   'Hagar and the Birth of Ishmael', in *The Meaning of the Book of Job and Other Biblical Studies: Essays on the Literature and Religion of the Hebrew Bible* (New York: Ktav), 69–70.

Yarbro Collins, Adela

　　1976　　*The Combat Myth in the Book of Revelation* (Missoula, Mont.: Scholars Press).

　　1984　　*Crisis and Catharsis: The Power of the Apocalypse* (Philadelphia: Westminster Press).

　　1997　　'The Early Christian Apocalypses', *Semeia* 14: 61–121.

　　1999　　'The Book of Revelation', in John J. Collins (ed.), *The Encyclopedia of Apocalypticism: The Origins of Apocalypticism in Judaism and Christianity* (vol. 1; New York: Continuum), 384–414.

Yarbro Collins, Adela (ed.)

　　1986　　(ed.) *Semeia* 36: *Early Christian Apocalypticism: Genre and Social Setting* (Decatur, Ga.: Scholars Press).

Zevit, Ziony

　　2002　　'Three Debates about Bible and Archaeology', *Biblica* 30/1: 1–27.

THE MOUNTAIN AND THE DESERT

David Parker

We have become habituated to forming different mental pictures from references to mountains in the Gospels from those to deserts. Expressing it at its crudest, we associate the desert with the place of lonely prayer and temptation, and the mountain with the theophany. Thus, for example, the commentary on Mt. 5.1 will draw a parallel between the Sermon on the Mount and the giving of the law on Sinai's height, while the desert will be the dwelling of unclean spirits or the place of withdrawal. However, the usage of ὄρος is not quite so straightforward. This becomes evident from the LXX of Josh. 8.24. The Hebrew reads בַּשָּׂדֶה בַּמִּדְבָּר. This is rendered in the LXX as ἐν τοῖς πεδίοις καὶ ἐν τῷ ὄρει (no variants recorded by Swete or Rahlfs). The contrast between the two terms indicates that the translators regarded ὄρος as a better translation of מִדְבָּר than ἔρημος or ἐρημία. Of course, the presence of such a phrase as σκεπάζουσαν πεδία καὶ ὄρη in the *Similitudes* of Hermas (at 8.1.1 see also 8.3.2) indicates that ὄρος can mean a hill or mountain as opposed to a plain, and this is not to be denied. Nor is the fact that particular named hills are found, most obviously the Mount of Olives. We find an apparently similar reference in Heb. 11.38, where it is said that those of whom the world was not worthy were ἐπὶ ἐρημίαις πλανώμενοι καὶ ὄρεσιν.[1] But it is less obvious here that the words are antithetical. It is worth considering whether they are synonymous, or at least complementary. A desert is not necessarily flat. It is uninhabited.[2] And a mountainous or hilly area[3] will generally have been a desert, that is, uninhabited, because people have always tried to live in as convenient a place as possible.

None of this opening paragraph is original, and the entries in the standard lexica are its evident sources. But whether full weight has been given to the exegetical significance of this information is another matter. Given the mountaineering disposition of the person for whom this volume is written, it seems apposite to take an upland stroll, and ask whether the reference to ὄρος in the Gospels indicates primarily the fact that it is a hill as opposed to a plain or valley, or whether it is the desert character of the location that is intended.

---

1. For ἐπί D Ψ M [black letter M] Cl Or Eus read ἐν (*teste* Nestle-Aland 27).
2. BAGD prefers to emphasize the scantiness of vegetation of an ἐρημία more than of an ἔρημος. But see 2 Cor. 11.26, where Paul describes himself as κινδύνοις ἐν πόλει, κινδύνοισ ἐν ἐρημία. Here the contrast is all about an inhabited area against an empty one.
3. See the references in BAGD. See also T. L. Donaldson, *Jesus on the Mountain: A Study in Matthaean Theology* (JSNTSup, 8; Sheffield: JSOT Press, 1985), who rejects this view.

One evident manner in which we might test this is by looking at the kind of motion indicated by the verbs of going into the desert or the mountain. Here is an overall view:

Mt. 4.8   παραλαμβάνει (λαμβανη K)…εἰς
   5.1   ἀνέβη εἰς
   8.1   καταβάντος/-άντι…ἀπό
  14.23   ἀνέβη εἰς
  15.29   ἀναβὰς εἰς
  17.1   ἀναφέρει (ἀνάγει D fˡ Origen)…εἰς
     9   καταβαινόντων/-ες…ἐκ
  24.16   φευγέτωσαν εἰς/ἐπί
  28.16   ἐπορεύθησαν…εἰς

Mk 3.13   ἀναβαίνει (ἀνέβη P 1 209) εἰς
   6.46   ἀπῆλθεν (ἀνῆλθεν 1 209) εἰς
    9.2   ἀναφέρει (ἀνάγει D 2)…εἰς
     9   καταβαινόντων (μεταβ. S)…ἐκ
  13.14   φευγέτωσαν εἰς

Lk. 4.29 ἤγαγον…ἕως
   6.12   ἐξελθεῖν/-θεν…εἰς
   9.28   ἀνέβη εἰς
    37   κατελθόντων (καταβαινόντων 69 , κατελθοντα D)…ἀπό
  21.21   φευγέτωσαν εἰς

Jn 6.3   ἀνῆλθεν (ἀπῆλθεν ℵ* D 124 433 a d q rˡ)…εἰς
    15   ἀνεχώρησεν (φεύγει ℵ* a aur c ff² j l Vg)…εἰς

If we compare this with the range of verbs used for going to or from the ἔρημος, we find the following:

Mt.
ἀνάγω εἰς 4.1
ἐξέρχομαι εἰς 11.7
ἀναχωρέω εἰς 14.13

Mk
ἐκβάλλω εἰς 1.12
ἀπέρχομαι εἰς 1.35; 6.32
δεῦτε εἰς 6.31

Lk.
ἐκπορεύομαι εἰς 4.42
ἐξέρχομαι εἰς 7.24

There is clearly some overlap between the usage for the two words. But it is more helpful to look in greater detail at the verbs used with ὄρος.

We start at Jn 6.3, where the Nestle-Aland text reads ἀνῆλθεν δὲ εἰς τὸ ὄρος Ἰησοῦς. For ἀνῆλθεν we find ἀπῆλθεν in ℵ* D 124 433, with support from the Old Latin witnesses a d q rˡ, which read *abiit*. Here the concept of climbing upwards is replaced by that of withdrawal by Jesus, a repeated theme in this episode. At 6.1 he has already 'gone away' (ἀπῆλθεν) and at 6.15 he does so again. Here most witnesses record ἀνεχώρησεν πάλιν. ℵ*, however, reads φεύγει. The reading is known also to much of the Latin tradition, where *secessit* is read by b d e f q r¹, and *fugit* by the remainder (that is, a aur c ff² j l and the Vulgate), while Tertullian is cited by Wordsworth and White in support of *refugit*. The Curetonian Syriac could also reflect this reading. As is often the case we find that the readings at verses 3 and 15 both have slight but widely diffused support. 124 is a member of the Ferrar Group. The reading will therefore have been current in South Italy in the eleventh century, the date of this manuscript. 433 is of a similar date. The versional support for the original reading of Codex Sinaiticus at verse 15 indicates that it once had a considerable currency in the Greek tradition.

Both the Greek readings at verse 15 treat the mountain as a place of retreat, the one emphatically so. The variation ἀπῆλθεν at verse 3 does the same. To treat this first variation as a choice between two for establishing an original reading would be to overlook the significance of the fact of the variation.[4] What is more significant is that some tradents of the text could regard ἀπῆλθεν as a preferable way of reading the passage.[5] This is the case even if we regard it as assimilation to the appearance of the word a couple of lines before.[6] The case of Codex Sinaiticus is particularly striking. It is an important witness to both the variants.[7] We are left with the fact of the mountain (or mountains?) here in John 6 being best understood as deserts, waste and uninhabited places.

The significance of this increases when we consider the Synoptic passages of which there are echoes in John. The traditional critical view is that whatever sources contributed to the composition of the Fourth Gospel, that of Matthew cannot have been one of them. This is certainly the orthodoxy which was taught in my generation. But I can no longer read John 6 and believe it. The chapter, in particular its beginning, seems to be rich with Matthaean allusions: the going onto the mountain, the crowd drawing near, Jesus sitting, with the disciples as an inner circle. At verse 15 there is another Matthaean event. In fact, the number of allusions differs in the manuscript tradition. At Mt. 14.13 the Nestle-Aland text reads

Ἀκούσας δὲ ὁ Ἰησοῦς ἀνεχώρησεν ἐκεῖθεν ἐν πλοίω/ εἰς ἔρημον τόπον κατ᾽ ἰδίαν (ΟΜ ἐν πλοίω Γ pc syˢ·ᶜ)

This, as we have already seen, is taken up by Jn 6.15, which in the Nestle text reads:

4. Tischendorf in fact prints φεύγει as his text. It is an example of his fondness for ℵ.
5. The word 'tradent' is used to avoid the facile 'scribe', or some more ponderous phrase. By it is intended any person contributing to the transmission of a text, such as a reader jotting down thoughts, an editor, a scribe or a corrector. I am grateful to Richard Goode for this word.
6. In the case of the Sinaiticus, the reading is in fact more extensive: the first hand wrote καὶ ἀπῆλθεν, which was corrected to ἀνῆλθεν δέ.
7. In each place, the text was corrected by the corrector known, in the nomenclature refined by Milne and Skeat, as Ca, that is, Hand a of the C group of correctors. They are dated to a period between the fifth and seventh centuries. At verse 3, corrector Cb2 rewrote the correction by Ca.

Ἰησοῦς οὖν... ἀνεχώρησεν πάλιν εἰς τὸ ὄρος αὐτὸς μόνος

We have here a prime case for the ὄρος being synonymous with the ἔρημος. But this is not all. The text of D reads as follows:[8]

ιη—σ ουν... ανεχωρησεν παλιν εισ το οροσ αυτοσ μονοσ κακει προσηυχετο

The final two words are another Matthaean allusion, this time to Mt. 14.23, where the Nestle text reads

ἀνέβη εἰς τὸ ὄρος κατ᾽ ἰδίαν προσεύξασθαι

The modern critical question of the sources of John is by the way here. According to this part of the manuscript tradition, the amplification of the Johannine text with a phrase from Matthew is perfectly credible. The implication is important: that the tradent read the ascent of the mountain in Mt. 14.23 as no different in kind from the departure to the desert in Mt. 14.13 and the withdrawal to the mountain in Jn 6.15.

At Mk 6.46 we find again that Jesus ἀπῆλθεν εἰς τὸ ὄρος προσεύξασθαι. And of course it is possible that the D text of John is influenced by that source. However, Mark was more frequently harmonized than used as a source for harmonizing, and Tischendorf is to be followed in finding the source of the D reading in Matthew.[9] It is worth noting that here 1 209, two members of the important group Family 1, reverse the trend we found at Jn 6.3 and report that Jesus ἀνῆλθεν.

But what about those places where the mountain seems to indicate a set-piece, with a reference to the law-giving of Sinai or some other theophany? The two passages which come first to mind as belonging in this category are Matthew's Sermon on the Mount and the Transfiguration. The latter seems to seal the case in the Markan and Matthaean narratives. But the textual data may suggest otherwise. In Mark the printed text of Nestle-Aland has

ἀναφέρει αὐτοὺς εἰς ὄρος ὑψηλὸν κατ᾽ ἰδίαν μόνους. καὶ μετεμορφώθη

The variants which concern us are as follows:

ἀναφέρει] ἀνάγει D 0131 565 (a usage reminiscent of the ἔρημος reference of Mt. 4.1)
ADD λίαν after ὑψηλὸν ℵ it
ADD εν τῷ / προσευχέσθαι αὐτούς after καὶ P45 W; with minor variations Θ f¹³ 565 pc

At Mt. 17.1 the same printed text reads

ἀναφέρει αὐτοὺς εἰς ὄρος ὑψηλὸν κατ᾽ ἰδίαν. καὶ μετεμορφώθη

The variants are

ἀναφέρει] ἀνάγει D f¹ Origen
ADD λίαν after ὑψηλὸν D

---

8.   Taken from the transcription made by the Principio Project for the International Greek New Testament Project's edition of the majuscule manuscripts of John. The data about Codex Sinaiticus is from the same source.

9.   *Editio octava critica maior, ad loc.*

Finally, Lk. 9.28 reads

ἀνέβη εἰς τὸ ὄρος προσεύξασθαι. καὶ ἐγένετο ἐν τῷ/προσεύχεσθαι αὐτὸν τὸ
ει\δος

The variants do not concern us here. In Luke, it appears that the primary purpose of the mountain is as a place of retreat to pray, and that the Transfiguration
happens in the course of the prayer and is not related to the place. And again we
find that the Markan form of this account has, in a number of witnesses, including one of our oldest witnesses, been easily adapted to the Lukan model. It may
be significant that Luke omits the ὑψηλὸν, with or without λίαν.[10]

And what of the adjective? We could understand it in two ways. Is it a stress
on the drama of the occasion, an emphatic statement of the particular height of
this mountain on which such an event occurred (so significant that to some
tradents this was stressed as ὄρος ὑψηλὸν λίαν)?[11] Or is it intended to indicate
that this ὄρος was not merely a desert of any kind, either flat or indeterminate,
but was indeed more significantly a mountain than it was a desert? That is, does
its status as ὄρος ὑψηλὸν lead us to suppose that ὄρος on its own was not so
certainly a mountain, could, indeed, be a waste and deserted place? Is this precisely the exception that proves the rule?

The particular use of the mountain in Luke is described by Conzelmann, who
notes the removal of any reference to a mountain from the temptation in which
Jesus is shown all the kingdoms of the world:[12]

> In Luke iv, 5 it is noticeable that, in contrast with Matthew, the mountain is not men-
> tioned, although the theme is suggested in the expression ἀναγαγών. Is this con-
> nected with the fact that in Luke 'the mountain' is more stylized than in the other
> evangelists and has a fixed meaning? It is the place of prayer, the scene of secret
> revelations, of communication with the unseen world. No temptation can take place on
> it nor any public preaching.[13]

The evidence in Luke, most markedly in the way in which he edits out the
mountain of temptation and the mountain of the sermon (Mt. 5.1),[14] indicates that

10. The IGNTP apparatus records one witness as amplifying ὄρος: *l*1056 (dated 1297) adds
υψιλον [*sic*].

11. The source of λίαν is not particularly obvious. The mountain in the temptation in Mt. 4.8 is
ὑψηλὸν λίαν, and it may be a recollection of that passage. In Mark's account (9.3), Jesus' clothing
gleams λευκὰ λίαν, and the word in verse 2 may be the result of a process of mental suggestion
along with an inclination to heighten the drama of the occasion. That is, there need not be any
connection or similarity of process in the introduction of the word in Matthew and in Mark.

12. The vast majority of witnesses do insert the phrase by harmonization to Matthew. Only a
very few manuscripts, of which Sinaiticus and Vaticanus are the oldest, and some of the Coptic
tradition omit it. This is an excellent example of the way in which Lukan characteristics were lost
until editions based on the fourth-century manuscripts (such as Westcott and Hort) began to be
made. See Parker, *The Living Text of the Gospels* (Cambridge, 1997), esp. ch. 4.

13. Hans Conzelmann, *The Theology of Saint Luke*, tr. G. Buswell (London, 1960), 29. At the
same time, Conzelmann sees the Transfiguration as being related both to the story of the Baptism
and to the story of the Passion (p. 58). Note the variant on ἀναγαγών, ἀγαγών found in S and
other witnesses (see Tischendorf, *op. cit.*, *ad loc.*

14. I accept the hypothesis that Luke had access to Matthew as well as to Mark, and discard the
hypothetical Q.

Wilderness

Conzelmann's interpretation is correct. That is, for Luke, as for John, the mountain is a place of retreat and not of theophany. It is its character as a deserted place that makes it suitable for this purpose, and the number of feet above sea level is not of primary significance.

To complete the picture, it is necessary to survey the other usages in the Gospels. With regard to the Mount of Olives, it is perhaps surprising that it is never *ascended*. Its *descent*, towards Jerusalem, is mentioned in Lk. 19.37. In Mt. 26.30, parallel Mk 14.26, we find ἐξῆλθον εἰς τὸ ὄρος τῶν ἐλαιῶν. We should doubtless understand εἰς in the sense of 'towards'. Luke 22.39 is also parallel, in a slightly different place in the narrative, and reads ἐπορεύθη κατὰ τὸ ἔθος εἰς τὸ ὄρος τῶν ἐλαιῶν. The passage Jn 7.53–8.11, which has a number of Johannine features, is very similar: Ἰησοῦς δὲ ἐπορεύθη (*ascendit* aur c ff2) εἰς τὸ ὄρος τῶν ἐλαιῶν. This turn of phrase suggests a trip to a well-known area. As a matter of fact the difference in height between Jerusalem and the top of the Mount of Olives is tiny (17 metres, according to BDAG). Whether this would have been known to the authors of these two texts is another question altogether.

The instance of the demoniac in Mk 5.1–20 is instructive. According to Mark, the man was continually crying out and hurting himself ἐν τοῖς μνήμασιν καὶ ἐν τοῖς ὄρεσιν. In verse 11 the herd of pigs is said to be πρὸς τῳ ὄρει. Neither of these references either makes sense or is in keeping with their own usage to Matthew or to Luke, who edit the first reference out completely, and alter the second (Mt. 8.30 – η\ν δὲ μακρὰν ἀπ' αὐτῶν; Lk. 8.32 – η\ν δὲ ἐκεῖ). The second reference, I suggest, is in the sense of sloping pasture or grazing land.

The parable of the lost sheep in Matthew and Luke is an important example. In Matthew (18.12) the rhetorical question runs οὐχὶ ἀφήσει τὰ ἐνενήκοντα ἐννέα ἐπὶ τὰ ὄρη...; The Lukan form (15.4) is οὐ καταλείπει τὰ ἐνενήκοντα ἐννέα ἐν τῃ ἐρήμῳ...;[15] Again, Luke has removed a Matthaean reference to the mountain where it does not suit his view, and brought out instead the mountain's character as ἔρημος.

Finally, there are a few places in the Gospels where the word ὄρος clearly refers to a hill or mountain as opposed to more level ground:

> Mt. 5.14, the city set on the hill
> Mt. 17.20 //? Mk 11.23, command to mountains to be moved
> Lk. 3.5, πᾶν ὄρος καὶ βουνός in citation of Isa. 40.4
> Jn 4.20f, where 'this mountain' refers to Mt Gerizim, whose lower slopes are visible from the Well of Jacob, according to Lagrange.[16]

The purpose of this brief survey has been to question the meaning of the word ὄρος as it is used by the evangelists. While it sometimes clearly refers to a moun-

---

15. 1443 reads επι τα ορη, and Lvt (l) reads *in montibus* (*teste* H. J. Vogels, *Codex Rehdigeranus (Die vier Evangelien nach der lateinischen Handschrift R 169 der Stadtbibliothek Breslau)* (Collectanea Biblica Latina 2; Rome, 1913); there is no indication of the reading in *Itala: Das Neue Testament in altlateinischer Ueberlieferung nach den Handschriften, herausgegeben von Adolf Jülicher, durchgesehen und zum Druck besorgt von Walter Matzkow† und Kurt Aland*, III: *Lucasevangelium*, 2nd rev. edn (Berlin/New York, 1976). Lvt (c ff²) conflate, reading *in montibus in deserto*. A similar phrase is found in Acts 7.30, ἐν τῃ ἐρήμῳ τοῦ ὄρους Σινᾶ.

16. M.-J. Lagrange, *Évangile selon Jean* (Études Bibliques; Paris, 1936, 5th edn), 111.

tain or hill, I suggest that there are also places where the meaning refers primarily to the ὄρος as desert. The significance of the high mountain may be not the height but the increased isolation and desolation as one gets ever further from human habitation. This is perhaps clearest in Luke, for whom the mountain is a place for retreat and prayer, and not for theophany. But it is worth at least asking whether the same applies in Matthew and John. I have presented evidence that it does for the latter. But what of the beginning of the 'Sermon on the Mount'? Does the evangelist have in mind the mountain as place of revelation or the mountain as place of desert retreat, where Jesus can teach without interruption? The debate continues. What one should not do is take too much for granted with regard to the mountain as a place of Wordsworthian grandeur,

> Characters of the great Apocalypse
> The types and symbols of eternity,
> Of first, and last, and midst, and without end.[17]

It seems to us very obvious that the Greek gods lived on Mount Olympus, that Moses received the law on Sinai, and so on, and it is very easy even to assume that these places are appropriate because they are closer to heaven, and that the higher the mountain the more mysterious it becomes. But such assumptions need to be scrutinized at regular intervals. They may project the commentator's point of view, they may underestimate the texts in question, and they may restrict the possibilities of language. This survey suggests that it is necessary to reconsider the assumption that it is its height *per se* that is significant about the Gospel mountain. The fact is that the higher the mountain, the more deserted, the more removed from civilization, it will be, and so the more suited to engagement with the divine, free from distraction of any kind. In addition, we have found evidence in the textual transmission of the Gospels which suggests that the uncertainty of usage which we have detected was recognized by ancient readers and transmitters.

---

17. William Wordsworth, 'The Simplon Pass', *Poetical Works*, ed. T. Hutchinson, rev. E. de Selincourt (Oxford Standard Authors; Oxford, 1936).

FINDING IDENTITY IN THE WILDERNESS

Lynne Wall

Introduction: Wilderness in Context

In Aotearoa New Zealand the concept of wilderness is expressed in terms of 'bush' – indigenous forests that offer opportunity for 'a wilderness experience' as the advertisers of bush walks put it. These can be as challenging as going it alone on Department of Conservation tracks or as luxurious as having someone carry your pack and prepare your meals for you in well-appointed 'huts' on the Queen Charlotte track.

The bush has its dangers for anyone miscalculating weather patterns, becoming lost or disoriented, or being ill-prepared in terms of food and clothing. But generally speaking the bush is seen as a place of beauty, where one can nourish one's physical and inner life primarily through walking or tramping for a few hours or several days. New Zealanders take pride in maintaining the pristine condition of native forests. The practice of conserving these wilderness areas in National Parks, under the direction of the Department of Conservation, is a high priority in national environmental policy.

The wilderness is also recognized as a place where a specifically Aotearoa New Zealand spirituality may be nurtured. Maori have long appreciated the *wairua* (spirit) present when Tane separated Papa, the earth mother, from Rangi, the sky father, at the dawn of time:

> At length the offspring of Rangi and Papa, worn out with continual darkness, met together to decide what should be done about their parents, that [humanity] might arise. 'Shall we kill our parents, shall we slay them, our father and our mother, or shall we separate them?' they asked... At last Tu matauenga, ... the god of war, spoke out. 'It is well. Let us kill them'. But Tane mahuta, god and father of the forests and all things that inhabit them, answered: 'No, not so. It is better to rend them apart, and to let the Sky stand far above us, but let Earth remain close to us as our nursing mother'. (Alpers 1964: 16–17)

Many *pakeha* New Zealanders, while affirming that they live in an increasingly secular culture, will nevertheless admit to the spiritual dimension or quality of life experienced in the context of the New Zealand landscape, whether in bush or mountain or coastline.

> Natural landscapes speak to us with a powerful voice, and over the years I have become convinced that the mere act of walking in nature is wonderfully therapeutic. On multi-day tramps, for reasons I can't explain, I find the rhythms of the wild soothe many of

my anxieties – I think clearer [*sic*] and sleep with fewer demons knocking on the door of my mind. (Potton 1997: 8)

This is engendered by the spectacular beauty of a unique and diverse landscape within the relatively small land mass which makes up these islands. We know we are blessed when we escape our towns and cities in search of a wilderness experience.

Yet our experience in the New Zealand landscape is not always so welcoming or beneficent. We too have our desert areas where lush vegetation is replaced by tussock and rock. The 'desert road' in the centre of the North Island reflects such dry barrenness yet has a harsh beauty. Cold winds blow over the bare plateau with three volcanoes dominating the surrounding basalt and scree. In winter, the road may be closed by heavy snowfalls, and even in summer it is not a place to have one's vehicle break down while negotiating the 70-kilometre uninhabited stretch of road. It is a rugged environment of emptiness and threat, of limits to human endurance and survival, of stark reminders that life is fragile and precious.

The Wilderness Motif in Biblical Literature

When we turn to the biblical landscape we find a similar ambivalence with regard to wilderness terrain. The wilderness became a place of transition for the people of Israel as they journeyed from the liberation of Egypt to the promise of Canaan. It was a testing environment, a place of punishment,[1] yet also a place of revelation. Hunger and thirst assailed them, but the giving of Torah was life-bearing. Though they were confused and bewildered, yet it was in the wilderness that the people of Israel claimed their identity as the chosen people of God.

So significant is this tradition that the wilderness becomes not a mere geographical location but a symbol of the formative events which shaped Israel's covenant relationship with God. It is this powerful symbolic use of the wilderness tradition that I believe provides an interpretive tool for our own physical and metaphorical experiences of wilderness today.

In the earliest of Israel's credal statements, there is no mention of the events attributed to the wilderness setting:

> Then you shall say to your children, 'We were Pharaoh's slaves in Egypt, but the Lord brought us out of Egypt with a mighty hand… He brought us out from there in order to bring us in, to the land that he promised on oath to our ancestors.' (Deut. 6.21–3)

and

> A wandering Aramean was my ancestor; he went down into Egypt and lived there as an alien, few in number, and there he became a great nation, mighty and populous. When the Egyptians treated us harshly and afflicted us… the Lord brought us out of Egypt with a mighty hand and an outstretched arm, with a terrifying display of power,

1. Talmon's thesis is 'that the theme of "disobedience and punishment" is of much greater impact on the subsequent formulation of the "desert motif" in biblical literature than is the concept of the desert as the locale of Divine revelation and of Yahweh's love for Israel' (Talmon 1966: 48).

and with signs and wonders; and he brought us into this place and gave us this land, a
land flowing with milk and honey. (Deut. 26.5–9)

This silence is remarkable since some 70 per cent of the Pentateuch is set in
the wilderness (Exod. 13.17 until the end). However, the impact of the wilderness tradition can be observed in a third credal affirmation:

Thus says the Lord, the God of Israel: 'Long ago your ancestors – Terah and his sons
Abraham and Nahor – lived beyond the Euphrates and served other gods… When I
brought your ancestors out of Egypt, you came to the sea… and your eyes saw what I
did to Egypt. Afterwards you lived in the wilderness a long time. Then I brought you
to the land of the Amorites…' (Josh. 24.2–13)

Yet even here, except for the statement that it was a long period of time, no
content is given to the wilderness tradition. Thus the evidence suggests that the
development of a wilderness tradition is the product of later, and certainly prophetic, reflection,[2] where the exodus theme has become united with the wilderness stories.

Typical is Amos's declaration: 'Also I brought you up out of the land of Egypt,
and led you forty years in the wilderness, to possess the land of the Amorite'
(Amos 2.10). Even in well-known texts such as Hos. 11.1: 'When Israel was a
child, I loved him, and out of Egypt I called my son', where there is no explicit
reference to the wilderness, yet the emphasis is not solely on the exodus. In the
verses following, wilderness traditions predominate:

Rebellion:
The more I called them, the more they went from me;
     They kept sacrificing to the Baals, and offering incense to idols.

(Hos. 11.2)

Teaching:
Yet it was I who taught Ephraim to walk,
     I took them up in my arms;

(Hos. 11.3a)

Nurturing of identity:
I led them with cords of human kindness, with bonds of love.
     I was to them like those who lift infants to their cheeks.
I bent down to them and fed them.

(Hos. 11.4)

It is Hosea's claim that the people of Israel were unaware of what was happening as a result of participating in the wilderness tradition: 'but they did not
know that I healed them' (Hos. 11.3b).

In Jeremiah's prophecy there is a more positive assessment of Israel's initial
wilderness experience:

Thus says the Lord: I remember the devotion of your youth, your love as a bride how
you followed me in the wilderness, in a land not sown.

(Jer. 2.2)

---

2.   Talmon traces the desert motif to the period of the First Temple where it is to be found in
non-historical literature such as Deuteronomy, the pre-exilic prophets and the Psalms (Talmon
1966: 47).

However, the same ambivalence we have seen before creeps in as the prophet speaks of Israel's later unfaithfulness:

> What wrong did your ancestors find in me that they went far from me?
>
> (Jer. 2.5)

Ezekiel is even more specific about the failings of Israel in the wilderness, despite God's gifts to them:

> So I led them out of the land of Egypt and brought them into the wilderness. I gave them my statutes and showed them my ordinances, by whose observance everyone shall live. Moreover, I gave them my sabbaths, as a sign between me and them, so that they might know that I the Lord sanctify them. But the house of Israel rebelled against me in the wilderness… (Ezek. 20.10–13)

The Deuteronomist summarizes the time in the wilderness as one of continuous judgment upon Israel in this way:

> Know then, that the Lord your God is not giving you this good land to occupy because of your righteousness; for you are a stubborn people. Remember and do not forget how you provoked the Lord your God to wrath in the wilderness; you have been rebellious against the Lord from the day you came out of the land of Egypt until you came to this place. (Deut. 9.6–7)

From this brief exploration, it becomes clear that the wilderness tradition is more usually presented in a negative light in the biblical tradition. Yet it cannot be denied that there is a positive subtext hidden within it. It is this subtext that some of the rabbis take up and continue to emphasize. For example, R. Eliezer insists on seeing the people of the wilderness in a positive light. In the *Mishnah* tractate Sanhedrin he claims that Ps. 50.5 about future judgment, 'Gather to me my faithful ones, who made a covenant with me by sacrifice!' is speaking of the generation of the wilderness (*m. Sanh.* 10.3). R. Akiva thought otherwise, but it is R. Eliezer's view which prevails in the subsequent midrashic tradition.

In a brief survey of three events associated with the wilderness tradition it is my intention to show that despite the failings of Israel, there is in each occasion an opportunity to see the people of Israel gaining voice and hence identity through participation in these events. The reflections of the prophets, and later the rabbis, reinterpret each event for adaptation to new situations in the life of the people of Israel, whether it be the exile, the post-exilic return, the destruction of the temple in 70 CE, or the later catastrophe of 135 CE. In this way wilderness experience becomes a creative if demanding process through which people may grow in self-understanding and faith in the life-bearing action of the God of Israel. An example is also given for each event to show how these dynamics continue to operate in my own context of Aotearoa New Zealand.

1. *Knowledge of God : Finding Wisdom in the Wilderness*
A major event in Israel's wilderness experience is the revelation of God's name and nature. It is in the wilderness that Israel struggles to understand who God is and how such knowledge of God will affect their own understandings of wisdom. For us too, growth in wisdom often emerges from a wilderness experience.

While in the priestly tradition, the revelation of God's name occurs in Egypt (Exod. 6.2), the elohistic revelation takes place in the wilderness, admittedly before the exodus takes place (Exod. 3.1). Janzen links Moses' own growing self-awareness ('Who am I?' (Exod. 3.11)) with both God's self-revelation and the accompanying presence of God (Janzen 1979: 234). At the same time Moses is challenged to take up the task of liberation and the search for identity on behalf of the whole people. The wilderness is 'the setting for encounter with the power of the possible' (Janzen 1979: 236). However, the yahwistic account of the revelation of God's name takes place in the wilderness of Sinai *after* the exodus (Exod. 33.19; 34.6) and in the context of the renewal of the covenant.

The significance of knowing the name of one's god is made clear in the biblical text. It reveals not only an appellation but also the attributes that the name signifies: 'I will be gracious to whom I will be gracious, and will show mercy on whom I will show mercy' (Exod. 34.19). Thus, within the yahwistic tradition, knowledge of the being and nature of Israel's God is made known in the wilderness. Such knowledge enables the possibility of communication. For Israel the name stands in place of the image of other Near Eastern gods and goddesses (Mauser 1963: 24–5).

Perhaps this growth in Israel's knowledge of God underlies the rabbinic tradition that the Israelites of the wilderness generation are called Darda 'for they had great knowledge' (*Mid. Prov.* 1.1).[3] The context here is a description of the nature and extent of Solomon's wisdom: 'He was the wisest of all men: [wiser] than Ethan the Ezrahite, and Heman, Chalkol and Darda, the children of Mahol. His fame spread among all the surrounding nations (1 Kgs 5.11)' (*Mid. Prov.* 1.1).[4]

In the *Pesikta Rabbati*, believed to have achieved its final form in the ninth century CE, but containing material from as early as the Amoraic period of the third and fourth centuries CE, there is a further midrash of this passage from 1 Kings.[5] In Piska 14, a discourse on the mystery and paradox of the red heifer, a purification rite, it is claimed that 'not even Solomon, who was privy to every kind of wisdom, could fathom the mystery of the red heifer'. His wisdom 'exceeded the wisdom of the children of the East (Pharaoh), Adam, Abraham, Moses, Joseph and the generation of the wilderness'. This claim is supported by an interpretation of 1 Kgs 5.11 (= 1 Kgs 4.31 NRSV) whereby 'wiser than all other men' is read to mean 'wiser than he who contained within himself all mankind, that is to say, wiser than Adam'. This reading continues:

> By 'Ethan' is meant our father Abraham (Ps. 89.1), by 'Heman' , 'the trusted one' is meant Moses (Num. 12.7), by 'Calcol', 'the sustainer' is meant Joseph (Gen. 47.12)

and finally,

---

3.   *Midrash Mishle* 1.1, tr. Burton Visotzky (New Haven: Yale University Press, 1992), 18.
4.   Cf. also *Lev. R.* 9.1 and *Num. R.* 19.3.
5.   Indeed Visotzky believes this to be the source of the Proverbs midrash – see *Mid. Prov.*, tr. Visotzky, 127 n. 12.

wiser... than Darda which was the generation of the wilderness and why does scripture speak of it as Darda? Because it was a generation (dor) of men everyone of whom was filled with knowledge (de'ah). 'Wiser... than... the sons of Mahol', is read to mean another name for the children of Israel to whom God's presence gave pardon (mohlah) for the making of the golden calf. (*Pesikta Rabbati*, Piska 14.7)

A footnote at this point states,

That the phrase 'sons of Mahol' is to be construed as the generation which received pardon for making the golden calf, is in keeping with a Rabbinic norm which assumes that identical series of names in two passages of scripture must be consistent. In this instant, Ethan, Heman, Calcol etc are identified in a genealogical list in I Chronicles 2.6 as being 'the sons of Zerah' whereas in I Kings 5.11 the same individuals are identified as 'sons of Mahol'. Hence the conclusion that 'sons of Mahol' intimates the generation which received pardon; and the further conclusion that the other names in Kings are likewise available for exposition. (Braude 1968: 274)

Thus it is clear that for the rabbis, the generation of the wilderness was gifted with knowledge and wisdom, comparable to that of Solomon, but surpassed by his. Nevertheless, their insight is legendary and is linked to the presence of God in forgiveness and reconciliation after the making of the golden calf. Perhaps such wisdom is consequent upon the failings of Israel and the recognition of those failings by the people in confession and repentance. In this way insight is the fruit of a reflective and contrite spirit.

But as Rowan Williams reminds us, it is necessary for community accountability to play its part in such introspection. We must be open to the position of vulnerability that an act of genuine remorse over past injustice or hurt will require, rather than ducking for cover as we stumble through the wilderness in protestations of denial and blame. We cannot control the past or how others will react to our initiatives of repentance. Williams makes clear the link between remorse and identity:

Remorse involves thinking and imagining my identity through the ways in which I have become part of the self-representation of others, groups or individuals; and so learning to see my (or our) present style of self-representation as open to question. It is in some degree to make *internal* to myself what I have been in the eyes of another. At the corporate level, this is, of course, a highly charged matter. (Williams 2003: 134–5)

Reflecting on New Zealand's corporate expressions of remorse through the Waitangi Tribunal, it is evident that all these responses of hurt, denial, blame and powerlessness have been played out on our national stage with regard to past grievances over land and resources unjustly taken and/or controlled by colonial powers. A clear example is the unjust confiscation of land after the wars of the 1860s. As a nation, New Zealand has had the opportunity to act on this knowledge of past grievances and present remorse through the Waitangi Tribunal, established in 1975. This tribunal has power to explore and rule on alleged breaches of the Treaty of Waitangi originally made between the Crown and Maori in 1840. While the process of putting right the injustices of the past is a protracted and sometimes frustrating one, yet it is a sign of growth in self-knowledge and repentance that a renewed relationship is now possible between *tangata whenua* (the people of the land) and those who arrived in Aotearoa New Zealand at a later date.

The painful facing of past wrongs and injustices bodes well for the building of a national identity based on truth and integrity. If our wilderness experiences, and reflection upon them, bring us face to face with our past in a way that triggers remorse and a desire for reconciliation, then there is an opportunity for creating communities of trust and hope into the future.

2. The Giving of Covenant and Law: The Finding of Voice in the Wilderness
The second event associated with the wilderness tradition is the renewal of the covenant and the giving of Torah, both of which take place in the wilderness (Exod. 24.3, 7). These two major and interrelated events are crucial to the future relationship between God and Israel and to the identity of Israel as the people of God. In later tradition Torah becomes the source of wisdom and it is through words and the interpretation of the words of Torah that the relationship is sustained and nurtured.

Of interest to our concerns is a passage in Hosea that has been taken up by the rabbis. Hosea 2.16 (2.14 NRSV) reads: 'Therefore I will now allure her [Israel] and bring her into the wilderness and speak tenderly to her.' The rabbis have noted the juxtaposition of 'wilderness' (*midbar*) and 'I will speak' (*vedibarti*) and the wordplay on the similar consonants *dbr* in both words. Despite there being no link in derivation (*midbar* is thought to derive from the Aramaic verb *dbr* 'leading sheep to pasture' rather than the Hebrew *dbr* 'word'), yet the rabbis have seen the two as identical. Fisch draws attention to this interpretation when he says that 'desert and speech are here joined by the wordplay of midbar …dibbarti' (Fisch 1990: 143). He compares the wilderness as 'a place of absence' with words in it, to the 'Voice crying out in the desert: Prepare the way of the Lord' (Isa. 40.3). Again Fisch claims that 'in the desert void the word is sounded; in the fullness of Canaan it is forgotten' (Fisch 1990: 144).

Similarly it is within formlessness and void that the creative word of God is heard in Genesis 1. God speaks into the silence and calls forth light and darkness, land and sea, plants and the incredible diversity of life forms on our planet. Such creativity is pronounced good and a blessing for all. It is also significant to note the earth creature's role in naming the creatures of the earth in Gen. 2.19–20, thus giving them identity.

Another positive evaluation of wilderness is found in *Exodus Rabbah*, where R. Joshua asks why Moses went with them to the wilderness. In answer it is claimed that

> he foresaw that the Israelites would be exalted from the wilderness…for from the wilderness they had Manna, the quails, the well, the Tabernacle, the Shechinah, priesthood, a Kingdom, and clouds of glory. Another explanation: God said to Moses: 'Thou wilt bring out Israel from Egypt by the merit of him with whom I spoke between the pieces' – that is Abraham. The word 'midbar' (wilderness) can only mean speech (dibbur) here, as it says: 'and thy speech (midbarek) is comely' (ib. 4.3). R. Levi said: God told Moses: 'Let this be a sign to you: In the wilderness wilt thou leave them, and from the wilderness wilt thou bring them back in the Messianic times, as it is said:

"Therefore, behold, I will allure her, and bring her into the wilderness (Hos. 2.16)"'.
(*Ex.R.* 2.4)

Is it that we hear more clearly in the wilderness because we are not distracted? Our minds are not cluttered and we can focus more easily on the words of wisdom and Torah made available to us in solitude. Certainly the wilderness sharpens our awareness of God's word addressing us and encourages us to respond to the call to renew the covenant with God. In the wilderness life choices are presented more starkly, priorities for life are clarified and the voice of a people is called forth.

The people of Israel found their voice in the wilderness:

On that day, says the Lord, you will call me, 'My husband,' and no longer will you call me, 'My Baal.' (Hos. 2.16)

With the promise of a renewed covenant and knowledge of God, the people can speak out and find their true identity as the people of God (Hos. 2.23). As Francis Landy has said, 'The barren place is cultivated through speaking it' (Landy 1995: 51). In the same way Jesus clarified his own identity and ministry in the wilderness by speaking the words of Torah. In a setting of deprivation and isolation Jesus is tested as to the way in which he will conduct his life. To each temptation he responds with words from Scripture which will define the quality of his life and ministry.

Similarly in the wilderness of a Western academic classroom in Aotearoa New Zealand, a young Samoan woman finds her voice as she asks the penetrating question, 'How do you let go in order to empower others?' She is speaking as a youth worker endeavouring to empower her own people within the multicultural context of church and society. She is also reflecting the wilderness situation of many young people who have been born in this land but whose parents have come from the Pacific Islands. In this liminal world where one does not belong fully in either place, it is hard to find one's voice and identity.

Yet it is these young people who so often see clearly the issues of identity and hear the words of Torah which speak into the void of homelessness. Their facility in both cultures enables them to express both the alienation and the *kairos* opportunity for discovering a new identity woven from the strands of their heritage and those of the new cultural environment they find themselves in. They speak out of a wilderness experience to challenge and question our understandings of identity and in them 'the Valley of Achor' does indeed become 'a door of hope' (Hos.2.15).

3. *The Election of Israel: Finding Transformation in the Wilderness*

As early as Exod. 4.22 Israel is declared to be God's 'first-born son' recalled by Hosea in the text already mentioned in Hos. 11.1 'Out of Egypt I called my son'. This identity, expressed in terms of the intimacy of a parent–child relationship is central to the biblical portrayal of the covenant between God and God's people, Israel.

The Deuteronomist reminds Israel of its failure to respond faithfully to its election as the people of God.

> Do you thus repay the Lord, O foolish and senseless people?
> Is not he your father, who created you, who made you and established you?
>
> (Deut. 32.6)

Here it is clear from the verbs 'created', 'made' and 'established' that Israel's whole identity rests upon the gracious action of Israel's God:

> The Lord's own portion [when dividing up the nations] was his people, Jacob his allotted share.
>
> (Deut. 32.9)

And then immediately we have the link with the wilderness:

> He sustained him in a desert land, in a howling wilderness waste;
> he shielded him, cared for him, guarded him as the apple of his eye.
>
> (Deut. 32.10)

Then, with the imagery of the mother eagle caring for its young, the wilderness is seen as the context for this nurturing and protecting guidance. Note too the link with creation through the use of the same word רחף at Deut. 32.11 and Gen. 1.2.

Thus while the Exodus is a pivotal moment in the liberation of Israel, it is the wilderness tradition which recalls the building of a nation, the shaping of an identity as the people of God. This understanding of the wilderness tradition is reinforced by the rabbinic interpretation of Song 3.6, which in the *Midrash Rabbah* reads:

> 'Who is this that cometh up out of the wilderness?' Israel's elevation is from the wilderness; her decline is from the wilderness; her death is from the wilderness, as it says, 'In this wilderness they shall be consumed, and there they shall die' (Num. 14.35). (*Song. R.* 3.6, 1)

Again the literal answer to the question raised at Song 3.6, of Solomon, is discarded for a more symbolic reading. Yet alongside this pessimistic view of the wilderness is the same ambivalence seen before: 'All the excellent gifts that God bestowed on Israel came from the wilderness' and these are listed as Torah, tabernacle, Sanhedrin, priesthood, the service of the Levites, royalty. Reference is also made to Exod. 19.6 that Israel shall be a priestly kingdom and a holy nation. This again reflects signs of a growing sense of identity and election in the wilderness as God's 'treasured possession out of all the peoples' (Exod. 19.5).

In the prophetic tradition we read of the transformation which takes place in the wilderness:

> The wilderness and the dry land shall be glad,
> the desert shall rejoice and blossom...
> Then the eyes of the blind shall be opened,
> and the ears of the deaf unstopped;
> then the lame shall leap like a deer,
> and the tongue of the speechless sing for joy.
> For waters shall break forth in the wilderness,
> and streams in the desert;
>
> (Isa. 35.1, 5–6)

Such transformation can be seen as the recovery of the original intention of God's creative word and it is in the wilderness that this new identity is forged both for Israel and for all creation.

There can be few wilderness situations as destructive and demoralizing of the human spirit as the criminal justice system as it is currently practised in most Western nations. It is perhaps the only area of human social order where we still use the same models that were used in the nineteenth century. These models of punitive retribution and isolation in a culture of imprisonment have generally not produced accountability and rehabilitation, but only ever-increasing levels of crime and recidivism, an ignoring of victims' needs and growing fear and insecurity in society. These in turn have resulted in calls for tougher sentencing, whether such sentences 'work' or not, issuing in a spiral of violence.

Yet, amazingly, the wilderness has indeed begun to blossom. The restorative justice movement is gaining momentum both in New Zealand and in other parts of the world. Here the central focus is on the hurt or injury sustained by the victim and his or her family, friends and community, rather than on an offence against the state or the breaking of a law. Restorative justice conferences allow both victim and offender to talk with one another in the presence of supporting family or friends and with the help of a skilled mediator. The aim is to bring about a resolution that is acceptable to all parties. Instead of vengeance, punishment, alienation and fear, the restorative justice process is characterized by apology, mercy, restoration, reconciliation and healing.

New Zealand became the first country in the world to reorganize its youth justice system on a restorative justice model in 1989 (Consedine 1995: 7; Marshall 2002: 83). By using family group conferences instead of criminal court proceedings for young offenders, numbers fell dramatically from 13,000 cases a year in court to 1800. But the really exciting statistic is that of the drop in offences by young people aged 17–20 as a result of this restorative process – 27 per cent in the first five years of operation (Consedine 1995: 168).

Despite this encouraging result over half of all men and two-thirds of women sent to prison in 1995 were Maori (Consedine 1995: 8). This again is a staggering statistic when one considers that Maori are only 14 per cent of the total population. It is highly significant therefore that restorative justice reflects values and processes which are far closer both to Maori traditions of justice and to the gospel than those of the retributive justice system.

A major contributing factor to the success of the restorative justice process is the placing of responsibility clearly with the offender and his family or supporters. This taking of responsibility is in terms both of the offence and in making restitution after hearing the effects of the offence on the victim. This power is taken away in the retributive system where such control is in the hands of the state. Restoring such power to the offender enables the possibility of genuine self-determination and the building of an identity which is responsive to the consequences and effects of offending. In this way transformation and rehabilitation become real possibilities.

Conclusion

Here in these three wilderness events – the revelation of God's name, the giving of the law and the covenant, and the election of Israel as God's people – we see their significance as defining moments in the identity of Israel. They are of such significance that the wilderness tradition is adapted and reinterpreted to meet other moments of transition in the journey of Israel, whether by the prophets before and after the exile or by the rabbis in the light of the catastrophes of 70 and 135 CE, and also in the journey of Aotearoa New Zealand as it adapts to a multicultural society in its nation-building.

Three factors seem to highlight the power of the wilderness tradition to offer life both for Israel and for ourselves:

1. The wilderness is a place of divine encounter, where defences are stripped away by the starkness of the landscape and the barrenness of human resources, where remorse and repentance are enacted in response to the truth of God's self-revelation and the truth of our own situation. Wisdom and understanding, both of self and others, are the fruits of such an encounter.

2. The wilderness is a place where a word is spoken and heard, where a voice is found. In the silence and emptiness of an alien environment, a creative word is spoken and becomes active in opening up new expressions of Torah-living.

3. The wilderness is a place of transformation where there are 'streams in the desert' and the recovery of God's original intention in creation. The wilderness is a place of hope, offering the resources for healing and the building of a new identity.

Sources

Midrash Mishle, tr. Burton Visotzky, 1992 (New Haven: Yale University Press).
Midrash Rabbah, tr. H. Freedman, and M. Simon, 1939 (London: Soncino Press).
Mishnah, tr. Philip Blackman, 1990 (Gateshead: Judaica Press; 2nd edn).
Pesikta Rabbati, tr. William Braude, 1968 (New Haven: Yale University Press).

BIBLIOGRAPHY

Alpers, A. (ed.)
  1964   *Maori Myths and Tribal Legends* (Auckland: Longman Paul).
Braude, W.
  1968   *Pesikta Rabbati* (New Haven: Yale University Press).
Consedine, J.
  1995   *Restorative Justice: Healing the Effects of Crime* (Lyttelton, NZ: Ploughshares).
Fisch, H.
  1990   *Poetry with a Purpose* (Bloomington and Indianpolis: Indiana University Press).

Janzen, J. G.
  1979   'What's in a Name? "Yahweh" in Exodus 3 and the Wider Biblical Context',
             Interpretation 33: 227–39.
Landy, F.
  1995   'In the Wilderness of Speech: Problems of Metaphor in Hosea', *Biblical Inter-
             pretation* 3: 35–59.
Marshall, C. D.
  2002   In *Overcoming Violence in Aotearoa New Zealand* (Wellington: Philip Garside),
             81–95.
Mauser, U.
  1963   *Christ in the Wilderness* (London: SCM Press).
Potton, C.
  1997   *Classic Walks of New Zealand* (Nelson, NZ: Craig Potton).
Talmon, S.
  1966   In A. Altmann (ed.), *Biblical Motifs* (Cambridge, Mass.: Harvard University
             Press), 31–63.
Williams, R.
  2003   *Lost Icons* (London and New York: Continuum).

The Wilderness Quotation in Mark 1.2–3

Steve Moyise

The beginning of the good news of Jesus Christ, the Son of God. As it is written in the prophet Isaiah, 'See, I am sending my messenger ahead of you, who will prepare your way; the voice of one crying out in the wilderness: "Prepare the way of the Lord, make his paths straight."' John the baptizer appeared in the wilderness, proclaiming a baptism of repentance for the forgiveness of sins. (Mk 1.1–4)

Introduction

There are a number of factors which come into play when seeking to interpret scriptural references in the New Testament. (1) The author may indicate how he wishes the words to be taken, either by an introductory or concluding formula, the exegesis that follows or the role the quoted words play in the new work. (2) Changes to the scriptural material might indicate the author's redactional interests. (3) The quoted text might bring with it connotations or associations from its original historical or literary context. (4) The quoted text might bring with it connotations or associations from significant subsequent contexts. (5) The commentator's own ideological stance and social location might influence how the evidence is evaluated (and more fundamentally, what is to be considered as evidence). One of the main difficulties with studying scriptural quotations in the New Testament is that there is no agreement on how these factors should be prioritized. For example, some would argue that a quotation from Isaiah 53 brings with it the whole context of the 'suffering servant', but are forced to deny that the quotation of Hos. 11.1 in Mt. 2.15 ('Out of Egypt I have called my son') brings with it *any* associations from the following verse ('The more I called them, the more they went from me; they kept sacrificing to the Baals, and offering incense to idols'). How does one decide whether the surrounding context is important or not?

In terms of Mark's opening quotation, interpretations largely fall into two camps. First, there are those interpretations that stress the importance of the scriptural background, importing key themes such as 'wilderness', 'exodus' and 'judgment' into a reading of Mark's text. Such interpretations are usually rooted in historical criticism, claiming that this is how Mark's first-century readers would have understood it. In short, Mark's exegesis is interpreted in the light of other first-century exegesis, notably the Dead Sea Scrolls. Second, there are those interpretations which stem from a narrative approach, where meaning is determined by the story world created by Mark. Such approaches focus on the internal dynamics of the narrative rather than events (or texts) external to it. The meaning of Mark's opening quotation is determined by its role in the developing narrative, not the meaning it may have had in some previous historical or literary context. It is the aim of this short article to discuss the 'wilderness' quotation in the light of these two methodologies and consider whether it is possible to adjudicate between them.

Meaning Derived Primarily from the Old Testament Context

Two factors have led to what we might call a 'maximal' interpretation of scriptural references in the New Testament. The first is the biblical theology movement, which sought to interpret the Bible on its own terms, using such concepts as covenant, salvation history or the people of God, to bridge the two Testaments. C. H. Dodd famously argued that references to Scripture in the New Testament are not limited to the actual words quoted but allude to major blocks of material, such as Daniel 7, Isaiah 40–55 and the royal psalms. He went on to assert that the themes from these major blocks of Scripture, together with the 'gospel facts', form the 'substructure of all Christian theology' (1952: 127). New Testament exegesis was not 'atomistic' but followed the contours of important salvation-history themes.

The second factor in establishing a 'maximal' interpretation has been the introduction of the literary concept 'intertextuality' into biblical studies (see Moyise 2001). Drawing on the work of Bakhtin, Julia Kristeva suggests a dialogical relationship between 'texts', broadly understood as a system of codes or signs. Moving away from traditional notions of agency and influence, she suggests that such relationships are more like an '*intersection of textual surfaces* rather than a *point* (a fixed meaning)'.[1] The notion was introduced to biblical scholars by two books in 1989. The first was a collection of essays entitled *Intertextuality in Biblical Writings*. In one of the contributions, Vorster states:

> First of all it is clear that the phenomenon text has been redefined. It has become a network of references to other texts (intertexts). Secondly it appears that more attention is to be given to text as a process of production and not to the sources and their influences. And thirdly it is apparent that the role of the reader is not to be neglected in this approach to the phenomenon of text. (1989: 21)

The other book was *Echoes of Scripture in the Letters of Paul*, by Richard Hays. Hays does not mention Kristeva but draws on John Hollander's work, *The Figure of Echo: A Mode of Allusion in Milton and After*. Hays is impressed by the subtlety of Hollander's analysis and asks why this has not always been so in biblical studies. He attempts to put this right in a number of highly regarded studies on Paul, claiming that 'the most significant elements of intertextual corre-

---

1. 'Word, Dialogue and Novel' was written in 1966 and first appeared in *Séméiotiké: Recherches pour une sémanalyse* (Paris: Le Sevil, 1969). It was translated in *Desire and Language: A Semiotic Approach to Literature and Art* (ed. L. S.Roudiez; New York: Columbia University Press, 1980) and is now conveniently found in T. Moi (ed.), *The Kristeva Reader* (New York: Columbia University Press, 1986). The quotation is taken from Moi 1986: 36 (emphasis original).

spondence between old context and new can be implicit rather than voiced, per-
ceptible only within the silent space framed by the juncture of two texts' (1989:
155). Despite the post-structuralist roots of intertextuality, many biblical scholars
now use the term to describe the way that a quoted text itself alludes to other
texts and thus the quotation presents itself to readers not as an isolated proof-text
but as part of a complex web of interlocking scriptural allusions. No text is an
island; it automatically brings with it connotations and associations from its
previous context(s).

Wilderness and the Isaian New Exodus

For Joel Marcus, the significance of the opening quotation in Mark lies in its
ascription to Isaiah. As is well known, the quoted words are a combination of
Exod. 23.20, Mal. 3.1 and Isa. 40.3. Matthew and Luke appear to have moved the
Exod. 23.20/Mal. 3.1 material to another location (Mt. 11.10; Lk. 7.27) and placed
it on the lips of Jesus. This allows the Isaiah ascription (Mt. 3.3; Lk. 3.4) to intro-
duce words that only come from Isaiah. Later scribes had a different solution,
changing the ascription in Mk 1.2 from 'Isaiah' to 'the prophets'.[2] Marcus deduces
from this that the composite quotation is the work of Mark, who associated Mal.
3.1 with Isa. 40.3 through the common phrase פַּנּוּ דֶרֶךְ ('clear away'),[3] which
only occurs in these two texts, plus two related ones (Isa. 57.14; 62.10). In effect,
what Mark is telling us is that the 'good news of Jesus Christ, the Son of God' is
written in Isaiah, which is therefore the key to understanding the Gospel. Marcus
says:

> John the Baptist and Jesus are set firmly within the context of Jewish apocalyptic
> eschatology by the citation of Isa. 40.3 in Mark 1.3. Their appearance on the scene
> fulfills the prophecies of old because it heralds eschatological events, because it is the
> preparation for and the beginning of the fulfillment of that end so eagerly yearned for
> since Old Testament times: the triumphant march of the holy warrior, Yahweh, leading
> his people through the wilderness to their true homeland in a mighty demonstration of
> saving power. (1992: 29)

This 'way' through the wilderness links with Mark 8–10, which has often been
characterized as 'following Jesus on the way' because of the occurrence of ἐν τῇ
ὁδῷ in Mk 8.27 and 10.52 (Best 1982: 5). The reader, says Marcus, would connect this 'way to Jerusalem' with the promised 'way' quoted in Mk 1.2–3 and so
deduce that 'the fearful trek of the befuddled, bedraggled little band of disciples
is the return of Israel to Zion, and Jesus' suffering and death there are the
prophesied apocalyptic victory of the divine warrior' (1992: 36). Of course, it
would be difficult to argue that this is what the historical Isaiah had in mind when
he spoke of a triumphant march through the wilderness but Mark is not simply
reproducing the thought of Isaiah 40, he is offering a 'radical, cross-centred
adaptation of it' (1992: 36).

---

2.   Ησαια is read by Χ Β L Δ 33 565 892 1241 2427 al sy[p. hmg] co; Or[pt]
3.   The piel of פנה is better translated 'clear' or 'clear away', despite the traditional rendering,
'prepare'. See BDB, 815.

Richard Schneck builds on this by asserting that a significant quotation or allusion to Isaiah can be found in each of Mark's first eight chapters. He begins by asserting that the prologue to Mark's Gospel, which he considers to be Mk 1.1–15, has a number of similarities to the prologue to Deutero-Isaiah (Isa. 40.1–11). These are: (1) The reference to a 'voice in the wilderness'; (2) The role both texts play as 'prologues' to a larger work; (3) The use of εὐαγγέλιον or εὐαγγελιζόμενος for God's joyful intervention; (4) Stress on the power of the one who is to come; (5) Focus on the rule or reign of God, especially in the Targumic reading of Isa. 40.9 ('The kingdom of your God is revealed'); (6) The word of God is to be jubilantly proclaimed; (7) Both are concerned with the forgiveness of sins (Isa. 40.2; Mk 1.4). Schneck concludes from this that 'the whole unit of Isa. 40.1–11 was intended by Mark to be taken into account for a full and proper understanding of the Markan prologue' (1994: 42).

He then seeks to show how there is a significant quotation or allusion to Isaiah in chapters 2–8 of Mark. In Mark 4 and 7, there is an explicit quotation (Isa. 6.9–10; 29.13). In Mark 2, he suggests that Isaiah 58 lies behind the discourse on fasting ('you fast only to quarrel and to fight… Is not this the fast that I choose: to loose the bonds of injustice…?'). On the surface, Mark 3 seems devoid of any obvious allusions to Isaiah but Schneck argues a case for Isaiah 49 as a background for the 'doing good on the Sabbath' sayings (Mk 3.4–7). For Mark 5, the story of the demoniac is clothed in imagery borrowed from Isa. 65.1–7 (pigs, demons, tombs, pagan territory). Mark 6 probably contains allusions to Isa. 55.1–3 (Mk 6.34–44) and Isa. 25.6 (Mk 6.39–40) but the strongest evidence is the reappearance of Isa. 6.9–10 in Mk 6.52. Lastly, Mk 8.17 also contains an allusion back to Isa. 6.9–10 and Mk 8.25 alludes to the first of the servant poems in Isa. 42.6–7. Schneck concludes that Isaiah was Mark's most important scriptural source and that by quotation and allusion, Mark intends to evoke this important salvation-history background.

Rikki Watts agrees with this but also wishes to do justice to the fact that the quotation is composite and includes a reference to Malachi. Mark's aim, he says, is to signal not only the salvation background of Isaiah but also the judgment theme of Malachi:

> Mark's opening composite citation is intended to evoke two different but closely related schemata. First, the appeal to Isaiah 40 evinces Israel's great hope of Yahweh's coming to initiate her restorational NE [New Exodus]. Second, the allusion to Malachi not only recalls the delay of this NE but also sounds an ominous note of warning in that the nation must be prepared or else face purging judgment… These twin themes of the fulfilment of the delayed INE [Isaian New Exodus] promise and possible judgment due to lack of preparedness are fused in Mark's opening citation and together seem to establish the basic thematic contours for his presentation of Jesus. (1997: 370)

Watts supports this by showing how the Malachi theme is picked up elsewhere in Mark's narrative. For example, the discussion in Mk 9.9–13 as to why Elijah must come first is clearly a reference to the final words of Malachi ('Lo, I will send you the prophet Elijah before the great and terrible day of the Lord comes'). The cleansing of the temple, cursing of the fig tree and the rent curtain can all plausibly be understood in the light of 'the Lord whom you seek will suddenly come to his temple' (Mal. 3.1), while the rejection of Jesus by the religious leaders could be seen as evidence of their unpreparedness and thus offers an explanation for the coming judgment. Watts believes that the composite quotation not only evokes the Isaian new exodus background but also the Elijah/judgment theme from the book of Malachi.[4]

Meaning Primarily from the New Context

Despite the apparent fruitfulness of this 'maximal' approach, a number of scholars have begun to question its basic assumptions. Christopher Stanley, for example, doubts that Paul's Gentile hearers would have had the facility to make the sort of intertextual connections proposed by modern scholars. It is one thing to claim that they would have been familiar with the basic story of Israel; quite another to claim that they were a walking concordance of scriptural cross-references (1997: 79–96). Christopher Tuckett makes a similar point. First, he notes that standards of literacy were not high in the ancient world. One estimate places it at no more than 20 per cent, and though it is now recognized that Christians were not drawn from the lowest strata, very few of them would have been in this top 20 per cent. Second, the production of texts was expensive and very few would have access to actual copies. Thus talk of evoking the original context is misleading. For the majority of Christians, context would mean either the 'lectionary' context (from the synagogue) or its contemporary application in the Christian community. In short, we cannot assume that a quoted text would immediately evoke the larger context in which we now find it, especially a modern construction such as 'Deutero-Isaiah' or 'The Suffering Servant'. That is not how the majority of first-century readers would have encountered the text (Tuckett 2002: 71–97).

The Meaning of the 'Wilderness' Quotation from the Narrative of Mark Alone

Thomas Hatina complains that instead of focusing on key themes of Mark's narrative, such as characterization and plot, the 'source-orientated practitioner subverts this process by assuming that the hermeneutical key is to be found in Mark's exegesis of Scripture' (2002: 46). For Hatina, the meaning of a scriptural quotation derives primarily from its narrative function in the Gospel, not from something outside of it. Whatever meanings and functions the text once had, the quoted material now takes its meaning from the contextual connections that the new author has established. Thus while Hatina acknowledges that Marcus's work contains many useful insights, he believes it is flawed on ideological grounds:

> Marcus's antagonism toward the view that Mark exegeted Scripture atomistically results in forcing too much of the context of the scriptural passage into the Markan context. Further, one wonders, given Marcus's acquaintance with the relevant Jewish primary literature, why he has not allowed for atomistic exegesis since this was the norm in early Jewish interpretation. (2002: 42)

4.   For the view that priority should be given to the Malachi theme because it comes first in the composite quotation, see Sankey (1985).

According to Hatina, Watts is even more guilty of this, for he assumes that the composite quotation is also intended to evoke the backgrounds of Exod. 23.20 and Mal. 3.1. Thus Watts argues that the judgment background of Mal. 3.1 prepares for the confrontations between Jesus and the Jewish leadership, particularly the incident in the temple. Now at first sight, the phrase, 'the Lord whom you seek will suddenly come to his temple' is certainly evocative, but there are two problems with importing the surrounding context into Mark's narrative. First, there is no indication in the immediate context of Mk 1.2–3 that this is what Mark intended. Had Jesus' announcement in Mk 1.15 alluded to Malachi, or had the temple incident immediately followed (as it does in John), this might be more plausible, but as it stands, the most natural reading is that the quotation refers to what immediately follows, namely, the ministry of John the Baptist.

Second, Hatina is able to show that Watts utilizes a highly selective understanding of the Malachi context, for Mal. 3.3 says, 'he will purify the descendants of Levi and refine them like gold and silver, until they present offerings to the LORD in righteousness'. Does Watts wish to suggest that Jesus' mission is to purify the descendants of Levi so that they may once again offer the prescribed sacrifices? Of course not. Watts knows the Gospel story and selects what he wants from Malachi to construct the so-called 'original context' of Mal. 3.1. Other aspects, such as Mal. 3.3, are simply ignored.

Hatina's objections to the 'maximal' interpretation of Marcus, Schneck and Watts can be summarized in four points (2002: 159): (1) It is based on modern Western understandings of quotation rather than ancient quotation techniques; (2) It fails to take into account that a quotation may have a range of rhetorical functions within the context in which it is now embedded; (3) It assumes that the original context of a quotation is more determinative in establishing its meaning than its function in the new work; and (4) It assumes that dictional and thematic links like εὐαγγέλιον and ὁδός can be traced back to a single source.

How then does Hatina understand the role and function of the composite quotation? First, the quotation is part of the prologue (Mk 1.1–15) which introduces the main theme of the Gospel, namely, the coming of Jesus to usher in the kingdom of God (1.14–15). In preparation for that, Mark introduces us to the role of the forerunner, mentioning his location ('wilderness'), actions ('baptizing'), diet ('locusts and wild honey'), clothes ('camel hair') and message ('one who is more powerful than I coming'). According to Hatina, the quoted material can be adequately understood in the light of this. Thus God is announcing that he will send a messenger (John) to prepare the way (the whole of John's ministry) for Jesus. In turn, John announces to the people that they are to prepare the way of the Lord by repenting of their sins and undergoing baptism 'as a public demonstration of their purification before the coming of the "Mighty One" who will baptize in the Holy Spirit' (2002: 182). The original meaning of 'clearing a path' through the wilderness is discarded in favour of identifying John as the messenger or forerunner. This becomes apparent when we observe the change in syntax between Isa. 40.3 and Mk 1.2–3:

> A voice cries out: 'In the wilderness prepare the way of the LORD, make straight in the desert a highway for our God.' (Isa. 40.3)
>
> As it is written in the prophet Isaiah, 'See, I am sending my messenger ahead of you, who will prepare your way; the voice of one crying out in the wilderness: "Prepare the way of the Lord, make his paths straight."' (Mk 1.2–3)

Thus the use of the Malachi material is not to provide another overarching framework for understanding Jesus (*pace* Watts) but to identify John as the returning Elijah (see Mk 9.12–13). This also initiates a change of meaning of Isa. 40.3, for John does not begin construction work in the wilderness but prepares people for the coming kingdom of God. The LXX had already begun the process of updating this prophecy by changing the singular 'highway' to the plural 'paths' (τρίβους) and rendering the piel of פנה ('to clear') by ἑτοιμάζω ('to prepare').[5] The readers of the LXX were not envisaging a return to Jerusalem by the construction of a single 'highway', for they were no longer in Babylon but dispersed. Furthermore, the choice of ἑτοιμάζω ('prepare') might already indicate that τρίβους is being taken figuratively (they are not thinking of literal highways at all). In this respect, it is interesting that the Qumran community appears to have taken the location in the wilderness literally but the construction of 'the way' figuratively, for it is explained as the study of Torah (1QS 8.13–18).

What then does Mark envisage when he has John the Baptist say, 'Prepare the way of the Lord, make his paths straight'? Marcus and Watts think that readers would immediately connect the 'highway' that signals the end of the exile with Jesus' 'way' to the cross. Hatina does not wish to dismiss the possibility of *some influence* from the Old Testament here but denies that it should be treated as a guiding metanarrative, for 'the correspondence does not extend to all the functions of these figures in their Old Testament contexts' (2002: 182). The fact that Mark (or his source) follows the LXX use of ἑτοιμάζω and τρίβους blunts the connection with a singular 'highway' and points to a more ethical interpretation, as at Qumran. John is 'preparing the people to travel along a road that the "Mightier One" will ask them to travel. By coming to baptism, the people metaphorically prepare for ethical (and even religious) transformation.' For Hatina then, Mark's narrative determines how he understands the scriptural quotations, not the other way around.

Analysis

In the light of the five factors mentioned at the beginning of this article, it is clear that the 'maximal' interpretation places the greatest emphasis on the third, namely, that a quotation brings with it connotations and associations from its original historical or literary context. By assuming this as a general principle, it searches (and finds) numerous parallels that link the prologue of Deutero-Isaiah

---

5.   Unless of course the LXX is witness to a different form of the Hebrew text. It is interesting that when מסלה is used in a similar sense in Isa. 62.10, the LXX omits it altogether. Nevertheless, as Hatina notes, it remains perplexing why the LXX did not also change the singular ὁδός to a plural.

with the prologue of Mark's Gospel. It also appeals to the first factor by high-lighting the importance of themes like ὁδός in the rest of Mark's narrative, thus seeking to demonstrate that this interpretation is clearly signalled by Mark him-self. On the other hand, it has to acknowledge that the story of Jesus takes quite a different turn to the 'highway to Jerusalem' envisaged by Isaiah. For Watts, this is solved by the composite quotation, where Mark fuses Malachi's threat of judgment through unpreparedness with Isaiah's promised new exodus, and this is what gives shape to Mark's narrative. For Marcus, there is a more dialectical understanding that Mark does not simply reproduce Isaiah's promise but offers a 'radical, cross-centred adaptation of it' (1992: 36).

Hatina also focuses on the first factor but in a different way. For him, it is the internal dynamics of characterization and plot that primarily determine meaning, not texts or events outside of the narrative. The parallels quoted by Marcus, Schneck and Watts are regarded by Hatina as deceptively selective, the product of a particular salvation-history ideology. Hatina subscribes to a different ideol-ogy, namely, that a narrative approach to the Gospels implies that Mark's story world provides the interpretative framework for understanding quotations, not their original or subsequent contexts. In order to support this, he draws on the second factor, namely, that changes to the quoted material might indicate the author's redactional interests. Thus he thinks the use of ἑτοιμάζω and τρίβους point to a more ethical interpretation of ὁδός than its meaning in Deutero-Isaiah. He also draws on the fourth factor (1) when he claims that first-century Jewish exegesis was atomistic, and (2) when he cites the Qumran interpretation that 'preparing the way' has an ethical meaning (Torah study). Hatina believes that the first-century context supports his narrative stance that Mark's story world determines the meaning of the wilderness quotation, not its meaning outside of the Gospel.

Though both interpretations use historical criticism to support their positions, their very different assessments of the evidence suggests that the fifth factor, the ideological stance of the commentator, deserves more consideration. For example, Hatina makes the sweeping statement that first-century Jewish exege-sis was atomistic. Some scholars have indeed argued for this but others, such as Brooke (1985) and Instone-Brewer (1992), have denied it. It is true that *pesher* interpretation often yields meanings that are surprising to us (as heirs of the Enlightenment), but is it true that the Qumran community had no interest in the overarching purposes of God (metanarrative) as revealed in Scripture? Clearly they were not concerned with 'original context' in the way that modern critics are but they were certainly interested in the metanarrative of God's scriptural plan, for they saw themselves as participating in its final chapter. Hatina's explicit adoption of a narrative approach, which by definition, marginalizes influences outside of the text, has affected his historical judgments.

Marcus, Schneck and Watts are less explicit about their ideological commit-ments but they are nevertheless detectable from their critical judgments. For example, Watts claims that the quotation of Mal. 3.1 evokes its original context and even includes references as far away as Mal. 4.5. However, he conveniently ignores Mal. 3.3, which would not have suited his argument. On what herme-neutical theory would readers import the meaning of Mal. 4.5 ('Lo, I will send you the prophet Elijah') but ignore the content of Mal. 3.3? It cannot be the general principle that quotations evoke their surrounding context since Mal. 3.3 is far closer to Mal. 3.1 than Mal. 4.5. In reality, Watts constructs the 'original context' of Mal. 3.1 to reflect the contents of Mark's Gospel. Similarly Schneck, although many of his parallels between Isa. 40.1–11 and Mk 1.1–15 are convincing, makes too much of what are only echoes or faint allusions to Isaiah in Mark 3 and 5. It is not that they are impossible, for allusions can indeed be the faintest of whispers (Hays 1989: 155). It is more that his conclusion from this evidence should have been that *sometimes* quotations and allusions point loudly to their previous contexts and *sometimes* they do not.

Conclusion

The ideological stance of the commentator is a significant factor in assessing the meaning of the wilderness quotation of Mk 1.2–3. Hatina's commitment to a narrative approach diminishes the influence of sources outside of Mark's story world, but is this true? Real readers inhabit many worlds, not just the world of the text. They are thus influenced by many things, one of which is other texts. On the other hand, Watts's commitment to biblical theology does not allow for the possibility that Mark *might* be giving new meaning to the wilderness text. After all, Mark is writing for a completely different audience in a different time and a different place. It would surely be surprising if we could maintain identity of meaning across such divides. In both cases then, it would seem that ideological commitments have led to blind spots when interpreting certain aspects of the evidence.

Does this mean that the interpretation of the wilderness quotation is a purely subjective affair? Not necessarily, for ideological commitments can be discussed and debated. In particular, I would suggest that neither a biblical theology that affirms identity of meaning nor a narrative approach that excludes external 'influence' are adequate for the task. At the very least, we need an ideology that can explain how Mark can both appropriate Isaiah's promise of exodus (itself a development of the original exodus tradition), while offering, in Marcus's words, a 'radical, cross-centred adaptation of it' (1992: 36). In terms of this debate, what we need is a more sophisticated biblical theology that can encompass discontinuity as well as continuity, and a more sophisticated literary theory that can combine insights from narrative criticism with insights from intertextuality (taking 'texts' in its broadest sense). Both concerns are present in the person to whom this volume is dedicated (Young: 1990, 1997) and were nurtured in me during my time of study at the University of Birmingham (1984–90).

BIBLIOGRAPHY

Best, E.
1981   *Following Jesus: Discipleship in the Gospel of Mark* (JSNTSup, 4; Sheffield: JSOT Press).

Brooke, G. J.
   1985   *Exegesis at Qumran: 4Q Florilegium in its Jewish Context* (Sheffield: JSOT Press).
Dodd, C. H.
   1952   *According to the Scriptures* (London: Fontana).
Hays, R. B.
   1989   *Echoes of Scripture in the Letters of Paul* (New Haven: Yale University Press).
Hatina, T.
   2002   *In Search of a Context: The Function of Scripture in Mark's Narrative* (JSNTSup, 232; Sheffield: Sheffield Academic Press).
Hollander, J.
   1981   *The Figure of Echo: A Mode of Allusion in Milton and After* (Berkeley: University of California Press).
Instone-Brewer, D.
   1992   *Techniques and Assumptions in Jewish Exegesis before 70 CE* (Texte und Studien zum antiken Judentum, 30; Tübingen: Mohr Siebeck).
Marcus, J.
   1992   *The Way of the Lord. Christological Exegesis of the Old Testament in the Gospel of Mark* (Edinburgh: T&T Clark).
Moi, T. (ed.)
   1986   *The Kristeva Reader* (New York: Columbia University Press).
Moyise, S.
   2001   'Intertextuality and the Study of the Old Testament in the New Testament', in S. Moyise (ed.), *The Old Testament in the New Testament* (JSNTSup, 189; Sheffield: Sheffield Academic Press), 14–41.
Sankey, P. J.
   1985   'Promise and Fulfillment: Reader-Response to Mark 1:1–15', *JSNT* 58: 3–18.
Schneck, R.
   1994   *Isaiah in the Gospel of Mark, 1–VIII* (Berkeley: BIBAL Press).
Stanley, C. D.
   1997   'The Social Environment of "Free" Biblical Quotations in the New Testament', in C. A. Evans and J. A. Sanders (eds.), *Early Christian Interpretation of the Scriptures of Israel* (JSNTSup, 148; Sheffield: Sheffield Academic Press), 79–96.
Tuckett, C.
   2002   'Paul, Scripture and Ethics', in J. M. Court (ed.), *New Testament Writers and the Old Testament* (London: SPCK), 71–97.
Vorster, W.
   1989   'Intertextuality and Redaktionsgeschichte', in S. Draisma (ed.), *Intertextuality in Biblical Writings* (Festschrift B.van Iersel; Kampen: Kok), 21.
Watts, R. E.
   1997   *Isaiah's New Exodus and Mark* (WUNT, 2.88; Tübingen: Mohr Siebeck).
Young, F. W.
   1990   *The Art of Performance* (London: Darton, Longman & Todd).
   1997   *Biblical Exegesis and the Formation of Christian Culture* (Cambridge: Cambridge University Press).

READING JESUS IN THE WILDERNESS

Judith Lieu

In her essay for the, then controversial, *Myth of God Incarnate*, Frances Young showed how the narrative of Jesus' 'testing' in the wilderness (Mt. 4.1–11; Lk. 4.1–13) itself constituted a distinctive locus of testing for the conflicting christological positions of the early Church. Were the temptations of Jesus a scene of genuine struggle, with the possibility of failure, or were they but a sham, a sham that might expose the limits of the divine involvement in human experience and in the world (Young 1977: 26–7).[1] Her own position is unequivocal: it has to be affirmed that God truly entered into human experience and that God dealt with it; we have to be able to tell two stories, '(a) the story of a *man* who lived as the "archetypal believer", who lived and died trusting in God ... [and] (b) the story of *God* being involved in the reality of human existence with its compromises, its temptations, its suffering, its pain, its injustice, its cruelty, its *death* ...' (37) Here 'temptations' become absorbed into a litany of the ambiguities of human existence, ambiguities that can only truly be recognized as such in the light of a belief in that same God as the creator not only of human existence but also of the totality within which it runs its course, and also in that same God as a God of justice, truth and love. They model what it is both for 'a man' to live trusting in God, and for God to accept involvement, but in so doing they fall under the shadow of the death in which both human trust and divine involvement most deeply intersect. Yet, we must conclude, their status is different: the death of which we can speak can only be that death; we cannot allow that Jesus died at some other time, in some other way than that remembered in both narrative and confession (1 Cor. 1.21–5). Can we, however, without loss replace the devil with the suppressed fantasies of the mind or of others' urging, the stones on the desert floor with the seduction of instant success, or the mountain-top vista with heady popular acclaim, both also attested in the Gospel narratives (Mk 8.11–13; Jn 6.14–15); still more, can we replace them with their mundane counterparts in our own lives? To explore the question we shall bring into dialogue Jesus' temptations as they are reflected on in theology, exegesis, and narrative in the earliest and in the most recent periods.

It was only with the christological disputes that were to lead to the doctrine of the two natures that the question of whether Jesus was tempted and triumphed as

---

1.   I had started my research with Frances the previous year, 1976; this essay is offered with deep respect and in appreciation of support and friendship since then.

man or as divine Logos could be posed in all its sharpness (Köppen 1961: 85–9). Yet Irenaeus already remarked on the fact that Jesus did not respond to the devil's address to him as 'Son of God', but by his reply, 'man does not live by bread alone', acknowledged his human nature (*Haer.* V.21).[2] Here it is the first temptation and Jesus' hunger that provides the strongest support against a docetic Christology. Tertullian will also use this to demonstrate the reality of Jesus' flesh (*Carn.* 9.7; *Prax.* 27.11).[3] On the other hand, if the devil himself acknowledges Jesus as the Son of God, there is little room for others to deny it.[4] The dilemma here that subsequent generations will wrestle over hardly clouds the sky; if some puzzle over the vulnerability displayed, Tertullian emphasizes that the temptation belongs to the first advent, not to the second, which is still anticipated (*Marc.* III.7.6; *Iud.* 14.7). Origen has no embarrassment in ascribing the Fourth Evangelist's failure to describe the temptations to the fact that he was speaking about God, and God cannot be tempted, but when commenting on Luke, he is content to say that Jesus was tempted as man 'for your sake', although this he interprets paraenetically rather than soteriologically (*Hom. in Luc.* 29.6).

However, as early as Justin the deeper resonances of the temptation stories can be exploited within a demonstration that 'he truly became man susceptible of sufferings', even to the extent of his prayer for escape and his submission to the will of God (*Dial.* 99.2). In his extended application of Psalm 22 (LXX 21) to the story of Jesus' passion, Justin suggests that an alternative reference of the 'roaring lion' of verse 14 is 'the devil, whom Moses calls "serpent", who in Job and Zechariah is called "devil", and who was addressed by Jesus as "satan"' (103.5).[5] He establishes the connection with the serpent of Gen. 3.1 through a spurious etymology of the apparently obscure (to him) *satanas: satan* means in Hebrew and Syriac 'apostate', from *nas* derives the translation 'serpent'.[6] This then produces a parallel between the devil's corruption of Adam and his attempt 'to achieve something' against Jesus in his invitation, 'Worship me'; it was an invitation given at the very moment that Jesus came up out of the Jordan after the heavenly words, 'You are my son, today I have begotten you' (103.6). This slightly cryptic formulation becomes more patent through Justin's earlier excursus on how Jesus can be called Son of God and Son of Man: there he draws a parallel between Jesus, born as man through the faithful virgin, and that other virgin, Eve, who, conceiving from the word of the serpent, gave birth to disobedience and death: the means of the origin of disobedience would become the means of its destruction, and of the destruction of the serpent and those angels and men like it (100.4–6).[7]

2.   A theme later more clearly developed as the deliberate deception of Satan as to the true identity of his antagonist.

3.   Later exegetes would debate whether Jesus' hunger was real or not.

4.   Irenaeus, *Haer.* IV.6.6; Tertullian, *Prax.* 16.4; 26.8.

5.   The exegesis runs from *Dial.* 97.3 to 106.2.

6.   In *Apol.* 28.1 Justin simply explains that 'serpent', 'devil' and 'satan' are the names given by us to the prince of demons.

7.   On this see Steiner (1962: 12–14).

Irenaeus offers a more developed form of this exegesis, explicitly rooting in it his doctrine of recapitulation (*Haer.* V.19.1; V. 21–4).[8] Here is fulfilled the prophecy of Gen. 3.15, as testified to by Paul in Gal. 3.19 and 4.4: as seed, born of a woman, after the likeness of Adam, Jesus recapitulates that ancient enmity and offers life and victory to those enthralled by the first defeat. How humanity appropriates that victory will, of course, provide subsequent theologians with new challenges. To prove his point Irenaeus, unlike Justin, discourses on all three temptations; as by food came the first transgression, so too comes victory over it; the infringement of God's command by Adam is cancelled by the Son of Man's obedience to God's command: it is this resolute obedience that lies at the heart of what the temptations are about. All this is also integral to Irenaeus' polemic against those whom he labels heretics, for it refutes any who suggest a division between the creator God or demiurge and the one whom Jesus calls Father, while Jesus' own appeal to the Law demonstrates that it was not rooted in ignorance and defect: there is here one continuous story.[9] Its soteriological significance extends beyond this: Irenaeus can now say, 'By summing up in himself the whole human race from the beginning to the end, he has also summed up its death' (*Haer.* V.24.2). M. Steiner observes that in this passage 'the scene of the temptation of Jesus is placed at the centre of the history of salvation'; noting that Irenaeus makes no reference to the death of Jesus, he asks whether we can see here 'an invitation, addressed by Irenaeus to his reader, to see in the scene of the temptation the revelation of this essential aspect of the whole work of the Saviour: his victorious encounter with Satan and the liberation of captive man?' (1962: 76). The temptations are not to be understood in the shadow of Jesus' death, but Jesus' death in the shadow of the temptations.

Justin provides a second reading of the devil's attempt to persuade Jesus to worship him that was to prove less influential (*Dial.* 125). This belongs to an extended argument claiming for Jesus, and for those who follow him, the title and privileges of 'Israel', an important theme in Justin's thought. 'Israel', he claims, means 'a man who conquers (*isra*) power (*el*)'; it was as man that Jesus conquered the devil who is 'that power which is also called serpent and satan', in a contest that was prefigured by Jacob's encounter with his mysterious antagonist (Gen. 32.23–33).[10] However, Justin is unable to resist finding Christ already present in so potent a theophany, also in that same assailant who is identified both as man and as God, and who blesses Jacob with his own name, Israel.[11] That others did not take up this use of the temptation narrative, should not then surprise us; however, that Jesus' fasting in the wilderness was prefigured in Scrip-

---

8. For a full discussion see Steiner (1962: 45–80).

9. It also provides a demonic ancestry for those who use Scripture to support their own deceptions.

10. For this interpretation of *el* see Aquila at Gen. 17.1 etc.; Justin does not refer to Mt. 12.29, the binding of the strong man, which Irenaeus does apply to Jesus' defeat of the devil (*Haer.* V.21.3).

11. Justin seems to deduce it is his own name since the blessing is in reponse to Jacob's request for his name.

ture, here by Moses and Elijah, is already noted by Irenaeus (*Haer.* V.21.2), although the link with Israel's wilderness wanderings favoured by contemporary exegetes does not appear to have struck the earliest interpreters.[12]

Yet even in these christological readings the paraenetic function of the narratives is never far away: it offers an encouragement to Christians when faced with temptations, the source of which is revealed as the deceit of the devil.[13] Jesus provides a model, of patience in his refusal to use more than words against the devil, but more particularly of enduring temptation immediately after baptism: for Christians, too, baptism is not the end of the struggle but its beginning and so must be accompanied by fasting, as it was by Jesus himself.[14] In these ways the story of the temptation of Jesus in the wilderness provides a new framework for understanding the experience of struggle and compromise that marks all human life, but particularly marks that of believers. Jesus was indeed tempted in his humanity, but believers can discover that their temptations belong to the struggle against the supernatural forces of evil.

Contemporary readings of Jesus' temptations adopt a very different starting point; even when labouring under the shadow of Athanasius and Arius, and perhaps more under that of the epigrammatic 'tested in every way in likeness without sin' of Heb. 4.15, they labour too under the spirit of Ernst Rénan's assertion, 'no angel of God comforted him, except his good conscience; no Satan tempted him, except that which each one bears in his heart' (1863: 310). Leonard Hodgson represents a traditional position in arguing that, although our temptations are 'due to our sinfulness, or to our incomplete detachment from worldly aims and cares', temptation as such 'is an integral part of human life, which no-one can escape, however close may be his communion with God', and so was possible for a Jesus who was none the less free from sin (Hodgson 1928: 399). Yet understandings of sin as well as the turn to theological anthropology will not rest here. John Macquarrie is less than happy with this distinction, and with traditional formulations of Jesus' sinlessness, even of a *posse non peccare*; he prefers to see Jesus' sinlessness as dynamic, as part of a 'progressive incarnation' within which Jesus was not only implicated in corporate sin, but also knew that alienation from God which is intrinsic to what it is to be human (Macquarrie 1990: 398). This means that he cannot accept the 'all-at once' implications of the Gospel temptation narratives: the sense of the cross, he believes, emerged only late during Jesus' ministry; and yet, 'one might venture to say that even at the beginning of his ministry he chose the way of non-violence, of service to his fellows, of teaching, discussion and communication, as we read about his methods in the gospels' (p. 396).

This turn to a historicizing interpretation of the temptation narratives for a theological purpose is widespread, and frequently the language of sin gets lost on the way. John V. Taylor prefers to speak of the struggle about making ethical decisions: 'The *context* of that withdrawal into the desert was political... The

---

12. For Moses see Exod. 34.28; Deut. 9.9, 18; Elijah 1 Kgs 19.8.
13. Tertullian, *Orat.* 8.4.
14. Tertullian, *Bapt.* 20.4; *Pat.* 3.2; Cyprian, *Bon.Pat.* 6.

content of the spiritual struggle which took place then was the right use of power' (1992: 260–4). Here, he asserts the inescapability of power in all human activity and its ever-present tendency to corrupt. There is in this a moral serious-ness and a realism that is missing from an earlier move in the same direction by H. E. W. Turner, who sees in the temptations Jesus' decision to be a 'spiritual messiah', rejecting the possibilities of an economic, a sign-giving, or a political style (1953: 98). Turner had conceded that 'there is little difficulty in believing that Jesus was really tempted. It is only the spiritually mature who can really feel the force and significance of moral evil'; but his somewhat equivocal assertion that the temptations belong to Jesus 'considered as the Christ and not merely to Jesus as a mere human being' reflects his discomfort with abandoning older formulations.

Yet the fundamental shift of focus is self-evident: the older questions were, given the God-ness of God, how can we speak of the temptations of Jesus, or, what does the temptation narrative say about the place of Jesus in relation to the rest of humanity? Now, the question is, what does the temptation narrative of Jesus, as icon of Jesus, tell us about God – in John Robinson's words, 'the human face of God' (1973)? Yet the implicit challenge of that question, and so the further function of the temptation narrative, will be: How does Jesus' response set up a new model for being human? Thus, for example, within liberation the-ology, Jesus' 'objective choice of service in the manner of the servant' will become a model not just of divine but also of human action (Sobrino 1987: 144–5). It is this that then sharpens the dilemma that, as we have already noted, is faced by Macquarrie. If our focus is on Jesus, is it more realistic to see the temptations as a continuing mark of his life, whether as Macquarrie's 'progressive incarnation' or in Robinson's presentation of a Jesus who can be changed by events (1973: 82)? Or are we better served by an initial decisive commitment to choose the way of service, a commitment integrally tied to Jesus' initiating experience of his divine vocation, in his baptism. Some ignore the question; others, like Macquarrie and Turner, seek to have it both ways.

Yet what also marks all these interpretations is that they are predicated, first, on the demythologization of the narrative, without asking why it takes this 'mythological form', and, secondly, on its historical contextualization, a histori-cal contextualization which is assumed to be unproblematic. Specifically, the details of the temptations are tied to models of messiahship which, it is supposed, were available to Jesus and to popular expectation (Turner); generally, with-drawal into the desert is related to the political situation and to patterns of response in first-century Judaea. In both cases the temptation is programmatic, whether or not we label that as specifically messianic; a picture of first-century Judaism, and of messianism, is taken very largely for granted without historical warrant. Here, as in other readings of Jesus (e.g. the entry into Jerusalem), one sometimes feels that there *must* have been active expectations of a political, wonder-working Messiah, just so that Jesus could, uniquely, reject them. What some would concede was the apologetic function of the temptation narratives in the life of the Church – to explain the unprepossessing life of the one proclaimed as God's representative – has become 'historical reality' in the experience of Jesus.[15]

However, those who approach the problem from the standpoint of a search for 'the historical Jesus' evince rather more caution. Many do find the retreat into the wilderness more than credible, given parallels in the accounts of Josephus, of Paul, and of the Dead Sea Community: 'It is intrinsically likely that from time to time Jesus sought solitude for prayer and meditation, that he sometimes felt tempted, and that he fasted before beginning his public activity' is something that even E. P. Sanders concedes (1993: 112). Others will go further and at least raise the question as to whether the narrative details allow us to speak of 'an experience of Jesus himself', or even of 'a profound personal crisis', presumably transmitted by him to his disciples (Dunn 2003: 379; Bockmuehl 1994: 80). Yet they find support for such a confidence in similar experiences reported by or of other spiritual figures: 'solitude and fasting, practices which produce changes in consciousness and perception, typical of what other traditions call a "vision quest"' (Borg 1987: 42–3).[16] The authenticity of the particularity of the temptations is preserved precisely by denying their particularity.

Moreover, some such historians find it difficult to locate such a decisive moment at the beginning of Jesus' public ministry. James Dunn presents an account of Jesus whose early ministry begins as a disciple of John the Baptist, and so he rejects a timing of the temptation experience immediately after Jesus' baptism, since this carries with it some degree of independence and a radical break with the Baptist (2003: 380). Here Dunn echoes John Robinson's briefer but more detailed argument that the temptation narratives reflect the critical turning-point that Jesus faced in the middle of his ministry in the events allusively described in Mk 6.45 and elaborated by Jn 6.15; according to Robinson, it was in this context of the pressure of popular acclaim that Jesus came to an understanding and an acceptance of the suffering and death that would be the outcome of his ministry as Son of Man (cf. Jn 6.66–9: Robinson 1988: 463–4). No less notable, however, is the number of 'historians of Jesus' who ignore the temptation narratives altogether in their reconstructions, presumably as being beyond the realm of historical investigation, both because of their personnel and because of the lack of witnesses.[17] Yet, with the exception of those who respond with silence, what unites the 'historical' and the christological approaches we have surveyed is their *episodic* treatment of the narratives: they function in some way as self-standing 'events'.

15. Here the 'divine man' can more reasonably take the place of the wonder-working Messiah.

16. Cf. Dunn (2003: 379–80) who speaks of 'typical religious experience and motivation', and, like others, uses the category of the shaman.

17. So Meier (1994: 272) notes that a withdrawal into the wilderness is not impossible, but that the story could be 'symbolic representation of the apocalyptic struggle between God and the devil which was prophesied for the last days': this note is his only reference in 3 volumes. Dunn also prefers to speak of the story as bearing witness to 'the impression Jesus made on his disciples'. Crossan does not refer to them in his narrative, while in his analysis of the strata of the tradition and its attestation he does identify the temptation narratives as 'a dramatic historicization of something that took place over a much longer period' (1991: 440).

It is here that we should turn to the exegetes, for before the temptation narratives can be lifted into the ministry of Jesus, losing their satanic antagonist in the
process, they must be read within the broader narratives of which they are a part.
We need to distinguish different levels of that exercise: first, they must be read
independently within the total narrative of Matthew and of Luke;[18] secondly,
there is the intertextual reading which acknowledges that the stories are shaped
by earlier stories, whether or not we feel that the particular Matthaean or Lukan
setting signals any one intertextual partner. Thirdly, we may ask about their place
in the earlier tradition, which many would initially identify as 'Q', and possibly
as a particular stage in the redactional history of Q. Only then can we begin to
ask what the story might mean in its earliest telling or experience – and what it
means to ask that question.

So, for example, many have noted in the *Matthaean* context the way that the
satanic invitation anticipates the repeated taunting of Jesus on the cross, 'If you
are the Son of God' (Mt. 27.40, 43: Matthew only); both Satan and the mocking
chief priests appeal to similar passages from the Psalms in their challenge to
Jesus to cast himself down or to come down from the cross (4.6; 27.42–3).[19]
Jesus' first words come from Scripture as do his last (4.4; 27.46); and he responds
to Peter, who had confessed him as Son of God but who then anticipates the
temptation implicit in the crowd's mockery, with the words that he had used to
the tempter, 'Go hence, Satan' (4.10; 16.23) (Graham 1997; Hasitschka 1997).
Martin Hasitschka also notes how the invitation to *worship* (*proskunein*) the
devil, and Jesus' non-septuagintal response, 'You shall *worship* the Lord your
God ...', carry a particular resonance in a Gospel where people do regularly
come and 'worship' Jesus, and he suggests that this demonstrates 'that Jesus
participates in God's might and honour' (1997: 490).[20] The temptation narrative
might also be read as putting into action Jesus' response to John's objection
when Jesus comes for baptism, 'it is fitting for us to fulfil all righteousness', a
distinctively Matthaean theme (3.15); after all, although the heavenly voice
acknowledged Jesus as 'my beloved son' at the baptism, this we already knew, as
readers, to be the case from the start, and particularly from 2.15, 'Out of Egypt I
called my son' (= Hos. 11.1). Perhaps, too, the three locations of the temptation,
desert, Jerusalem, and mountain, anticipate the role these latter will also have in
the continuing story of Jesus.[21]

18. We shall not explore the Markan reference here, although the wilderness theme in Mark has
been richly (perhaps too richly) explored by Mauser (1963).

19. In Luke the taunts focus on Jesus as king of the Jews or as Christ, and invite him to save
himself, not to come down from the cross; the mocking appeal to Ps. 22.9 (LXX 21.9) comes only in
Matthew. Gerhardsson (1996: 306) makes much of the triple taunts (including the bandits in 27.44,
although they are given no words).

20. The verb *proskunein* comes 11 times in Matthew besides these two; in Luke only one other.
LXX Deut. 6.13 reads 'you shall fear' (*phobesthai*). Justin (see above) follows the Synoptic text and
also introduces it into the Great Commandment in *Apol.* 16.6. On this see Bellinzoni (1967: 37–43);
Prigent (1987: 37–43).

21. Mauser (1963: 144–5) emphasizes the different use of the wilderness theme in Matthew from
that he traces in Mark and suggests that these three localities may purely serve as topographical
settings.

In the Lukan context, we are struck by the sequence of the temptations – probably a piece of Lukan redaction – which now climax with Jesus' equivocal words. 'You shall not tempt the Lord your God' (Lk. 4.15). Here, Jesus' final temptation in Jerusalem foreshadows the place that Jerusalem will continue to fill in the Lukan narrative, and especially in Jesus' passion which culminates in its own climax of Jesus' commitment of himself into his Father's hands (22.46; cf. 4.11).[22] The statement that follows, that 'the devil left him for a while', has rightly provoked debate as to how this prepares us for the course of Jesus' ministry, as a Satan-free period (until 22.3, 31), or as a sequence of such efforts?[23] Yet the opening words of the account, where Jesus 'returned full of the Holy Spirit', are resumed in the episode that immediately follows, where once again 'he returned in the power of the Spirit' (4.1, 14), a signal that all happens under the Spirit's guidance, a favourite Lukan theme. Further, in Luke the temptations are separated from Jesus' baptism by the genealogy which ends with 'Adam (son) of God'; this has led many to find Jesus here enabling 'the restoration of the image of God in people which Adam's disobedience had lost' (Franklin 2001: 931), so bringing us quickly to the intertextual echoes of the narrative.

As we make that move we need to remember that we are now no longer tracing the surface of the narrative and its internal symbolism, but are adopting a reading mechanism that looks outside the narrative, even though many would argue that it only makes explicit something that is inherent in the creation, and so in the reading, of any text. Yet in Luke it must be questioned whether the sequence of genealogy and temptation is really enough to warrant an Adamic reading without the hindsight of patristic interpretation.[24] In fact it is Mark's 'he was with the wild beasts' (Mk 1.13), which is adopted by neither Matthew nor Luke, and possibly the ministering angels (also in Mt. 4.11), that may suggest the restoration of paradisal conditions, but it is difficult to see what is being made of this. More evident is the intersection with the story of Israel through Jesus' three citations of Deuteronomy; the first of those citations, Deut. 8.3, comes in a context that recalls how God led them in the wilderness (echoed by Lk. 4.1), and tested them (*ekpeirazein*) 'for forty years ... as a man disciplines his son' (Deut. 8.2–5). More specifically, Gerhardsson (1996: 1–23) has argued for an interplay in Matthew with the Shema (Deut. 6.5), and with its interpretation in Jewish exegesis (e.g. *m. Ber.* 9.5), namely the tripartite command to love God with all one's heart, with all one's soul, and with all one's mind. Israel is God's son (cf. Hos. 11.1 cited by Mt. 2.15), and as Israel was tested (not tempted) in the wilderness, so too is Jesus.[25] Where, then, does this take us? Are we to see Jesus as

22. The Matthaean order is generally seen as the 'original' (Q). For a sensitive reading of the narrative in the Lukan context see Radl (2003: 222–40).

23. Conzelmann (1960: 28) followed by Mauser (1963: 148), who finds this confirmed by the reference to the wilderness as a symbol of the old epoch at the beginning of the narrative indicating 'the event of transition from the old epoch to the new'.

24. Attempts to relate the three temptations to the seductions of the tree in Gen. 3.6 involve too much imagination; Fitzmyer (1981: 512) denies any Adamic motifs, but they are accepted by Talbert (1982: 47–8) and Nolland (1989: 178–83).

25. But in Matthew the desert is not the only place of temptation; see above.

the representative of Israel or of the new Israel? Are we invited to continue that where Israel failed, Jesus succeeded? Is there here an antithesis to Israel that will move smoothly into the polemic against her? Each of these positions can and has been taken, and one might argue for one reading in Matthew – whose 'forty days and forty nights' also more clearly recalls Moses (4.1, see n. 12), but where we have also observed the echoes of Satan's taunts in those of the chief priests – and another one in Luke with its emphasis on divine guidance; but such readings only become possible when each narrative reaches its end.[26] The problem may be that when the narrative provides no clues, intertextual echoes are easier to detect than they are to interpret, and that interpreters are liable to elide the different possibilities.

Moreover, it is evident that there are further intertextual possibilities. A number of scholars have pointed to the more extensive traditions of the testing of the righteous in Jewish thought, particularly that of Job where Satan first makes an appearance.[27] Also to be brought into the picture is the righteous sufferer of Wisdom 2, whose opponents determine to test him: 'for if the righteous is a son of God, God will help him and will deliver him from the hand of his opponents' (Wis. 2.18). But the presence of the devil moves such opposition onto another plane.

Whether with these intertextual readings we have already moved to the pre-Gospel tradition of the temptation narratives, to Q, is hard to say, for with Q we lack a context. Some would argue that a narrative context for the taunt, '*If* you are the Son of God', is unavoidable, and that something like the baptismal account seems the most obvious candidate, even though we have no certain traces of a 'Q' version of this; yet an appeal to Wisdom 2 may suggest that that need not be so. Further, given the character of Q as hypothetically a Sayings Source, how would the temptation narrative be read? Its 'mythic' character, its appeal to Scripture, and the echoes or anticipations of the passion narrative have seemed to many to present a problem, indicating that it belongs only to the latest stage, and that it sits uncomfortably with the rest. Others, however, have pointed to the rejection of signs (11.29–30) and to absolute reliance on God as Father, the ultimate source of protection and provision of all that is necessary (11.11; 12.30–1), as key themes elsewhere in Q (Kloppenborg-Verbin 2000: 152, 212–13; Tuckett 1992). In this framework the narratives present Jesus as a paradigmatic figure in his obedience as God's son and in his trust in God's word: those who follow Jesus are also sons of God (6.35) and so are able to share in the struggle and the victory which may still be uniquely Jesus' own. The devil's claim to the kingdoms of the world anticipates Jesus' own teaching about the Kingdom of God and its mani-

26. So Gerhardsson (1996) finds in Matthew Jesus as the firstborn of a new Israel, and an implicit polemic that only becomes explicit in the passion narratives; in Luke, Kimball (1994: 96) sees an 'antithetical Israel–Christ typology', while Bock (1994: 289) speaks only of Jesus as the representative of Israel.

27. However, Satan appears to be introduced into the Matthaean temptation narrative, perhaps from Mk 1.13 or by retrojection from 16.23 = Mk 8.33; otherwise Matthew and Luke speak of 'the devil' here although they know Satan elsewhere.

festation in his casting out of demons (11.20). In these ways, the temptation narratives would admirably set the stage for Q, both by authenticating Jesus as teacher and because they would expose the fundamental issues lying behind all that followed – the need to make a decision, and what that decision was for or against (Tuckett 1992: 2000; Kirk 1998).

To push back further than these narrative functions would be to move away from the text into the realm of conjecture. Many have pointed to an apologetic dimension – the justification of why Jesus, once he was confessed by the early Christians to be Son of God, did not act in ways that might have demonstrated his divine status and rescued him from his ignominious death. Gerd Theissen suggests a socio-political context at least for the third (Matthew) temptation, in the Emperor Caligula's demand for worship and assertion of absolute power which were diametrically opposed to any acknowledgment of God (1992: 206–21). Yet these belong to another level of reading, where the world behind the text shapes the text that we have. Certainly they remind us that what we do have is the product of the experience of the Church, and of specific influences and contexts, important among which must be a Hellenistic setting, the determinative use of the Septuagint, and the conventional tripartite pattern of oral and written tradition.[28] As such they warn against too simplisitic a projection of precisely these, and only these, 'temptations', once 'demythologized', onto the historical person of Jesus.[29] Yet all such readings also entail a certain provisionality about the actual text(s) that we do have: the same concerns could have produced a different text, either in discourse or in narrative form.

We do not encounter Jesus' clash with the devil in the wilderness in any other form than that which it takes in the text. To demythologize it into discarded strategic options for ministry, or even into 'a visionary or inward, spiritual experience' (Kimball 1994: 84), is to produce a different text, an episode in the history or in the psychology of Jesus. Yet we cannot ignore its textual positionings, in Matthew and in Luke, as well as in the greater narratives to which intertextual readings point us. Here we recognize that the temptation narratives can only have the form that they do, and that their meaning inheres in this and not in some supposed reference that lies outside them. The stones on the desert floor, the parapet of the Temple, and the mountain-top vista cannot be exchanged, but neither can the devil; the mythic dimensions are integral.[30] Here contemporary exegesis recognizes what the earliest patristic interpreters also saw; for what characterizes their exegesis is, as Köppen notes, that it is rarely episodic, predominantly salvation-historical (1961: 79). We may be more aware than they of the multi-

28. Theissen (1992: 206–8) notes that form-critically the third temptation differs, lacking the opening formula, 'If you are the Son of God ...'

29. We tread a fine line between not wishing to deny that they may 'bear vivid witness to the impression Jesus made on his disciples', and tying to them alone that 'he was remembered as firmly rejecting populist or merely eye-catching options and as resolutely refusing to compromise on the whole-hearted devotion which God alone could command' (Dunn 2003: 380); but, more importantly, the text we have is other and more than this.

30. So rightly Luz (1989: 191).

plicity of stories within which the temptation narrative may be told, and so of the different forms it may take, the different echoes that may be heard; we will also be more aware of the dangers in the telling, when the devil becomes incarnated in particular people (see Graham 1997: 509–11). Driven to find new retellings, we must find a mythology or a theology that speaks not only of God and man, this man, but of a pattern in the experience of humankind, in their dealings with God and in God's dealings with them; even in the 'offence of particularity', in the story of *this* people without which *this* man cannot be understood, and, perhaps, without which humankind's story cannot be understood.

Bibliography

Bellinzoni, A. J.
    1967   *The Sayings of Jesus in the Writings of Justin Martyr* (NTSup, 17; Leiden: Brill).
Bock, Darrell L.
    1994   'Proclamation from Prophecy and Pattern: Luke's Use of the Old Testament for Christology and Mission', in C. A. Evans and W. R. Stegner (eds.), *The Gospels and the Scriptures of Israel* (JSNTSup, 104; Sheffield: Sheffield Academic Press), 280–307.
Bockmuehl, Markus
    1994   *This Jesus: Martyr, Lord, Messiah* (Edinburgh: T&T Clark).
Borg, Marcus
    1987   *Jesus, a New Vision: Spirit, Culture and the Life of Discipleship* (San Fransisco: Harper).
Conzelmann, Hans
    1960   *The Theology of St. Luke* (ET; London: Faber).
Crossan, John D.
    1991   *The Historical Jesus: The Life of a Mediterranean Peasant* (San Francisco: Harper).
Dunn, James D. G.
    2003   *Jesus Remembered* (Christianity in the Making, 1; Grand Rapids: Eerdmans).
Fitzmyer, J.
    1981   *The Gospel according to Luke (I–IX): Introduction, Translation and Notes* (AB, 29; Garden City, NY: Doubleday).
Franklin, Eric
    2001   'Luke', in J. Barton and J. Muddiman (eds.), *The Oxford Bible Commentary* (Oxford: Oxford University Press), 922–59.
Gerhardsson, Birger
    1996   *The Shema in the New Testament* (Lund: Nova Press).
Graham, Susan L.
    1997   'A Strange Salvation: Intertextual Allusion in Mt. 27,39–44', in Tuckett 1997: 501–11.
Hasitschka, Martin
    1997   'Der Verwendung der Schrift in Mt. 4,1–11', in Tuckett 1997: 487–90.
Hodgson, Leonard
    1928   'The Incarnation', in A. E. J. Rawlinson (ed.), *Essays on the Trinity and the Incarnation* (London: Longmans), 361–402.
Kimball, Charles A.

1994   *Jesus' Exposition of the Old Testament in Luke's Gospel* (JSNTSup, 94; Shef–
            field: Sheffield Academic Press).

Kirk, Alan
1998   *The Composition of the Sayings Source: Genre, Synchrony, and Wisdom
            Redaction in Q* (NTSup, 91; Leiden: Brill).

Kloppenborg-Verbin, John
2000   *Excavating Q: The History and Setting of the Sayings Gospel* (Minneapolis:
            Fortress Press).

Köppen, Klaus-Peter
1961   *Die Auslegung der Versuchungsgeschichte unter besonderer Berüchsichtigung
            der Alten Kirche: Ein Beitrag zur Geschichte der Schriftauslegung* (Beiträge
            zur Geschichte der Biblische Exegese, 4; Tübingen: Mohr Siebeck).

Luz, Ulrich
1989   *Matthew 1–7: A Commentary* (ET; Edinburgh: T&T Clark).

Macquarrie, John
1990   *Jesus Christ in Modern Thought* (London: SCM Press).

Mauser, Ulrich W.
1963   *Christ in the Wilderness* (SBT, 19; London: SCM Press).

Meier, John P.
1991, 1994,
2001   *A Marginal Jew: Rethinking the Historical Jesus* (vols. 1–3; Anchor Bible
            Reference Library; New York: Doubleday).

Nolland, John
1989   *Luke 1–9:20* (WBC; Dallas, Tex.: Word Books).

Prigent, Pierre
1987   'Les citations des évangiles chez Justin (Apologie 14–17)', in *Lectures
            anciennes de la Bible* (Cahiers de la Biblia Patristica, 1; Strasbourg: Centre
            d'Analyse et de Documentation Patristiques), 137–51.

Radl. W.
2003   *Das Evangelium nach Lukas. Erster Teil: 1,1–9,50* (Freiburg: Herder).

Rénan, Ernst
1863   *The Life of Jesus* (ET; London: Trübner).

Robinson, John A. T.
1973   *The Human Face of God* (London: SCM Press).
1988   ' "His Witness is true": A Test of the Johannine Claim', in E. Bammel and
            C. F. D. Moule (eds.), *Jesus and the Politics of His Day* (Cambridge: Cam-
            bridge University Press), 453–76.

Sanders, E. P.
1993   *The Historical Figure of Jesus* (London: Penguin).

Sobrino, Jon
1987   *Jesus in Latin America* (Maryknoll, NY: Orbis Books).

Steiner, M.
1962   *La Tentation de Jésus dans l'interprétation patristique de Saint Justin à
            Origène* (Études Bibliques; Paris: Gabalda).

Talbert, Charles
1982   *Reading Luke: A New Commentary for Preachers* (London: SPCK).

Taylor, John V.
1992   *The Christlike God* (London: SCM Press).

Theissen, Gerd
1992   *The Gospels in Context: Social and Political History in the Synoptic Tradition*
            (ET; Edinburgh: T&T Clark).

Tuckett, Christopher
   1992   'The Temptation Narrative in Q', in F. van Segbroeck, C. M. Tuckett, G. van
             Belle and J. Verheyden (eds.), *The Four Gospels 1992: Festschrift Frans
             Neirynck* (3 vols.; BETL, 100; Leuven: Peeters), vol. 1, 479–507.
   1997   *The Scriptures in the Gospels* (BETL, 131; Leuven: Peeters).
   2000   'Q 22:28–30', in David G. Horrell and Christopher M. Tuckett (eds.), *Christol-
             ogy, Community and Controversy: New Testament Essays in Honour of David
             R. Catchpole* (NTSup, 99; Leiden: Brill), 99–116.
Turner, H. E. W.
   1953   *Jesus Master and Lord: A Study in the Historical Truth of the Gospels*
             (London: Mowbray).
Young, Frances
   1977   'A Cloud of Witnesses', in John Hick (ed.), *The Myth of God Incarnate*
             (London: SCM Press), 13–47.

THE POOR WISE MAN AND THE CACOPHONY OF VOICES

Paul M. Joyce

Among her many other roles, Frances Young is known both as a creative interpreter of the Bible and also as one who has reflected a good deal on the nature of
biblical interpretation (cf. Young 1990a). In this short piece in honour of Frances,
I want to explore two biblical passages, each highlighting a theme close to her
heart and experience: that wisdom is more often found in weakness than in
strength and that tears and joy belong together.

First some intriguing verses from the book of Ecclesiastes:

> I have also seen this example of wisdom under the sun, and it seemed important to me.
> There was a little city, with few people in it. A great king came against it and besieged
> it, building great siegeworks against it. Now there was found in it a poor wise man,
> and he by his wisdom delivered the city. Yet no one remembered that poor man. But I
> say that wisdom is better than might – though the poor man's wisdom is despised, and
> his words are not heeded. (Ecclesiastes 9.13–16)

The Book of Ecclesiastes (otherwise known as Qoheleth) has had a mixed
reception over the centuries. If this book can sometimes be depressing for the
reader, it seems that it was somewhat taxing for the writer too; for having concluded he writes, 'of making many books there is no end, and much study is a
weariness of the flesh' (Eccl. 12.12). The Jewish rabbis were at times unsure
whether this sceptical and occasionally even cynical book deserved its place
among the scriptures of orthodoxy. 'Do not be too righteous, and do not act too
wise', writes the author at one point, 'why should you destroy yourself?' (Eccl.
7.16) The book swings between sceptical and more conventional statements; in
modern times various scholars have tried (none too successfully) to render it
more consistent by arguing that the more positive verses have been added to an
original entirely sceptical text. (For an account of approaches to the book, see
Whybray 1989.) But there is surely a place in the Bible for this honest and forth-
right book, expressing the frustrations and injustices of life without pretence. The
tensions and swings between doubt and faith are to be seen as reflecting the
wrestling of a shrewd, if perhaps jaded, believer.

One of the real gems of the book is the story cited above: the poor wise man
delivers his city from the attack of the great king – but he is despised and forgotten. In ancient Israel, as in other places such as Egypt and Mesopotamia, there
was a lively intellectual tradition concerning wisdom. Although we cannot recon-
struct the history of the tradition in ancient Israel with any confidence, there is
much to suggest that it moved from early rather confident assertions about life

and the world (there is much of this kind in the book of Proverbs) to later doubts and uncertainties, reflected in Job as well as in Ecclesiastes. Early on, there was an emphasis on wisdom as a matter for kings and their courtiers. The book of Ecclesiastes does maintain the traditional link between wisdom and Solomon (Eccl. 1.1, 12; 2.9), but here in this sober and down-to-earth story true wisdom is found not with the mighty king but, mysteriously, with the insignificant and ignored poor man.

That the true wisdom of God is to be found among the poor is an insight that has been stressed passionately over recent decades by various liberation theologians. Jon Sobrino, in *The True Church and the Poor* writes, 'What we are saying is that the Church of the poor is the true way of being a Church in Jesus – this provides the means of becoming more and more the Church of faith' (Sobrino 1985: 124). But while the work of Sobrino and others has challenged many assumptions, for the most part Christians still fail to take seriously the shocking idea that the wisdom of God is to be found among the broken and the marginalized more often than among the secure and the powerful. In fact, some of the appeal of liberation theology can amount to little more than a superficial attraction to the exotic beyond our shores, rather than a profound conversion of expectations and priorities. It is all too easy to leave unscrutinized many of our deep-rooted reactions, to pay lip-service to ideas about 'the Church of the Poor'. But we can be made to feel very awkward when our day-to-day dealings with people are examined. Whose letters are answered promptly and whose are left to gather dust? Whose opinion do I value and to whom do I defer? It can be alarming and embarrassing to realize how far our reactions are shaped not by a sense of the wisdom of the poor and weak – but rather by the conventional notions of power, status and authority.

And yet at the very heart of the gospel is a stark inversion of the usual expectations and assumptions of the world. There is a striking passage in St Paul's first letter to the Corinthians where he speaks of Christ as the power and the wisdom of God: 'Where is the one who is wise? Where is the scribe? Where is the debater of this age? Has not God made foolish the wisdom of the world?' (1 Cor. 1.20). Paul goes on to speak of Christ crucified as a stumbling-block to Jews and foolishness to Gentiles: 'for God's foolishness is wiser than human wisdom and God's weakness is stronger than human strength' (1 Cor. 1.25). How we insulate ourselves against the shocking impact of this central truth of the Christian faith! We continue to order our lives in society and even in the Church according to values of power and status that are in fact contradicted and overturned by the gospel. The implications of the central symbols of the Christian faith are profound: the cross, on which the wisdom of God is stretched and broken, like the millions in our world racked by hunger or by torture; and the eucharist, which speaks of a body broken and blood shed and claims that these are the things of God.

We turn to another book from post-exilic Israel, the book of Ezra, and its account of the laying of the foundation of the restored Jerusalem Temple:

And all the people responded with a great shout when they praised the Lord, because the foundation of the house of the Lord was laid. But many of the priests and Levites and heads of families, old people who had seen the first house, wept with a loud voice when they saw the foundation of this house being laid, though many shouted aloud for joy, so that the people could not distinguish the sound of the joyful shout from the sound of the people's weeping, for the people shouted so loudly that the sound was heard far away. (Ezra 3.11–13)

In 587 BCE the Babylonians razed to the ground the great Temple of Solomon in Jerusalem. Half a century or so later, the Persians succeeded the Babylonians as world rulers and permitted the return to Jerusalem of many of those Judaeans who had been exiled. Here we have an account of this restoration from a historian writing perhaps several generations after these events. The precise dating of the laying of the foundation of the Temple here referred to is much debated – as are the many other historical and literary questions raised by the work of the historian in question. (For an account of these debates, see Blenkinsopp 1988.) But I do not propose to explore these issues in detail in this context, rather to focus on the striking motif of the loud cacophony in which rejoicing and weeping were indistinguishable. Like Ecclesiastes, Ezra is a book that has had a mixed reception. Indeed with its exclusive, priestly concerns, it has been regarded as a rather alien work by many in the modern world. But it would be difficult not to be moved by this particular passage.

Some commentators have understood the reference to weeping here as a weeping for joy at the laying of the foundation of a new temple, or as an expression of the intensity of the prayers being offered, rather than as a sign of mourning at the contrast between the old temple and the new. But these verses are better understood as indicating two divergent reactions (rejoicing and regret) to the one event. It may be that they reflect an awareness of some words attributed to two prophets contemporary with the events being described, namely Haggai and Zechariah. We are reminded of the words of Haggai, 'Who is left among you that saw this house in its former glory? How does it look to you now? Is it not in your sight as nothing?' (Hag. 2.3) and of Zechariah, 'Whoever has despised the day of small things shall rejoice' (Zech. 4.10). Moreover, unless the author of Ezra 3 intends a contrast between joy and weeping, it is very hard to see why he should emphasize the difficulty in distinguishing between the two.

The image of the loud cacophony in which rejoicing and weeping are indistinguishable is a powerful one indeed, and provides a fertile ground for reflection. A first thought relates to youth and old age. In the mixture of joy and regret we see highlighted in turn the strengths and the weaknesses of the young and the old. In the shout of joy, we hear the exuberant response of the young who see the new beginning and whose joy at this hope of better things is fresh and untainted by cynicism, and who nevertheless in their superficiality lack the sense of historical perspective to appreciate the full significance of what they are witnessing. On the other hand, the elderly who actually remembered seeing the great Temple of Solomon before 587 are fully aware of all that this restoration represents and yet their joy is clouded by regret for a lost past. The memories of the past, distorted no doubt by a rosy nostalgia, rob them of the freedom to enjoy to the full the good gifts of God in the present.

The second reflection prompted by our picture from Ezra is about the ambivalence and complexity of all human experience, in a world in which one person's joy is the next person's sorrow. How readily we assume that we know what the other person is experiencing, and how easy it is to fail to respond to them in the appropriate way! This passage from Ezra always puts me in mind of that brief poem by Stevie Smith, 'Not Waving but Drowning'. Of a drowned man the witness of the tragedy may well say, 'Poor chap, he always loved larking', and yet his own truth may be very different: 'I was much too far out all my life, and not waving but drowning' (Smith 1978 [1975]).

But a third and still more telling insight is prompted by the cacophonous scene of Ezra 3, and this concerns the inseparable nature of joy and sorrow. The events of restoration described in Ezra 3 could never have happened without the disaster of conquest and exile that had taken place earlier in the sixth century (that catastrophe still mourned by the old people). Moreover, awareness of that loss and trauma is precisely what earths, and gives meaning to, the restoration that is now at long last possible. There can be no authentic hope for human beings (which is more than merely shallow optimism) unless the loss and pain of the past, and indeed of the present, is taken with full seriousness.

The proclamation of the resurrection, which is at the very heart of the gospel, stands for the affirmation of hope and meaning, of new life for humankind and for the world. Believers do well to respond to the gospel with great rejoicing. And yet its message of hope will lack all power and authenticity unless rejoicing is accompanied by an acute awareness that behind the resurrection stands the cross. As we greet the resurrection, we should not be surprised to hear – ringing in our ears – the tortured cries of the crucified Jesus, the anguished pleas of drowning humanity.

It is a privilege to be able to honour Frances Young in this volume. Few readers will need telling that she is a scholar notable not least for the breadth and range of her work. A senior academic, bemoaning the paucity of omnicompetent external examiners, exclaimed recently: 'What we really need to do is to clone Frances Young!' But Frances is remarkable in ways other than scholarship. She has taught me much: that good administration is good pastoral care, that one needs to snatch research time as precious in a busy life, and little things too, such as that dates are not to be feared but rather seized eagerly and entered at once into one's diary. But she has helped me learn more important lessons than any of these, that wisdom is more often found in weakness than in strength and that tears and joy belong together, insights that run against the tide of the culture of the times in the university world. Frances Young has long been a member of the elite of the academy. But one knows that in Frances this role is also conditioned by her awareness of the ambiguous nature of power, her recognition that it is more often in weakness than in strength that the things of God are to be found, a truth reinforced for her in her work with the L'Arche community and in her life with her son Arthur. And the inseparable nature of sorrow and joy is something

Frances knows much about too. She has written movingly on all these themes (e.g. Young 1990b, 1997), but she has also lived them and enabled others to live them.

The wilderness, which provides the overall theme for this volume, is symbolically a place both of bleakness and of fruitfulness. The wilderness experience can be one of weakness and of tears, but it can also become a journey of discovery of the God who leads us on, out of brokenness and loss to new life:

> The Lord your God, who goes before you, is the one who will fight for you, just as he did for you in Egypt before your very eyes, and in the wilderness, where you saw how the Lord your God carried you, just as one carries a child, all the way that you travelled until you reached this place. (Deuteronomy 1.29–31)

Bibliography

Blenkinsopp, J.
　1988　　*Ezra–Nehemiah: A Commentary* (Old Testament Library; London: SCM Press).
Smith, S.
　1978 [1975]　*Selected Poems* (Harmondsworth: Penguin).
Sobrino, J.
　1985　　*The True Church and the Poor* (London: SCM Press).
Whybray, R. N.
　1989　　*Ecclesiastes* (New Century Bible; Grand Rapids, Mich.: Eerdmans; London: Marshall, Morgan & Scott).
Young, F. M.
　1990a　　*The Art of Performance: Towards a Theology of Holy Scripture* (London: SCM Press).
　1990b　　*Face to Face: A Narrative Essay in the Theology of Suffering* (Edinburgh: T&T Clark; 2nd edn).
Young, F. M. (ed.)
　1997　　*Encounter with Mystery: Reflections on L'Arche and Living with Disability* (London: Darton, Longman & Todd).

Mimēsis, Typology and the Institution Narrative: Some Observations on *Traditio Apostolica* 4 and its Afterlife

Alistair Stewart-Sykes

Traditio apostolica 4 directs the manner in which the bishop should pray when making the offering on the occasion of his ordination. Among its points of interest is the occurrence of an institution narrative within the anaphoral frame; on the assumption that the prayer is indeed a product of the early third century this is the first occasion that a narrative of institution is to be found within an anaphora. The purpose of this paper is to explain the developments which led to the appearance of such a narrative and to explore the possible significance of this development in later eucharistic prayer. In doing so I shall expand some comments made in the published version of my doctoral thesis, completed under Frances Young.[1]

Approximately fifty years prior to 'Hippolytus', Justin, discussing the eucharist in his *Apology*, explains that the elements of bread and wine become the Body and Blood of Christ *di' euchēs logou par' autou*.[2] He then goes on to cite the institution narrative. Although this has led to the supposition, most recently supported by Cuming[3] and Yarnold,[4] that the anaphora known to Justin actually contained these words, the following observations militate against such a conclusion:

(a)   The inclusion of the words of institution within the prayer is inconsistent with the earlier description of the prayer given by Justin.[5]

(b)   The words of institution are not a *prayer* formula at all.[6] Although they might be recognized as such once the expectation that these words are to be found within the prayer has been established, in the second century, when there is no such expectation, they simply cannot be described as a word of prayer without qualification.

---

1.   Stewart-Sykes (1998: 193–6).
2.   1 *Apol.* 66.2.
3.   Cuming (1980). The argument here depends on an interpretation of *logos* which is without lexical support. So Gelston (1982: 172–5) points out that Cuming's attempt to justify this understanding of *logos* through a citation of Addai and Mari is fundamentally flawed. The most recent discussion of this passage of Justin is that of Heintz (2003). Heintz suggests that there is no institution narrative, but perhaps an epiklesis addressed to the *logos*.
4.   Yarnold (1997: 407).
5.   McGowan (1999: 81).
6.   Gelston (1982: 173).

Yarnold notes that the prayer is said to have been handed down (*paredōken*) and suggests that since, later in the chapter, the rites of Mithras are said to have been handed down, the reference must be to a prayer formula. However, earlier in the chapter the same verb appears not with reference to a formula of prayer but to teaching concerning the meaning of baptism. Thus the use of *paredōken* more probably refers to a tradition of teaching. In view of this, and since the command of repetition is placed first, implying that the point of the citation is to justify the action, the function of the citation of these words in the *Apology* is therefore, as McGowan suggests, to provide an example and rationale for the eucharistic action, and the locus of their transmission that of instruction.[7] That Justin is an exemplar of a scholastic type of Christianity provides a context for this explanation of the manner in which the words are repeated and retained, but it leads to the question of why a catechetical explanation and justification for the eucharistic rite should find its way into a eucharistic prayer, as it does in *Traditio apostolica*, a document which derives from a community which, like that of Justin, might be described, as a scholastic household. I have argued elsewhere that the prayer in the extant *Traditio apostolica* has been redactionally extended, and that the original product read:

> We give thanks to you God, through your beloved child Jesus Christ. When he was handed over to voluntary suffering, in order to dissolve death and break the chains of the devil and harrow hell and illuminate the just and fix a boundary and manifest the resurrection, he took bread and giving thanks to you he said: take, eat, this is my body which will be broken for you. Likewise with the cup saying: this is my blood which is poured out for you. Whenever you do this, you perform my commemoration. Remembering therefore his death and resurrection, we offer you bread and cup, giving thanks to you because you have held us worthy to stand before you and minister to you as priest, that we may praise and glorify you through your child Jesus Christ, through whom be glory and honour to you, with the Holy Spirit in your holy church, both now and in the ages of the ages. Amen.[8]

Even without removing any material, Mazza had already observed that the institution narrative is within a subordinate clause,[9] and McGowan suggests that its function thus remains catechetical.[10] However, once the material provided by the secondary redactor is removed, the logic of the appearance of the narrative in this anaphora is easy to explain. As it did in Justin's writing, the institution narrative provides an exemplum and rationale for the action of offering which the bishop is making, namely that it is the *mimēsis* of Christ. The prayer, like several other prayers in this collection, thus has the shape of a collect. It is quite possible that this is an allusion to an explanation passed on through catechesis, in line with McGowan's suggestion, but we may now see the purpose to which it is included, for what is lacking in McGowan's hypothesis is a reason for the inclusion of this catechetical material within a prayer. I have suggested elsewhere that the whole purpose of the first redactor of *Traditio apostolica*, in which the first

---

7.   McGowan (1999: 83).
8.   Stewart-Sykes (2001: 75) in summary of the previous discussion.
9.   Mazza (1983: 445).
10.   McGowan (1999: 84).

version of this anaphora, including the institution narrative, is to be found, is the legitimation of the bishop's ministry;[11] in this light the inclusion of this narrative, employed already as an aetiology for the rite within a scholastic community, may be seen as a means of legitimating the bishop's action of offering with reference to Christ. The ordination prayer which immediately precedes the offering has characterized the bishop as a high priest, and so the anaphora places the bishop into the place of that high priest through making an offering in the same way that the Lord did. Thus, although catechesis might be the means by which the narrative of institution was transmitted, its presence in this prayer is more than simply a reflection of catechetical activity but is an attempt to justify the bishop's action and position.

This is the first example of a eucharistic anaphora which includes an institution narrative. However, the institution narrative is present in all classical eucharistic prayers except Addai and Mari, into which in time it also made its way. We should therefore enquire whether the transmission of the narrative of institution through catechesis led to inclusion of that narrative in those other rites, and what the function of the narrative in these other rites might be.

Fenwick indeed suggests that the catechetical tradition of linking the eucharist to its foundation in the last supper led to the inclusion of eucharistic words in the rite of Jerusalem, on the grounds that the liturgy known to Cyril of Jerusalem lacked an institution narrative, whereas the Liturgy of St James has one.[12] Problematic, however, is absence of any rationale for such a proposed transference from catechesis to liturgy in fourth-century Jerusalem. In a scholasticized Roman community of the second century such a transference is understandable, though not inevitable, but when catechumens were excluded from the ritual action as they were in Cyril's Jerusalem, and when there is no internal need to legitimate the eucharistic action or the celebrant's role within it, it is hard to see how, let alone why, this transference might have taken place.

It is, however, true that Cyril employs the narrative of the last supper in a catechetical context in his mystagogy,[13] and that this catechetical context may be the basis on which the words are transmitted, but this does not of necessity lead to the inclusion of these words in the canon. The citation of these words stands at the head of a catechetical homily intended to establish that the bread and wine received are the very Body and Blood of Christ, but a series of other texts follow which are said to establish the same point, such as Ps. 22.5 (23.5) and Eccl. 9.7. Yet these texts were never transferred from their catechetical setting to the eucharistic prayer. Theodore of Mopsuestia likewise deals with the last supper in his catecheses at a point separate from his treatment of the canon,[14] which may be taken as further evidence that the tradition of seeing the foundation of the eucharist in the last supper is indeed a catechetical tradition,[15]

11. Stewart-Sykes (2001: 38–45).
12. Fenwick (1992: 138–9). This assumes that Cyril's liturgy lacked an institution narrative, an assumption which has been questioned by, e.g. Yarnold (1997).
13. *Cat. Myst.* 4.
14. *Cat. Hom.* 15.7.
15. One might add, as an aside, that this catechetical tradition finds its way into Eusebius, *Demon-*

but again this poses the question of how the catechetical tradition found its way into prayer.[16]

Cyril cites the words of Jesus at the last supper to make the point that, whatever the outward appearance and taste of the bread and wine, they are indeed the Body and Blood of Christ, because that is what the Lord had said that they were. He goes on, however, to state that the Body is given *en tupō ... artou* and the wine *en tupō oinou*. This is ancient liturgical language, for the language of type to refer to the eucharistic gifts is widespread in the earlier period. The *locus classicus* is *Adversus Marcionem* 4.40, when Tertullian paraphrases the words of Christ as 'this is the *figura* of my body', but there are many other examples of the use of figurative or typological language to refer to the eucharistic elements from the third to the fourth century, among which we may particularly notice *Adversus Marcionem* 1.14, where Tertullian states that the bread *representat* the body of Christ, *Adversus Marcionem* 5.7, in which we read that there is a relation of similitude between the blood of the paschal lamb and that of Christ, and the directions concerning eucharistic meals at *Traditio apostolica* 21 and *Traditio apostolica* 38, both of which refer to the elements received as types and antitypes.

The language of type is not the language of liturgy alone, but it is also the language of exegesis. As Frances Young has shown, central to ancient interpretation of Scripture, and so to the employment of the language of type to describe this exegesis, is the idea of *mimēsis*; the text is a *mimēsis* of reality, which becomes reality in the process of being heard. Beyond this she suggests that liturgy might be a theatre in which mimetic exegesis is played out, that it might be possible to mimic the *mimēsis* in order to represent the reality other than by reading.[17] Given, then, that the liturgy might be a context for the *mimēsis* of Christ, is this the basis on which this text found its way into so many eucharistic prayers? In other words, might the inclusion of these words come about not by the catechetical tradition through which they were transmitted but through the extension of *mimēsis* from Scripture to liturgical action? If this is the case, then the inclusion of the words of institution in the eucharistic prayer might be seen as a reflection of exegesis, an attempt to imitate directly the action of Jesus at the last supper as described in Scripture, in order to conform the liturgical action to Scripture itself, going beyond fulfilment of the command of Jesus to imitate his actions to imitate his words.

If we understand the language of type to apply to the eucharistic action in the same way that it might be applied to a text we can see that in earlier discussion of

stratio evangelica 7.1.28. (Cf. Wallace-Hadrill (1953), who attributes the similarity of Eusebius' version of the dominical words to those of Cyril to their presence in the anaphora.)

16. Although Yarnold (1997: 407–8) suggests that words of institution were present in the rite known to Theodore, and Mazza (1995: 308–10) countenances this possibility, at 304–5 he makes it clear that this was not the case in the *ordo* on which Theodore comments. Insofar as the *ordo* derives from a catechetical tradition, rather than the liturgical actuality of Theodore's community, it is possible that an institution narrative was present in Theodore's rite, but was a very recent introduction.

17. Young (1997: 234–5).

the eucharist the emphasis is on the mimetic action performed in conformity to the command of the Lord. So Irenaeus states that the Church, taught through the apostles, continues Jesus' offering.[18] However, although he cites the narrative of the last supper, the text in which he is more interested is Mal. 1.11. Cyprian, arguing against wineless eucharists, states that the sacrifice should correspond to the passion of Christ,[19] by which we may deduce that the eucharistic action was seen as a typical representation of Christ's passion, in the same way that the eucharistic elements typified Christ himself. In other words, the eucharistic action and elements were like scriptural texts, which imitated the realities and brought them home to the Church. But far from necessitating the transfer of the words of institution into the eucharistic prayer, it makes them redundant, as the act itself is sufficient *mimēsis*.

Quite apart from literary theories of *mimēsis*, however, Syria had long known a liturgical theory of *mimēsis*. This differed from the extension of the literary to the liturgical which we have hypothesized here in that, in this Syrian tradition, the mimetic actant is not the rite, but the individual who performs the rite. This may perhaps be extended back as far as Ignatius, who in his desire to be an imitator (*mimētēs*) of the suffering of Christ is anxious to be ground by the teeth of wild beasts into the bread of the eucharistic sacrifice,[20] and as a prophet facing death is become the word of God.[21] Tatian applies this language to teaching. To explain the begetting of the Word without diminution of the Godhead he employs the image of the spoken word, which while issuing forth from the speaker does not diminish the speaker's power of speech. He goes on:

> Just as the Word begotten in the beginning in turn begot our creation by fabricating matter for himself, so I too, in imitation of the Word, having been begotten again and obtained understanding of the truth, am bringing to order the confusion in kindred matter. (*Or. ad Graec.* 5.3)

Subsequently we find the concept of *mimēsis* central to the narrative of *Acta Thomae*, as Thomas proves to be the twin of Jesus, readily exchanging identity with Jesus, demonstrating that the one reborn is another Christ through imitation of him, through becoming a twin to the Lord like Thomas himself.[22] Finally, it is given explicit liturgical expression in the *Mystagogical catecheses* widely attributed to Cyril of Jerusalem, which speak of baptism as the *mimēsis* of Christ, undertaken by the candidate.[23]

It is this tradition which appears in Chrysostom's homily on Judas, in the statement that the priest takes the place of Christ in saying the words of institution,[24] and in the *Catecheses* of Theodore of Mopsuestia when, in connection with the action of the bishop at the eucharist, he states that the bishop, in imitat-

18. *Adversus omnes Haereses* 4.27.5.
19. *Ep.* 72.9.
20. Rom. 6.3; 4.1–2.
21. Rom. 2.1.
22. See the discussion of Gerlach (1998: 136–9).
23. *Cat. Myst.* 2.2, 2.5–7. See Cutrone (1978: 53–4).
24. Chrysostom *De Proditione Judae* 1.6.

ing the actions of Christ, corresponds to the High Priest, Christ himself.[25] But if the performer is the *mimētēs*, then the elements which are the Body and Blood of Christ cannot themselves be types. Thus in expounding the Lord's words at the last supper Theodore explicitly states that the Lord did not say that the bread was the type (the Syriac *twps'* is a transliteration of the Greek *tupos*) of his body and that the cup was a type of his blood, but that he said, 'This is my body' and 'This is my blood.'[26] Similarly, when Ephrem finds Marcionites using the language of type and likeness to refer to the consecrated elements he assumes that they have no doctrine of the real presence of Christ.[27] Theodore's statement that the words of the Lord draw the attention of the hearer away from the outward form of the bread and wine runs counter to the Antiochene insistence on the integrity of the literal signification of the scriptural text, but we may see that this Syrian rejection of the language of type applied to the eucharistic elements derives from an ancient Syrian tradition of understanding liturgy as *mimēsis*, which, once the Lord's words are part of the rite, leads inevitably to a naive somatic realism becoming attached to the eucharistic elements.

But although this Syrian tradition might open the way for an inclusion of an institution narrative, by which the eucharistic prayer might be a *mimēsis* of the last supper, and despite the obvious connection between doing what the Lord did and saying what the Lord said, it does not do so of necessity. Thus it does not occur to Aphraahat that the fulfilment should be carried out in such a literal way. In the 12th *Demonstration* we have what Gerlach recognizes as a description of the liturgy as direct *mimēsis* of the Lord's actions.[28] Paschal baptism is a *mimēsis* of the footwashing, and the eucharist a *mimēsis* of the (synoptic) meal. But although the words of Jesus are quoted, there is no liturgical development of the words, as there is a treatment of the footwashing as baptismal. The same observation may be made of the eucharistic meals described in *Acta Thomae*: for all that there is such a thoroughgoing *mimēsis* of Jesus by Thomas that he is a twin of Jesus, not once is allusion made to the last supper in a eucharistic context; indeed the ritual meals are wineless, celebrated with bread and water. Finally it is to be observed that Cyril's own sacramental theology, which is concerned with seeing the believer as enacting an identification with Christ, would lead one to anticipate that this would find expression in the anaphora, but the very absence of such material leads Cyril to discuss the last supper in an earlier catechesis.[29]

Thus, although it may seem obvious to us that a transference of an institution narrative from the catechetical tradition to the eucharistic prayer might take place as a result of an understanding of the eucharist as mimetic, this simply did not happen until late in the fourth century. The conditions for such a transfer existed, but some external factor needs to be sought to explain the development.

25. *Hom. cat.* 16.12.
26. *Hom. cat.* 15.10.
27. *Hymn. c. haer.* 47.1.
28. Gerlach (1998: 239–43).
29. Cutrone (1978: 62–4).

One possible factor for the transfer of these words might be the influence of *Traditio apostolica* itself. That *Traditio apostolica* was circulating in Syria in the fourth century may readily be demonstrated through the existence of two reworkings of the document, *Testamentum Domini* and the eighth book of the *Constitutiones apostolorum*. What is odd about both of these reworkings, however, is that the account of the institution in the reworking of the anaphora of *Traditio apostolica* 4 is the same in neither, and neither is the same as the institution narrative of the Latin version of *Traditio apostolica*. Pitt suggests that the text underlying the Latin version (which also underlies the Ethiopic version) and the redactor of *Constitutiones apostolorum* 8 independently expand an original, brief, institution narrative, which was close to that of *Testamentum Domini*.[30] It is equally possible that the narratives of *Testamentum Domini* and *Constitutiones apostolorum* 8 have each substituted a Syrian form of the narrative, passed down through catechesis, for the form found in *Traditio apostolica*.[31]

That the form found in the Verona Latin may be Italian, however, may be suggested by comparison with the form cited by Ambrose.[32]

AT (Latin):	*Amb:*

Accipiens
panem
 	
gratias tibi agens
 	
dixit:
'Accipite, manducate: hoc est
corpus meum quod pro vobis confringetur'
        Similiter et calicem
 	
dicens:
 	
        Hic est   sanguis meus qui pro vobis
effunditur; quando hoc facitis, meam
commemorationem facitis.
	…in sanctis manibus suis accepit panem, respexit ad caelum, ad te, sancte pater, omnipotens, aeterne deus, gratias agens benedixit, fregit, fractumque apostolis et discipulis suis tradidit, dicens, accipite et edite ex hoc omnes: hoc est enim corpus meum quod pro multis confringetur
	        Similiter etiam calicem, postquam cenatum est, pridie quam pateretur, accepit, respexit ad caelum, ad te, sancte pater, omnipotens aeterne deus, gratias agens benedixit, apostolis et discipulis suis tradidit dicens: accipite et bibite ex hoc omnes:
	        hic est enim sanguis meus…

Ambrose's narrative is longer than that of the Verona palimpsest, but these expansions are to be anticipated in what is a later text. Fenwick sums up the difficulty of comparing texts of the institution narrative thus:

> Textually, the institution narrative is one of the most complex sections of the anaphora. Not only does it exhibit signs of the influence of one anaphora on another, but each anaphora (or, indeed, at times almost each MS) has been further influenced by the four New Testament accounts, which themselves show considerable divergences.[33]

---

30. Pitt (1953: 6–7).
31. As suggested at Stewart-Sykes (2001: 72).
32. *De Sacramentis* 4.21–2.
33. Fenwick (1992: 132).

Given these difficulties it is all the more remarkable that the only substantial difference between the two, apart from the expansions and minor differences of wording which might be put down to the fact that the Verona version is translated directly from Greek, are the statements that the body is broken 'pro vobis' (in *Traditio apostolica*) and 'pro multis' (in Ambrose). The distinction may be assigned to the influence of Mt. 26.28 on the Ambrosian version. Thus if the Verona form is Italian, it is likely to be close to that found originally in *Traditio apostolica*, whereas the redactors of the Syrian versions each substituted a form known to them. The probability is that these forms were not known to them from eucharistic prayer but from catechesis. It is thus reasonable to suggest that the institution narratives occur in a eucharistic context in *Constitutiones apostolorum* 8 and *Testamentum Domini* only because their redactors found such a narrative in *Traditio apostolica* first.

The question then becomes one of whether the influence of *Traditio apostolica* exercised influence on eucharistic prayer beyond these literary exercises. Was the presence of an institution narrative here the cause, whether direct or through the mediation of *Constitutiones apostolorum* 8, of the insertion of such a narrative in Ur-Basil, from which it spread to other eucharistic prayers, given that the conditions were already right for such a narrative to find a place in eucharistic prayer? That the institution narrative is an insertion into the Basilian framework is clear from the words *katelipen hēmin* with which the formula is introduced.[34] There must be a source, the source is not catechesis, and so *Constitutiones apostolorum* 8 is the obvious candidate.

To sustain the case we must accept that *Constitutiones apostolorum* 8 is prior to Egyptian Basil (as the earliest extant version of the Basilian family). Although this was the position adopted by Lietzmann,[35] and has been widely followed,[36] Fenwick suggests that the anaphora of *Constitutiones apostolorum* 8 is too developed to be a source for the West Syrian material in *James*,[37] and is therefore secondary. However, Ur-Basil was entirely independent, and so the question of influence is solely restricted to the inclusion of an institution narrative. The West Syrian material in *James* is another issue entirely.

It is impossible to discuss here the possible relationship between the extant anaphora of *Constitutiones apostolorum* 8 and the various hypothetical original versions of other anaphoras;[38] the only suggestion made here is that the anaphora of *Constitutiones apostolorum* 8 pre-dates Sahidic Basil, which is the earliest extant version of the Basilian anaphora, and therefore that it may be the source for the inclusion of an institution narrative, even if other Basilian material pre-dates it.[39] If we examine the two anaphoras we may note that the intercessions

34. Fenwick (1992: 134).
35. Lietzmann (1926: 24–8).
36. By, e.g., Yarnold (1992: 234), Bouley (1981: 232).
37. Fenwick (1992: 46).
38. Bates (1975), for instance, leans towards the influence of Ur-Basil, Fenwick (1989) a distant predecessor of the Liturgy of St John Chrysostom.
39. As Bates suggests. To an extent he is followed by Graves (1997: 191, 194).

are comparable in length and complexity, and that whereas the anamnesis and oblation formula of *Constitutiones apostolorum* 8 is longer this can largely be explained through the inclusion of Hippolytean material alongside the forms inherited in West Syria. The main difference of development is in the history of salvation which precedes the institution narrative; whereas this is clearly much more extensive in *Constitutiones apostolorum* 8, this will be explained below and can be allowed as an exception to the guideline that a shorter text is generally more primitive. The institution narratives differ, but the replacement of the narrative of *Traditio apostolica* by the redactors of *Testamentum Domini* and *Constitutiones apostolorum* 8 alike indicates that a redactor would be free to use the version alive in the catechetical tradition known to him.

If *Constitutiones apostolorum* 8 is the prior text then we may suggest that it mediated the institution narrative to the classical anaphoras. Thus we may see that Hippolytus' *exemplum* is the basis on which the institution narrative is extended not only to Italian rites but, through the mediation of *Constitutiones apostolorum*, to Syrian rites as well. It is also possible, given that the institution narrative in the Sacramentary of Serapion is an evident interpolation, that *Traditio apostolica*, either directly or through an intermediary, lies at the root of this likewise, though here we have no literary evidence. However, its entry to Egypt was assured in any event through the influence of the Basilian anaphora.

Another aspect of the anaphora of *Constitutiones apostolorum* 8 which is noteworthy is the extraordinary length of the history which prefaces the institution narrative, encapsulating the *sanctus*.[40] Although thanksgiving for food is one of the roots of eucharistic prayer, and although this thanksgiving might readily extend itself to thanks for creation and for redemption, this preface is in itself a complete summary of salvation history.

This, likewise, may ultimately result from Hippolytus' inclusion of an institution narrative in the anaphora of chapter 3. For although the purpose of the inclusion of these words is to provide a legitimatory *exemplum*, they have another result: namely, by anchoring the eucharistic action in the action of the last supper, 'Hippolytus' has anchored the eucharist in the paschal celebration. The second redactor of *Traditio apostolica* united the Hippolytean community with other Roman Christian communities in part through the solution of the vexed issue of the date of the Pascha by transferring the Pascha to the Sunday immediately following the 14th Nisan. In doing so, however, he effectively made the paschal celebration indistinguishable from a Sunday eucharist. A similar strategy of transference may be found in Asia and Syria in the same period, with the same result. Thus we may observe the conformity of the Pascha to the eucharist elsewhere, as in the third century the early variety of ritual meals begins to coalesce. So, the anonymous author of *In Sanctum Pascha* quotes the words of institution as the fulfilment of the Old Testament figures which typified the Pascha:

> This was the Pascha which Jesus desired to suffer for us. His suffering has freed us from sufferings, his death has vanquished death, the visible nourishment has procured

40. The alert reader will spot that the analysis of the West Syrian form is that of Bouyer (1968: 143), preferred to that of Shepherd (1961: 37–8).

his eternal life for us. Such is the salutary desire of Jesus, such his love which is the Spirit; to show the figures as figures and no more, to offer in their place his holy body to his disciples. 'Take and eat: this is my body... drink of this for this is my blood of the new covenant which is being shed for many unto the remission of sins.' Therefore he desires not so much to eat (*phagein*) as he desires to suffer (*pathein*), so that he might deliver us from suffering in eating. (*In Sanctum Pascha* 49)

In the same way *Vita Polycarpi* describes the Pascha as 'the new covenant of the offering of the bread and the cup'.[41] Like the Hippolytean school, the schools which produced *In sanctum Pascha* and *Vita Polycarpi* have emerged from Quartodeciman communities and have so introduced the idea of an annual commemoration to the wider Church.

Mazza suggested that the tradition of paschal homiletic was one of the sources of the anaphora of *Traditio apostolica* 4, and although Mazza stretches the parallels somewhat,[42] we may nonetheless accept that the mental world of the original author of the rite, a Quartodeciman, is formed in the same tradition of paschal homiletic, as the whole salvific work of Christ is announced as a preliminary to the provision of Christ's example at the last supper. The second redactor in turn expands the salvation history in part to make some doctrinal clarifications, but also expanding the statement in line with the model of the haggadah, or statement of salvation.

In time, when *Traditio apostolica* is reread, and the inclusion of an institution narrative in the anaphora is taken up, the way is open for a Pascha which has already become marked by a eucharist in turn to paschalize the eucharist, and to turn the Sunday celebration into a commemoration of the last supper. The redactor of *Constitutiones apostolorum* thus does what the second redactor of *Traditio apostolica* had done, and includes a typically paschal commemoration of salvation history in the anaphora. We may be assured that this was not an isolated example since the same process may be observed in the Anaphora of the twelve apostles, the preface of which was originally a free-standing commemoration.[43] The paschal origin of much of this may be noted through certain lexical similarities with Melito's *Peri Pascha*,[44] and it is because the redactor is acutely aware of incorporating a paschal summary of salvation that the material before the institution narrative is so lengthy.[45]

If the paschalization of the eucharist is a result of a reading of *Traditio apostolica*, this answers the question posed by Frances Young of why, if the eucharist

41. *Vita Polycarpi* 2.

42. Stewart-Sykes (1998: 194). See also, for a more extensive critique, with which I would now largely concur (this work not being available when my work went to press), Bradshaw (1997: 10–14).

43. So Engberding (1937). The same process is suggested with regard to other anaphoras by Cuming (1984).

44. Discussed by Stewart-Sykes (1998: 133–4) following Bonner (1940: 144–5, 147).

45. For a much more extensive discussion of the sources of this anaphora see Graves (1997). The hypothesis suggested here, that the preface is partly constructed using material from the tradition of paschal commemoration, does not conflict with any of Graves's suggestions. Graves himself suggests that there is material here from other (unknown) anaphoras.

was a memorial of the Passover, it was not an annual occasion.[46] That is to say, Pascha was an annual occasion, and its celebration, while generically eucharistic, was not simply eucharist, and the eucharist was not simply a commemoration of Pascha. She further observes that the linkage between Passover and eucharist is not made in the earliest period, is first found in Origen, and even then represents Origen's own viewpoint and is hardly representative of thinking throughout the Church.[47] We may suggest that the linkage is made in the earliest period simply because it is a product of the fourth century, and comes about through a reading of *Traditio apostolica*.

The presence of the institution narrative in the classical anaphoras has yet satisfactorily to be explained. Three previous justifications have been proposed:

1. That it originally formed an embolism, either in the *birkath haMazon*[48] or in the paschal haggadah.[49] The paschal version of this thesis fails on the grounds set forth by Frances Young and on the grounds that the one Christian version of the haggadah extant, Melito's *Peri Pascha*, makes no reference to the last supper. We note here that the paschalization of the eucharist is caused by the inclusion of an institution narrative, rather than the innate paschal nature of the eucharist bringing about the inclusion of an institution narrative.

2. That it is a result of concentration on the elements, rather than thanksgiving.[50] This assumes a transfer of the focus of the eucharist from the offering of thanksgiving to the offering of gifts, an assumption which, apart from remaining unproven, seems to assume a linear development. We may note, moreover, that this would not automatically bring about the inclusion of an institution narrative. Theodore's concentration on the reality of the Body and Blood of Christ, as opposed to the typical value bestowed on the bread and wine, is based not on the presence of the institution narrative in the anaphora, but on the words of distribution.

3. That it is a result of catechesis. While we have accepted that catechesis was the means by which the narrative was transmitted, and is the reason for its connection with the emerging eucharist, we have noted here that of itself it cannot bring about the transfer of the narrative into the eucharistic prayer.

---

46. Young (1979: 306–9).

47. Young (1979: 306–9).

48. So Ligier (1973: 179–81). Ligier does not seek to explain *why* the narrative was included. A festal embolism, such as that known at Pesach, would fall prey to the same objections as the idea that it is haggadic. Bouyer (1968: 157), who refers to the institution narrative as a *haggadah*, suggests that it was originally recited separately from the *birkath haMazon* in the course of the meal, and is subsequently incorporated in the anaphora when the *birkath haMazon* are rearranged in the course of anaphoral construction. However, this is all undertaken on the assumption that the eucharist was always linked with the last supper, a hypothesis which seems to run contradictory to the evidence of the *Didache* of a eucharistic celebration which has no contact with a last supper tradition.

49. There are various versions of this theory. Note Felmy (1983); Rouwhorst (1996).

50. Cuming (1982: 127).

We have suggested therefore that a more complex path led to this phenomenon. First the mimetic reading of Scripture naturally led to the search for a mimetic outcome of the reading of the narrative of the last supper. Since, for catechetical reasons, this was already linked to the eucharist, it was natural to see the eucharist as a *mimēsis* of that scriptural event. But this did not bring about the general inclusion of an institution narrative, it simply provided the conditions under which such a narrative, once included, might readily take root. A further prior condition was the catechetical transmission of the institution narrative as the foundation of the eucharist, but this of itself was not sufficient to enable the narrative to cross over from catechesis to prayer: but the efficient cause lay in the reading of *Traditio apostolica* in fourth-century Syria, as in fourth-century Italy. 'Hippolytus' had included an institution narrative in order to justify the bishop's action. When an expanded version of the anaphora of *Traditio apostolica* 4 is read in conditions far removed from its production, and in which there was already an understanding that the last supper was the foundation of the eucharist and that the eucharist might be a *mimēsis* of that foundational event, so Hippolytus, through his anonymous interpreter, provided the model by which such an inclusion might come about. A model which readily commended itself was readily imitated, in an uncanny echo of the adoption of the Hippolytean anaphora in the liturgical reform of the twentieth century.

Beyond this, as the scriptural narratives of the last supper find themselves in a paschal frame, so there is a fusion of pascha and eucharist which conforms the prayer to the setting of the narrative, and turns a large part of the anaphora into a typically paschal narrative of salvation.

Bibliography

Bates, W. H.
   1975   'The Composition of the Anaphora of Apostolic Constitutions VIII', in E. A. Livingstone (ed.), *Studia patristica* 13.3 (TU, 116; Berlin: Akademie): 343–55.

Bonner, C.
   1940   *The Homily on the Passion by Melito Bishop of Sardis and Some Fragments of the Apocryphal Ezekiel* (London: Christophers).

Bouley, Allan
   1981   *From Freedom to Formula* (Washington, DC: CUA).

Bouyer, L.
   1968   *Eucharist* (ET; Notre Dame: Notre Dame University Press).

Bradshaw, P. F.
   1997   *Essays on Early Eastern Eucharistic Prayers* (Collegeville, Minn.: Liturgical Press).

Cuming, G. J.
   1980   'Di' euchēs logou', *JTS* (NS) 31: 80–2.
   1982   'The Anaphora of St Mark: A Study in Development', *Le Muséon* 95: 115–29.
   1984   'Four Very Early Anaphoras', *Worship* 58: 168–72.

Cutrone, E. J.
   1978   'Cyril's Mystagogical Catecheses and the Evolution of the Jerusalem Anaphora', *Orientalia Christiana Periodica* 44: 52–64.

Engberding, Hieronymus
    1937   'Die syrische Anaphora der zwölf Apostel und ihre Paralleltexte', *Oriens Christianus* 34: 213–47.
Felmy, Karl Christian
    1983   'Was unterscheidet diese Nacht von allen anderen Nächten?', *Jahrbuch für Liturgie und Hymnodik* 27: 1–15.
Fenwick, J. R. K.
    1989   *The Missing Oblation* (Bramcote: Grove).
    1992   *The Anaphoras of St Basil and St James: An Investigation into their Common Origin* (Orientalia Christiana Analecta, 240; Rome: Pontificium Institutum Orientale).
Gelston A.
    1982   'Di' euchēs logou', *JTS* (NS) 33: 172–5.
Gerlach, Karl
    1998   *The Ante-Nicene Pascha: A Rhetorical History* (Leuven: Peeters).
Graves, Raphael
    1997   'The Anaphora of the Eighth Book of the *Apostolic Constitutions*', in Bradshaw 1997: 173–94.
Heintz, Michael
    2003   'Di' euchēs logou tou par' autou', *Studia Liturgica* 33: 33–6.
Lietzmann, H.
    (1926)   *Messe und Herrenmahl* (Bonn: Marcus & Weber).
Ligier, L.
    1973   'The Origins of the Eucharistic Prayer', *Studia Liturgica* 9: 161–85.
Mazza, E.
    1983   'Omelie pasquali e birkat ha-mazon: fonti dell' anafora di Ippolito?', *Ephemerides Liturgicae* 27: 409–81.
    1995   *The Origins of the Eucharistic Prayer* (Collegeville, Minn.: Liturgical Press).
McGowan, A. B.
    1999   'Is There a Liturgical Text in this Gospel? The Institution Narratives and the Early Interpretative Communities', *JBL* 118: 73–87.
Pitt, W. E.
    1953   'The Anamneses and Institution Narrative in the Liturgy of *Apostolic Constitutions* Book VIII', *JEH* 8: 1–7.
Rouwhorst, G.
    1996   'La célébration de l'eucharistie dans l'église primitive', *Questions Liturgiques* 77: 152–73.
Shepherd, M. H.
    1961   'The Formation and Influence of the Antiochene Liturgy', *Dumbarton Oaks Papers* 15: 23–44.
Stewart-Sykes, A.
    1998   *The Lamb's High Feast: Melito, Peri Pascha and the Quartodeciman Paschal Liturgy at Sardis* (VigChr supplement, 42; Leiden: Brill).
    2001   *Hippolytus: On the Apostolic Tradition* (Crestwood, NY: Saint Vladimir's Seminary).
Wallace-Hadrill, D. S.
    1953   'Eusebius and the Institution Narrative in the Eastern Liturgies', *JTS* (NS) 4: 41–2.
Yarnold, E.
    1992   'The Liturgy of the Faithful in the Fourth and Early Fifth Centuries', in C. Jones *et al.* (eds.), *The Study of Liturgy* (London: SPCK).

1997   'Anaphoras Without Institution Narratives?', in E. A. Livingstone (ed.), *Studia Patristica* 30 (Leuven: Peeters): 395–410.

Young, F. M.

1979   *The Use of Sacrificial Ideas in Greek Christian Writers from the New Testament to John Chrysostom* (Cambridge, Mass.: Philadelphia Patristic Foundation).

1997   *Biblical Exegesis and the Formation of Christian Culture* (Cambridge: Cambridge University Press).

'INCENSE IN OUR LAND'
JULIAN SABA AND EARLY SYRIAN CHRISTIANITY

Susan Ashbrook Harvey

The career of the fourth-century holy man Julian Saba marked a crucial turning-point in early Syrian ascetic tradition. Julian had turned to his vocation as a young man, making his abode in the wilderness of Osrhoene and following an austere prayer discipline. He soon gained disciples (around the year 320), and eventually the leadership of a large monastic community formed on his model: settled in wilderness caves, and practising an elaborate system of continual psalmody. While his own practice alternated between prayer in the context of this community and periods of withdrawal into the desert, he also took his monks on pilgrimage to the Holy Land (where he is said to have built a church on Mount Sinai) and entered Antioch in 365 to intervene in the Arian crisis there. He died in 367 (Chron. Ed. 28, Guidi 1903), after an ascetic career lasting perhaps 50 years (Griffith 1994; Vööbus 1960: I, 42–51).

Julian represents two important developments in the history of Syrian asceti-cism. First, he marks a change in ascetic location. Until the second half of the fourth century, Syrian ascetic tradition had been primarily focused on a way of life enacted within the church community in service to the parish and the church hierarchy. This tradition was best represented by the Sons and Daughters of the Covenant, consecrated laypeople who took vows of poverty and celibacy and assisted the bishops and parish priests; or by Ephrem the Syrian (d. 373), whose tireless efforts on behalf of the Nicene bishops of Nisibis and Edessa served to stabilize the Christian community in those areas (Griffith 1995). Julian Saba's career marks the turn to an ascetic life pursued in distinct separation from the civic church community while yet tied to its service. We first see the tendency in Julian's older contemporary Jacob of Nisibis (d. 337/8), a signatory of the Coun-cil of Nicaea in 325 who had lived as a recluse in the wilderness before assuming the episcopacy of Nisibis (Theodoret, *HR* 1). But Jacob's years of withdrawal were an individual instance and only the preface to his ecclesiastical career; Julian's led to the formation of a sizeable monastic community living well away from the city. For the first time in Syrian ascetic tradition, the poles of wilderness and city were distinctly visible.

Second, Julian marks the growing predilection in the Syrian Orient of this time to pursue a more extreme ascetic practice. According to Theodoret of Cyrrhus, Julian lived in a cave and ate once a week a stringent diet of barley, bran, salt and water. Even his disciples had to elaborate slightly on this regime, adding pickled vegetables to their fare (Theodoret, *HR* 2.2, 4). In its extremity of discipline, Julian's career initiates the golden age of Syrian ascetics who lived on pillars, in cages, in trees, naked in the wilderness as 'grazers', or in other notably dramatic forms of *askesis*. If we are to understand the religious impetus of this extreme tradition, epitomized in the stylite's vocation on his pillar, we must look not only to the changing location and form of Syrian asceticism as evidenced in the career of Julian Saba, but also at the way that career was understood by his contemporaries.

While information on Julian is sprinkled across a variety of ancient texts, both Greek and Syriac, two sources stand apart as particularly important for considering these issues. Scholars generally begin with the account of Julian's career narrated in Theodoret of Cyrrhus' *History of the Monks of Syria* (or, *Historia Religiosa*), chapter 2, written in the 440s (Canivet and LeRoy-Molinghen 1977; Price 1985).[1] Although the text is self-consciously hagiographical, Theodoret was an astute and scrupulous historian. His account is an interpretive narrative that frames the events of Julian's career within the larger ecclesiastical history of his time. While Theodoret did not know him personally, he knew several of Julian's disciples, and these were central resources for his presentation of the holy man and his accomplishments.

Rarely studied but no less important for understanding the work of this saint is a cycle of 24 hymns composed in Syriac soon after the saint's death and attributed to Ephrem the Syrian (Beck 1972).[2] Although only the first four hymns hold any possibility of such authorship, the entire cycle shows clear signs of coming from Ephrem's immediate disciples (Melki 1983: 58–60; Griffith 1994).[3] While the question of Ephrem's authorship must remain open, there is nonetheless a marked difference between the first four hymns and the rest of the cycle. This is less a difference in time (earlier as opposed to later), than a difference again of location. The first four are written from the vantage point of the city of Edessa: the self-referent repeated here is the term 'our land'. These hymns take as their task the interpretation of the changes marked by Julian's choices, and the reconciliation of the ascetic life – in Julian's practice, now physically separated from the life of the civic community – with the ongoing life of the Church in the city. The rest of the cycle is located rather in the community of Julian's disciples. Here the self-referent in addition to 'our land' is the term 'our congregation', and it is clearly the monastic congregation which is summoned thereby. These hymns speak to the trials faced by the community as it continued in the wake of Julian's death – a different challenge than that posed for the city. It is the first four of these hymns that are especially relevant to the concerns of this study.

Theodoret's Greek narrative and the Syriac hymn cycle represent distinct literary forms in contrasting languages. What is striking, however, is the degree to

1. Abbreviated here as Theodoret, HR (=*Historia Religiosa*). I follow the translation of Price (1985).
2. Translations here are my own.
3. Beck is inclined against Ephremian authorship, though he would place the hymns in the first or second generation after Ephrem's death; Beck 1972: CSCO 323/Scr. Syr. 141: xv.

which both focus on devotional practices as the means by which the work of the desert recluse and the activities of the Christian in the world could be seen as intimately linked within a larger liturgical frame. My purpose here is to examine how this focus on religious practices enabled Julian's changed ascetic location and form to be integrated back into the central life of the civic ecclesiastical community. How did Julian Saba, hermit and 'Father of Monks', become the great 'treasure without price' for the people of Edessa?

Theodoret's account is framed by the way in which he introduces Julian's place and mode of life. Having explained the desolation of the desert at the edges of Osrhoene where Julian would live, Theodoret describes the cave in which the young ascetic settled: 'not made by hands, nor well and beautifully dug out', yet Julian thought it 'of more value than palaces shining with gold and silver'. There,

> [a]s his luxury, indulgence, and elaborate banquet he had the hymnody of David and perpetual intercourse with God. ... For Julian received such a firebrand of longing that he was intoxicated with desire, and while seeing nothing of earthly things dreamt only of the Beloved [Christ] at night and thought only of him by day. (*HR* 2.2)

In the bleak desert landscape Julian pursued a perpetual liturgy, chanting the biblical psalms in continuous prayer. Theodoret draws his imagery of intoxicated love from both classical and biblical models: from Plato's *Symposium*, and from the biblical Song of Songs, thereby anticipating the sumptuous mystical imagery that would flower with the growth of Christian contemplative tradition.[4]

Drawn by the simplicity and beauty of Julian's life, disciples began to appear. Soon, Julian found himself presiding over a large monastic community (one hundred monks, according to Theodoret). Julian accepted his new role while insisting on preserving his original desire for solitary prayer. For days at a time he would go off alone into the desert, 'like some new Moses'. If a disciple chose to follow, he would find the saint's beatific contemplation conducted in a desert landscape of harrowing mortal danger – dangers quietly averted by the saint's prayer. But just as Moses returned to the Israelites after communing with God on Sinai, so, too, did Julian return every few days to his monks, his 'choir'. These he taught to practise 'common hymnody' in their cave dwelling before dawn. After daybreak, they would go to the desert in pairs, one to worship God kneeling while the other sang fifteen psalms standing. Back and forth the two monks would alternate posture with silence or song, from early morning until late afternoon; after a short rest, all gathered back in the cave to sing the evening hymns in unison. Thus did the lifeless desert become a sanctuary adorned with ceaseless song, according to a 'new law' given by a 'new prophet' (*HR* 2.4–5).

Theodoret continues his narrative to number Julian's mighty feats, all of which he presents as possible and effective because of Julian's (and his monks') musical prayer practice. By Julian's prayer a dragon could be slain, or water made to appear in the desert (*HR* 2.6–7); pilgrimage was undertaken, and a church was built (*HR* 2.13). Hearing of dire straits in the city of Antioch, Julian went to help, 'unalarmed at the unpleasantness of civil tumult' (*HR* 2.17). The dead were raised

---

4.   See also Theodoret's essay 'On Divine Love', with notes (Price 1985: 190–207).

and the sick healed (*HR* 2.17–20); heresy was laid to rest, and paganism defeated (*HR* 2.14, 16, 21). By Julian's prayer, then, the Church – indeed, the world – was healed of every woe, even as the bodies of the sick whom his touch restored. Body and soul, individual and collective: Julian healed and sanctified the human condition. Nor did he confine his blessings to works by his own hands. Theodoret stresses that Julian's vocation bore an immense harvest of fruits: the solitary recluse produced a thriving monastic community to continue his work. From this community came disciples who went on themselves to become monastic founders and leaders, or even bishops (notably Asterius, abbot of a monastery in Gindara, and Acacius, bishop of Beroea from 379 to 436), guiding the churches of Syria aright even as they returned, repeatedly, to visit their spiritual father Julian Saba (the 'Old Man'). Hence the ecclesiastical order of Theodoret's own day was held firm, he claimed, by those who carried on their master's vocation of prayer and hymnody, transposed from the desert into village monasteries and city cathedrals. By this most practical link were desert and city joined: the common voice of congregations, monastic and civic, led by monk bishops trained at the same source.

The Syriac hymns on Julian Saba present a different perspective altogether. Written in the near aftermath of the saint's death, they approach their task through a sequence of images that repeatedly stress the saint's continuing presence for the city of Edessa. That presence was vividly concrete, in the first place, by the burial of the saint's bones in Edessa itself. Joyously depicted at the start of the hymn cycle as 'the treasure of his bones' (Hymn 1.2), Julian's relics now adorned Edessa with the splendour of his works: the glory of his ascetic feats, and the continuing miracles that were their fruits. Hymn 4 is a passionate celebration of the presence of these relics in the civic community and the riches bestowed by the saint through them, naming Julian's grave 'a great harbour' summoning merchants (= pilgrims) to Edessa (Hymn 4.3). Julian was the one who had wearied himself labouring everywhere (a reference to his travels to the Holy Land and to Antioch), yet 'he did not rest and sleep in just any place / but in our land. Blessed are you, our land, / because of the gift that was given to us, the treasure of his bones' (Hymn 4.5).

Hymn 4 indicates further that Julian's bones were buried in the tomb of the great Edessan martyrs Shmona, Guria and Habib, and alludes to the addition of his festival to theirs. For the city of Edessa, such a holy configuration would have carried dramatic force. Perhaps because of its late annexation into the Roman empire, Edessa and its territories had not suffered persecution of Christians until the final Great Persecution instigated by the Emperor Diocletian early in the fourth century. Sometime between 309 and 312, the Christians of Edessa witnessed the heroic deaths of these three martyrs: two laymen Shmona and Guria, and a deacon Habib. All three were from villages near the city. Their deaths were commemorated in two fine passion accounts, and the veneration of their relics was a cherished part of the city's identity (Burkitt 1913; Harvey 1990; Doran 2000).[5] Hymn 4 portrays Julian Saba, worn out at the end of his life, seeking 'a

---

5. Jacob of Serug (d. 521) wrote important homilies in their honour (Bedjan 1890: 131–43, 160–72); and they were popular in Greek tradition (Halkin 1962).

companion for himself, kindred to him', to share his burden. Thus were joined together

> ...The martyr [Habib] who was burned
> for the sake of our Lord, and [Julian] Saba who conquered for the sake of Jesus.
> Rise up, our land, fulfil your vows with your feasts!
> For lo, feasts resound in you like trumpets
> [the feasts] of Guria and Habib and Shmona
> the comely Saba is given also to you
> for the song of his trumpet – behold! – sings a new festal gathering for you.
>
> (Hymn 4.6–7)

During the second half of the fourth century, Edessa like other cities of the empire had gloried in the rising cult of relics (Delehaye 1933: 24–99; 1927: 122–61, 196–207; Segal 1970: 174–8, 182).[6] Gradually, her saints were moved from their graves outside the city walls, into new shrines and churches inside. The bones of Shmona, Guria and Habib, buried outside the northern end of the city near the place of their deaths, were moved inside during the episcopacy of Abraham, bishop in the city between 345 and 361, when he had a martyrion built for this purpose (Chron. Ed. 18).[7] The Christians of Nisibis, exiled to Edessa in 363 when their city fell to the Persians, brought the bones of Jacob of Nisibis with them (Theodoret, *HR* 1.14). Later again, on 22 August 394, the bones of the Apostle Thomas would be transferred from their martyrion outside Edessa to a church in the south-west corner of the city by Bishop Cyrus (Chron. Ed. 38).[8]

In this context of piety, the burial of Julian's bones in the shrine of the Edessan martyrs offered a concrete reconciliation of wilderness and city: the saint had come back to the civic church community, into its very heart. Further, the move established in literal, physical terms the equation of monk and martyr, alluded to, for example, in the *Life of Antony* of Egypt, when Athanasius spoke briefly of Antony 'martyred daily' by virtue of his ascetic discipline (*Life of Antony* 47, Gregg 1980). The action of burying Julian in the martyrs' shrine left no question as to the place of the ascetic in the life of the church, nor to the accomplishment of the ascetic's vocation. As great a witness to Christian truth as the martyrs' deaths had been, so great, again, was the witness proclaimed by the monastic saint's life. Indeed, just as Julian's prayers had sanctified the land while he was alive, so now the strength of that prayer continued to be present in his bones, in the city. So Hymn 2.17: 'A protector / is separated from us [by death]. May our Lord be willing / that just as [Julian] was our protector in his life / again he may

---

6.   Ephrem celebrates the cult of relics in his *Hymns against Heresies* 42.9–10 (Beck 1957); and especially in his *Hymns on Nisibis*: 13 (Jacob of Nisibis); 33.13 (St John the Baptist and the martyrs); 42 (St Thomas and Elisha); 43 (Moses carrying the bones of Joseph) (Beck 1961).

7.   For the burials of Shmona, Guria and Habib, see Burkitt (1913), *Shmona and Guria*, sec. 67, and *Habib*, sec. 38.

8.   Egeria visited the martyrion with the bones of Thomas when she went to Edessa in 384; Egeria, *Travels* 17.1; 19.1. The question of the location of the building in which she saw the bones remains open (Wilkinson 1971: 223–5; Peeters 1940). On the date of Egeria's visit to Edessa, see Devos (1967).

be for us a wall by his bones, like Joseph.'[9] Here, too, we may understand the references in Hymns 1 and 3 to the 'signs' (*athwotho*) worked by Julian: the healings accomplished by the 'medicine' of his prayers, healings worked both in life and still, after death, through his relics. These 'signs', the hymns stress, 'possess a force with which no one can contend' (Hymn 1.9).

The placing of Julian's bones evidenced the reconciliation of wilderness and city. So, too, did the imagery used in these hymns for Julian's prayer serve to reconcile the extremity of his physical *askesis* with the inherited traditions of prayer practice that would continue as classic for Syrian Christianity. Thus Julian is shown in Hymn 2 both to enact and to embody the image of God, painting it on his heart with the pigments of good works (Hymn 2.8). Moses and Christ had taught humankind about the Godhead by painting its image for us; this image Julian had 'put on by his way of life / with prayer and not with pictures / … paint[ing] Jesus at every moment in his ascetical practices' (Hymn 2.9–13). The crucifixion is mentioned only once in these first four hymns, briefly and in passing (Hymn 2.2). It appears as a major image first in Hymn 7, where the cross is a treasury of wealth, sumptuously described, which Julian 'fastens inside his body' (Hymn 7.12–15). As always in Syriac literature prior to the sixth century, the cross is used here not so much to denote pain as to reveal glory.

While emphasis is placed on Julian's long-suffering endurance, the impetus of these hymns is repeatedly toward the transformative, even transfigurative, nature of prayer. When our hymnwriter speaks of the 'purity' or 'luminous clarity' of Julian's will (*shafyo/shafyuto*; Hymns 2.10, 16; 3.11), or uses the image of a highly polished mirror to convey the radiant nature of Julian's prayer (Hymns 2, 14, 16), he uses terms employed from our earliest Syriac writers on the contemplative life right through the history of Syriac Christianity (Brock 1987). It is not the harshness of Julian's chosen vocation that the hymnwriter sees, but its transfigurative results: 'while [Julian's] light enlightened him / his rays shone forth in our land / for his ascetical practices like his disciples shone out in our region' (Hymn 3.1). The manner in which these hymns characterize Julian's practice of prayer place that practice at the centre of Syrian Christianity as it can be seen before and for centuries after Julian's life. Thus the hymnwriters diminish the importance, or jarring effect, of his extreme physical *askesis*, subordinating it to the interior quality of his prayer. As the *Odes of Solomon* had urged two centuries earlier, such luminous prayer (articulated in sacred song!) might be the offering of any believer (Charlesworth 1977).

The radiance of transfiguration leads to the image of incense. Like the bones with which these hymns begin, incense is used in this cycle to convey a concrete practice of piety as well as an emerging metaphor for the ascetic life and its place in the larger worshipping community.

---

9. The allusion is to Gen. 50.25; Exod. 13.19. The bones of Joseph were a common topos for the power of relics. Evagrius Scholasticus, *Ecclesiastical History* 1.1.3, records how the city of Antioch refused to part with the relics of Simeon the Stylite when the Emperor Leo had requested them, saying, 'Because of the fact that our city does not have a wall, since it collapsed in an earthquake, we have brought the all-holy body [of Simeon] so as to be a wall and protection for us' (Whitby 2000: 37).

In Hymn 1, Julian's prayer practice is described as incense, spreading the sweet scent of his sanctity throughout the land, announcing the 'news' of his holy activity by its perfumed presence:

> Who needs to ask about you [Julian],
> for lo! your ascetical practices are like heralds in creation.
> A great censer [is] in our land,
> whose strong perfume [is] with those nearby
> and whose lovely fragrance [is] with those far off
> who have heard the news of him.
>
> (Hymn 1.15)

But is the incense of the image a metaphor for Julian's prayer, or is it the incense actually offered by the faithful with prayers at his tomb? In Hymn 4, we seem to have the latter:

> Rich is the incense from his pure censer,
> Its fragrance billows and wafts to every corner.
> How much indeed would our land give thanks that it is worthy,
> for behold, in it is laid a treasure of sweet spices,whose fragrance goes out to people
> that they might come to it.
>
> (Hymn 4.2)

Finally, in Hymn 7, Julian himself becomes the very incense he images, sanctifying his disciples by his transfigured presence, even as the Holy Spirit had shed the perfumed sweetness of divine presence on him:

> Your spirit, my Lord dwelt in him, sweet-smelling
> and by his converse he delighted us greatly.
> Because I have dealt from the treasure of his incense
> may the fragrance of his sweet-spices spread in me.
>
> (Hymn 7.18–19)[10]

Incense imagery in these hymns represents a turning-point in both of its usages – both in the practice of piety and in the understanding of extreme asceticism. Not until the fifth century was incense explicitly and commonly included as part of Christian worship ceremonial. The pilgrim Egeria mentions the use of incense in Jerusalem *c*.381, only in the Resurrection matins service on Sunday mornings where it is part of the liturgical drama of the myrrh-bearing women at the tomb (*Travels* 24.10). Hers is the only liturgical use of which we can be certain this early. Occasional references speak of Christians using incense during the fourth century, in paraliturgical settings: at funerals, or in civic processions, for example in the transference of relics, following the custom from the imperial cult of incense as a sign of veneration and honour (Dix 1945: 425–30; Bradshaw 1982: 76–7, 84, 87, 112; Taft 1975: 149–62; Atchley 1909: 97–101). Among our earliest references to the Christian use of incense, however, whether in collective ceremonial or private prayer, those from the Syrian Orient are the most common.

---

10. Throughout the ancient Mediterranean world, religions presumed that divinity smelled sweet: fragrance was often the form in which divinity was present to the human person. See Classen, Howes and Synnott (1994); Detienne (1994).

Indeed, as incense piety developed subsequently in the fifth and sixth centuries, evolving into a lavish Christian practice throughout the Roman empire and beyond, Syriac Christianity remained notable for the richness of its incense usage both in practice and in theological imagery.[11]

The references to incense in the Hymns on Julian Saba correspond to several other contemporary Syriac passages. Ephrem in his Nisibene Hymns, written in 363 (not long before the hymns on Julian Saba), refers to Bishop Abraham of Nisibis using incense: 'May your fasting be a defence for our land, your prayer a shield for our city / May your incense acquire reconciliation! Blessed is he who has hallowed your offerings' (*Hymns on Nisibis* 17.4.4–6, Beck 1961). Ephrem does not tell us the context of Abraham's use, whether it was liturgically or in the private devotion of his prayer practice. Similarly, the censer referred to at Julian's tomb is clearly there as a prayer offering, quite apart from liturgical worship. Soon, in the first years of the fifth century, Simeon the Stylite while a young boy would be gathering storax to burn as incense while tending his father's sheep, in his first attempt at prayer. In time, after his unsuccessful years as a coenobitic monk, Simeon would establish himself as a recluse living in a small hut, where he kept a plain altar with a censer on it: the scene of the vision that would call him to take the place of the incense on the altar, and so lead to his vocation on the pillar when Simeon became the living embodiment of incense rising heavenward in prayer (*Syriac Life*, sec. 112, Doran 1992).

These three early examples of the use of incense in Syriac literature represent not the mimetic action of the Jerusalem worship service, but rather a practice of piety that embodies the image from Ps. 141.2: 'Let my prayer arise in thy sight as incense.' And it is this image that will offer the profoundly poignant terms by which the piety of the stylites will soon come to be articulated in action and in text, for incense piety was a form of devotion heavily associated with veneration of the stylites as with their own practices (Vikan 1982; Van den Ven 1962–70). Indeed, the development of Christian incense piety from its first usage as a practice to accompany prayer, into an integral element of the late antique eucharistic liturgy – a shift occurring between the late fourth and early fifth centuries – is paralleled by the evolution of incense imagery for Syriac ascetic texts. By the fifth century, Syriac writers would present the ascetic life as a liturgical celebration enacted in the temple of the body, upon the altar of the heart, adorned with an incense of tears and prayers.[12]

The references to incense usage at the shrine of Julian Saba tie together both the devotional practices of the Christians of Edessa, and the ongoing work of the saint, as present through the miracle-working power of his bones. The offering of incense by the faithful at Julian's tomb, in supplication and as an honorific, is

---

11. Examples abound, but the Syrian cult of stylite saints is a case in point (Vikan 1982; Van den Ven 1962–70). Again, Syriac liturgical prayers developed a complex structure around incense offerings, with prayers chanted before, during and after the incense was burned (Taft 1986: 242–3; Mateos 1962; Thekeparampil 1975–6). For other examples, see Harvey (forthcoming).

12. e.g., *Book of Steps* 12.12 (Brock 1987: 45–53); 'On Hermits and Desert-Dwellers', esp. lines 97–108, 485–96 (Amar 1990).

paralleled to the offering of prayer by the saint during his lifetime: just as the fragrance of the incense wafts across the land now, announcing the (hoped-for) efficacy of his relics, so, too, did the reputation, and the efficacy, of Julian's prayer spread throughout the region during the years of his desert practice. Hymn 4 extols the paradox that neither withdrawal to the desert, nor death itself, could separate Julian from the heart of the Church. The hymnody which Julian had practised has become the hymnody in his honour sung by the Edessan congregation; his bones continue his power of healing; his separation in the desert yielded the growth of monastic assemblies, just as now, the feast days in his honour yield congregational celebrations of his life.

> [Julian's] mouth which was silenced extols praise for us
> so that even his silence is for us a cause of song.
> And his death is the cause of life
> And his separation the cause of congregations
> And his sleep the cause of vigil for praising.
>
> (Hymn 4.4)

In Hymn 6, the adornment of Edessa by the growth of the saint's cult is likened to the adornment of the desert through his monastic foundation: 'Through you our land which you have adorned has become beautiful, / and the desert has become beautiful, through your monastic communities' (Hymn 6.21). Thus Julian's work is seen to have spread throughout the whole of the Christian community: civic and monastic, city and desert. The practices of incense piety, the veneration of relics, shared hymnody, and fervent prayer join the Edessan congregation to Julian's desert vocation, both in his life and in his death. Neither his physical withdrawal, nor his severe asceticism, separate him from the life of the Church in its broadest sense: rather, all are woven together by the concrete practices of piety, common to Christians as a whole.

Both Theodoret's chapter and the Syriac cycle of hymns are noteworthy for their efforts to tie Julian's asceticism and holy activities into the devotional and liturgical life of the larger ecclesial community. Concrete links are drawn between what Julian and his disciples undertook as disciplinary practices and devotional actions, and the related religious rituals that would be engaged by clergy and laity in their daily civic lives. Thus a kind of ritual dialogue is established between hermit and citizen, monk and layperson, bishop and pilgrim, while the various locations of Christian piety – monastic, civic, domestic – are woven together in a tapestry of shared practices that yield a common religious identity: a Church made whole by the joining of its different members (Bell 1992). By focusing on this linkage of practices, both sources succeed in rendering Julian central to the continuing life and health of the worshipping community, thus relocating and reconfiguring the place and form of his asceticism.

Theodoret's hagiographical narrative and the Hymns on Julian Saba show us a bridge in the changing piety of late antique Syrian Christianity. They bridge from the way things had been, to the way things were coming to be. By that bridging, they reconcile what was changed (or new) with what had been and would remain constant: wilderness reconciled to city, extreme asceticism to the practice of prayer, the use of incense to the image of worship. Standing on that bridge, we can see not only what lies ahead, but also why it is there.

Bibliography

Amar, Joseph P.
    1990   'On Hermits and Desert Dwellers', in Vincent Wimbush (ed.), *Ascetic Behavior in Greco-Roman Antiquity: A Sourcebook* (Minneapolis: Fortress Press), 66–80.
Atchley, E. G. C. F.
    1909   *A History of the Use of Incense in Divine Worship* (London: Longmans, Green & Co.).
Beck, Edmund
    1957   *Des heiligen Ephraem des Syrers Hymnen contra Haereses* (CSCO, 169: Scriptores Syri, 76; Louvain: Durbecq).
    1961   *Des heiligen Ephraem des Syrers Carmina Nisibena* (CSCO, 218–19, 240–1: Scriptores Syri, 92–3, 102–3; Louvain: CSCO).
    1972   *Des Heiligen Ephraem des Syrers, Hymnen auf Abraham Kidunaya und Julianos Saba* (CSCO, 322–3: Scriptores Syri, 140–1; Louvain: CSCO).
Bedjan, Paul
    1890   *Acta Martyrum et Sanctorum*, vol. 1 (Paris: Harrassowitz; 1968 Hildesheim: Georg Olm).
Bell, Catherine
    1992   *Ritual Theory, Ritual Practice* (New York: Oxford University Press).
Bradshaw, Paul
    1982   *Daily Prayer in the early Church* (New York: Oxford University Press).
Brock, Sebastian P.
    1987   *The Syriac Fathers on Prayer and the Spiritual Life* (Kalamazoo: Cistercian Publications).
Burkitt, F. C.
    1913   *Euphemia and the Goth with the Acts of the Martyrdom of the Confessors of Edessa* (London and Oxford: Williams & Norgate).
Canivet, Pierre, and A. Leroy-Molinghen
  1977, 1979 *Théodoret de Cyr, Histoire des moines de Syrie* (ed. and tr. Sources Chrétiennes, 234 and 257, 2 vols.; Paris: Beauchesne).
Charlesworth, James H.
    1977   *The Odes of Solomon* (Missoula: Scholars Press, 2nd edn).
Classen, Constance, David Howes, and Anthony Synnott
    1994   *Aroma: A Cultural History of Smell* (New York: Routledge).
Delehaye, Hippolyte
    1927   *Sanctus: Essai sur le culte des saints dans l'antiquité* (Subsidia Hagiographica, 17; Bruxelles: Société des Bollandistes).
    1933   *Les origines du culte des martyrs* (Subsidia Hagiographica, 20; Brussels: Société des Bollandistes, 2nd edn).
Detienne, Marcel
    1994   *Gardens of Adonis: Spices in Greek Mythology* (Princeton, NJ: Princeton University Press).
Devos, P.
    1967   'Égérie à Édesse. S. Thomas l'apôtre. Le roi Abgar', *Analecta Bollandiana* 85: 381–400.

Dix, Gregory
    1945   *The Shape of the Liturgy* (London: A. & C. Black).
Doran, Robert
    1992   *The Lives of Simeon Stylites* (Kalamazoo: Cistercian Publications).
    2000   'The Martyrdom of Habib the Deacon', in Richard Valantasis (ed.), *Religions of Late Antiquity in Practice* (Princeton, NJ: Princeton University Press), 413–23.
Gregg, Robert
    1980   *Athanasius, the Life of Antony and the Letter to Marcellinus* (New York: Paulist Press).
Griffith, Sidney H.
    1994   'Julian Saba "Father of the Monks" of Syria', *Journal of Early Christian Studies* 2: 185–216.
    1995   'Asceticism in the Church of Syria: The Hermeneutics of Early Syrian Monasticism', in Vincent Wimbush and Richard Valantasis (eds.), *Asceticism* (New York: Oxford University Press), 220–45.
Guidi, I.
    1903   'Chronicon Edessum', ed. and tr. in idem, *Chronica Minora* (CSCO, 1–2: Scriptores Syrii, 1–2; Louvain).
Halkin, F.
    1962   'L'éloge des Trois Confesseurs d'Edesse par Aréthas de Césarée', *Mélanges de l'Université Saint Joseph* 38 (Beirut): 269–76.
Harvey, Susan Ashbrook
    1990   'The Edessan Martyrs and Syrian Ascetic Tradition', in R. Lavenant (ed.), *V Symposium Syriacum* (Orientalia Christiana Analecta, 236; Rome: Pont. Institutum Studiorum Orientalium), 195–206.
    Forthcoming *The Scent of Salvation: Ancient Christianity and the Olfactory Imagination* (Berkeley: University of California).
Mateos, Juan
    1962   '"Sedre" et prières connexes dans quelque anciennes collections', *Orientalia Christiana Periodica* 28: 239–87.
Melki, J.
    1983   'S. Ephrem le Syrien, un bilan de l'édition critique', *Parole de l'Orient* 11: 3–88.
Peeters, Paul
    1940   'Glanures Martyrologiques, ii: La basilique des confesseurs à Édesse', *Analecta Bollandiana* 58: 110–23.
Price, R. M.
    1985   *Theodoret of Cyrrhus: A History of the Monks of Syria* (Kalamazoo: Cistercian Publications).
Segal, J. B.
    1970   *Edessa: The Blessed City* (Oxford: Oxford University Press).
Taft, Robert
    1975   *The Great Entrance: A History of the Transfer of the Gifts and Other Pre-anaphoral Rites of the Liturgy of St. John Chrysostom* (Orientalia Christiana Analecta, 200; Rome: Pont. Institutum Studiorum Orientalium).
    1986   *The Liturgy of the Hours in East and West* (Collegeville, Minn.: Liturgical Press).
Thekeparampil, Jacob
    1975–6   'Prayers After Incense', *Parole de l'Orient* 6/7: 325–40.

Van den Ven, Paul
 1962, 1970 *La vie ancienne de saint Syméon Stylite le Jeune (521–592)* (Subsidia
     Hagiographica, 32 (2 vols.; Brussels: Société des Bollandistes).
Vikan, Gary
 1982 *Byzantine Pilgrimage Art* (Washington, DC: Dumbarton Oaks).
Vööbus, Arthur
 1960 *History of Asceticism in the Syrian Orient* (vol. 2; CSCO, 197: Subsidia, 17;
    Louvain: CSCO).
Whitby, Michael
 2000 *The Ecclesiastical History of Evagrius Scholasticus* (Liverpool: Liverpool
    University Press).
Wilkinson, John
 1971 *Egeria, Travels* (London: SPCK).

Part II
Theological Explorations

WILDERNESS, REVELATION AND THE NEW JERUSALEM IN RADICAL CHRISTIAN WRITINGS

Christopher Rowland

In the Spirit follow the Angel into the Desert
(Joachim of Fiore, *Liber de Concordia* 2.1)

There is a dramatic moment in the Apocalypse where John is taken for one of his visions to a desert place (17.1–6):

> Then one of the seven angels who had the seven bowls came and said to me, 'Come, I will show you the judgment of the great harlot who is seated upon many waters, with whom the kings of the earth have committed fornication, and with the wine of whose fornication the dwellers on earth have become drunk.' And he carried me away in the Spirit into a wilderness, and I saw a woman sitting on a scarlet beast which was full of blasphemous names, and it had seven heads and ten horns. The woman was arrayed in purple and scarlet, and bedecked with gold and jewels and pearls, holding in her hand a golden cup full of abominations and the impurities of her fornication; and on her forehead was written a name of mystery: 'Babylon the great, mother of harlots and of earth's abominations.' And I saw the woman, drunk with the blood of the saints and the blood of the martyrs of Jesus.

This is the third time in his vision that John has described being in Spirit, a moment of ecstatic experience (cf. 1.10; 4.2; 21.10; Ezek. 8.2).

Down the centuries the images of Revelation 17 have resonated with many as they have sought to discern the role of Babylon, and in the wilderness of the contemporary life to look forward to, and even embody, the life of the New Jerusalem. Nowhere is this more true than in the seventeenth century, a veritable 'golden age' of the interpretation of the Apocalypse, when many ordinary readers, men and women, had recourse to this book to read the signs of the times and to understand themselves better before God. (Mack 1992; Hobby 1988; Hinds 1996).

This essay concerns the way in which exponents of a radical religion used the wilderness and the end of a period of exile and alienation to describe both the spiritual journey and the opportunity for political change. Fell and Winstanley are the exceptions in that they think of the immediately present possibility of social change in ways which had become difficult for writers a couple of decades later. Blake, while ever anxious to stress the need for Albion to repent and be restored to its true vocation, is sanguine about the prospects for change, and, like Jane Lead before him, underlines the way in which the wilderness can be a place of individual spiritual growth.

Mary Cary (fl. 1649) in 'The Little Horne' and 'The New Mappe of the New Jerusalem' expounded a doctrine which was to become extremely influential among revolutionary groups: namely, that the succession of world empires predicted in Daniel 2 and 7 had come to its end and that the reign of King Jesus was about to be established (Hill 1972; 1993; Capp 1972). In the process of the establishment of this 'fifth monarchy', Cary gave the saints an active role in the establishment of the kingdom on earth. Cary carefully applies passages in Daniel and the Apocalypse to contemporary events and to their elucidation of them in the divine economy. According to Cary, the reign of God which will be set up on earth will be a happy condition for the Saints. Her belief in an imminent dawning of a new age brings to an end a situation of loneliness and exile for God's people, represented by the period the woman spent in the wilderness. There is a sense of anticipation in her writing that a period of exile and the wilderness are imminently to be brought to an end:

> That the woman fled into the Wilderness from the persecution of the Dragon, where she was nourished for a time, times, and half a time; and in the sixth verse of that Chapter where there is another mention of the woman's flying into the Wilderness, where she was to be fed or nourished; it is said to be for a thousand two hundred, and sixty days... Now by this one thousand two hundred and sixty days, is to be understood so many years as it is usual in the Prophets to put a day for a year. So that when the one thousand two hundred and sixty years, in which the Romish beast, (of whom that Prophesy speaks) was to continue prevailing against the Saints, did expire, then the One thousand two hundred and sixty years. Or, Forty two months, or Time, times, and half a time: (For so it is variously expressed) of the Saints suffering persecution, did expire also ... That is, they shall be given into his hand, until the end of the one thousand two hundred and sixty years, in which the Romish Beast was to be permitted to persecute the Church or Saints of God, and to overcome them, and tread them under foot. So that, so long, this horn was to go on speaking great words against the most High, and wearying out the Saints; and endeavouring to change times and laws, and to have them given into his hand, even until that time was to be expired. Now that this one thousand two hundred and sixty years, in which the Romish Beast was to be permitted to persecute the Church, and to tread it under foot, is very near come to a period: In the concurrent judgment of all the learned, and godly men that have written, and published any thing of it: and also the judgment of many private, faithful, and precious Christians in these times. But that it is not only very near, but is already fully expired. (*The Little Horns Doom & Downfall* [1651], 8[r])

In *The Daughter of Sion Awakened* (1677) Margaret Fell, the mother of Quakerism, sees the wilderness as a place of exile and yet also of hope, whence the longed-for redemption will come, and where will be a return to the spiritual power of the earliest days of the Church's life. For her, like her earlier contemporary Gerrard Winstanley, the coming of the New Jerusalem is no eschatological event only but a real possibility in the transformation of the lives of men and women. Fell sees the time of darkness to be at an end and the last days to be upon her. Spiritual regeneration and structural change are for her intimately linked. The new heaven and earth is something to be seen here and now. The kingdom of God is, as for all these radical writers, very much a this-worldly kingdom and to be entered into here and now. God is not far above the heavens; God is to be found in the lives and experiences of men and women.

> And now, in these last days, since there hath been a falling away, and a Night of Dark-
> ness, and a Night of Apostasy from the true, spiritual and glorious Appearance of the
> Resurrection of Jesus, in the Apostles and primitive Christians days, since which time
> the Woman, that brought forth the man-child, hath been fled into the Wilderness, a
> Place prepared of God for her, and had the two Wings of the great Eagle given her:
> But she is now returning out of the Wilderness, leaning upon her Beloved; and the
> Holy City, New Jerusalem, is coming down from God out of Heaven, prepared as a
> Bride for her Husband, having the Glory of God; and her Light is like a Jasper Stone,
> most precious, clear as Crystal, which shines forth in its Glory, and clearly makes
> manifest all the power and body of spiritual Darkness. (*The Daughter of Sion Awakened*,
> 12)

There are very similar themes in the writings of Gerrard Winstanley (Bradstock and Rowland 2002; Hill 1972). From April 1649 to March 1650 Winstanley's career and writing were intimately bound up with the Digger commune
set up in Surrey. Winstanley was prompted by a revelation that he and his companions should dig the common land and claim what they regarded as their
rightful inheritance. Winstanley and a few others moved to St George's Hill
Cobham in 1 April 1649. They were finally driven off the land in the spring of
1650. Fundamental to the communal experiment of the Diggers was the belief
that the earth was a common treasury. Winstanley was concerned to expose the
way in which the preoccupation with private property reflected a fundamental
characteristic of humanity after the Fall of Adam. The struggle between the
Dragon and Christ is now linked to the advocacy of communism and in dealing
with the opposition to it. The perfect society will come when there takes place
what Winstanley calls 'the rising up of Christ in sons and daughters, which is his
second coming'.

In the writings written round about the period when the Digger commune was
set up, Winstanley stresses the reality of eschatological fulfilment as the period of
exile and wilderness comes to an end, as he anticipates a time of eschatological
change in English society when King Jesus reigns in the establishment of a
communist society. This sense of fulfilment is apparent in the extract from Winstanley's long work *The New Law of Righteousness*, which offers the most extended vision of his theological and political ideas (Sabine 1941: 198–9).

> For every one shall know the Law, and every one shall obey the Law; for it shall be
> writ in every one's heart; and every one that is subject to reason's law, shall enjoy the
> benefit of sonship. And that is in respect of outward community, to work together and
> eat bread together; and, by so doing, lift up the creation from the bondage of self-
> interest, or particular propriety of mine and thine; which is the Devil and Satan, even
> the God of this world, that hath blinded the eyes of covetous, proud flesh, and hath
> bound them up in chains of darkness. Acts 4.32.

> The universal spirit of righteousness hath been slain by covetous, proud flesh; this
> 1649 years ago: but now that spirit begins to rise again from the dead and the same
> Beast seeks to hinder his rising; or else watches to kill the man child after he is
> brought forth. Covetous proud flesh will kill a Tyrant, but hold fast the same Tyranny
> and slavery over others in his own hand; he will kill the traitor, but likes well the trea-
> son, when he may be honoured or lifted up by it. Rev. 12.4, 3 Kings 20.16.

Look upon the mountains and little hills of the earth, and see if these prickling thorns and briers, the bitter curse, does not grow there: Truly Tyranny is Tyranny in one as well as in another; in a poor man lifted up by his valour, as in a rich man lifted up by his lands: And where Tyranny sits, he is an enemy to Christ, the spreading spirit of righteousness: He will use the bare name, Christ, that he may the more secretly persecute, and kill his power. Tyranny is a subtle proud and envious Beast; his nature is selfish, and full of murder; he promises fair things for the public; but all must be made to centre within himself, or self interest not the universal liberty.

Well to be short, let every one know, if they wait upon their Maker they will know, that the universal power of righteous Community, as I have declared, is Canaan, the land of rest and liberty, which flows with milk and honey, with abundance of joy and peace in our Maker, and in one another. Zach. 8.3. to 12.

But the condition of the world, that upholds civil interests of mine and thine: Is Egypt the house of bondage; and truly Pharaoh's task masters, are very many both teachers and rulers.

In this passage Winstanley picks up on themes from Christian eschatology which stretch back to the New Testament itself (e.g. 1 Cor. 2.10–16), in which the external moral code is seen as obsolete, to be replaced by the law written on the heart. This would enable the establishment of an egalitarian society, in which there would be an absence of 'particular propriety'. The era which Winstanley believed had dawned in 1649, in the aftermath of the execution of Charles I, was a fulfilment of Revelation 12, when the apparent defeat of Christ would be overcome 1649 years later. Even then the dragon who threatened the woman with child would also threaten the fledgling society (as indeed it did in the case of Winstanley's communist experiment). He was not naive about the way in which self-interest affected rich and poor alike, for 'wherever tyranny sits, he is an enemy to Christ'. Winstanley in his vocation as a prophet of the practice of a different sort of society sees in the establishment of the Diggers' communes a practical demonstration of the liberation of Israel and a challenge to the bondage of the Pharaohs of his day.

Many, like Winstanley, Cary and Fell, in the middle decades of the seventeenth century in England, entertained hopes of a change in society, and the restoration of the monarchy led to huge disappointment. Milton and Bunyan both reflect in their greatest writing a retreat from the political as a sphere of radical change to the world of literature and spiritual and inward renewal. In *The Pilgrim's Progress* the quest for individual salvation in a Promised Land beyond this world compensates for the disappointments of not experiencing it in this. Their concern with inner transformation provided a resource for that generation to seek for the light within and engage in an inner struggle when the prospects for engaging in it in the world at large seemed to lead only to defeat. Christopher Hill has written of 'the experience of defeat' (Hill 1975), and that was shared by many who looked for a new order. The egalitarian spirit of the Quakers was kept alive through the concern for inwardness and the eschewing of hierarchy and force. This quiet, silent protest was the path taken by those who sought to keep alive the flame of radicalism of the 1640s as exemplified in the work of Mary Cary and others of her generation.

One of the most remarkable examples of this kind of spirituality is the career of Jane Lead, whose influence was felt and is still looked to as the fountainhead of a line of prophets, mainly women, of whom Joanna Southcott at the end of the eighteenth and the beginning of the nineteenth centuries is an example (Ruether and McLaughlin 1979: 183). Jane Lead's works were intended to bring spiritual teaching for the little groups of seekers who were yearning for the 'renewal of the Mind and Heart that is absolutely necessary to achieve a walk with God'. In *The Revelation of Revelations* (1683) she interprets the symbols of the Apocalypse in connection with the spiritual journey, in a way that is parallel to, but more abstruse than, we find in Bunyan's *Pilgrim's Progress*. The opening of the Seven Seals, the coming of the New Jerusalem State, are to be found in the lives of the readers themselves. The writing is shot through with the conviction that the life of Paradise is to be attained before death, if the believer can see what hinders spiritual progress and is aware of the Prince of this World who tempts the Soul:

> A Fountain is opened in the Desert, of which the Soul, which is in union with the Virgin, shall drink, instead of the muddy Waters of the Earth, which she loathes: Pleasant Food is provided in this Wilderness by God himself, and his Christ. The Lord affords these Dainties to the abstracted Life, where the Virgin-Spirit is a stranger to sensitive Self within, as well as to the enchanting World without. Here it wants no good company, for it is never without heavenly Visitants because it reserves it self chiefly for converse with the Deity, from whom she expects all her Blessing and Increase: And thus the Soul shall spring and multiply, where the Virgin hath realized her self. Her Wilderness shall become a rich Sharon-Pasture, a Land of unknown Plenty, where Gold, Silver, and precious Stones shall be as the Dust under the Feet of these holy separated Virgins: Also within and without, their feeding shall be on Power, Joy, and Peace, till the division of Time shall come to an end, in which a further Mystery will be understood. But oh! let all this be first fully witnessed.

Several of the themes considered above converge a century later in the poetry of William Blake, who came from an artisan background and was apprenticed to an engraver in London, a skill which he refined and perfected so that he evolved a way of producing the creations of his own prophetic imagination. Though his inspiration lies in the Bible, he became disillusioned with some of the minority groups in which he discerned the stratified society and the bondage of a religion of law which he so much abhorred. This Blake sought to challenge in his illuminated books. Blake's sense of prophetic vocation and insight equipped him to offer the meaning of contemporary events. His work probes the roots of humanity's disaffection and alienation from God and from one another. Because of the way the Bible seemed harnessed to an oppressive religion and morality, Blake evolved his own mythology, rooted in the symbols and images of the biblical prophecies and apocalypses, to challenge the domination of deference to the old words and phrases and to seek to enable the expression of a different, more humane, conception of human life. Blake realized that for Scripture to speak there had to be found ways to enable that imagery to be reborn by word, picture, myth and artistic ingenuity, so the Scripture and the spiritual experiences of previous generations could become present truth and words of life. In addition to preoccupation with the letter of the Scripture Blake inveighed against a theology which viewed God as a remote divine monarch and law-giver.

In his early works he saw himself as a 'voice in the wilderness' (actually quoted on the title page of *All Religions are One*, Plate 1). At the opening of *The Marriage of Heaven and Hell* Blake conjures up the image of the just man walking through perilous paths along the vale of death: 'The just man rages in the wilds where lions roam'. Here, as a John the Baptist-like figure in the midst of a world of rationalistic philosophy and the dominance of empire, Blake, and those who think like him, conduct the 'mental fight'. A different approach to the wilderness and desert emerges in the following quotation, which comes from the deceptively simple *Songs of Innocence and Experience*, in which Blake uses his perception of what he calls 'minute particulars' to juxtapose the contrary situations of human life to provoke imaginative engagement with hope and injustice, lofty ideals and brute reality.

'The Little Girl Lost'	'The Little Girl Found'
In futurity I prophetic see, That the earth from sleep, (Grave the sentence deep)	All the night in woe, Lyca's parents go: Over vallies deep, While the desarts weep.
Shall arise and seek For her maker meek: And the desert wild Become a garden mild.	Tired and woe-begone, Hoarse with making moan: Arm in arm seven days, They trac'd the desart ways.
In the southern clime, Where the summers prime. Never fades away; Lovely Lyca lay.	Seven nights they sleep. Among shadows deep: And dreamt they see their child Starv'd in desert wild.
Seven summers old Lovely Lyca told, She had wandered long. Hearing wild birds song.	Pale thro' pathless ways The fancied image strays. Famish'd, weeping, weak With hollow piteous shriek
Sweet sleep come to me Underneath this tree; Do, father, mother, weep. – 'Where can Lyca sleep.'	Rising from unrest, The trembling woman prest, With feet of weary woe; She could no further go.
Lost in desert wild Is your little child. How can Lyca sleep. If her mother weep.	In his arms he bore, Her arm'd with sorrow sore; Till before their way, A couching lion lay.
If her heart does ake, Then let Lyca wake; If my mother sleep, Lyca shall not weep.	Turning back was vain, Soon his heavy mane Bore them to the ground; Then he stalk'd around.

Frowning frowning night,
O'er this desert bright,
Let thy moon arise,
While I close my eyes.

Sleeping Lyca lay:
While the beasts of prey,
Come from caverns deep,
View'd the maid asleep

The kingly lion stood
And the virgin view'd,
The he gambold round
O'er the hallowed ground:

Leopards, tygers play,
Round her as she lay;
While the lion old,
Bow'd his mane of gold,

And her bosom lick,
And upon her neck,
From his eyes of flame,
Ruby tears there came;

While the lioness,
Loos'd her slender dress,
And naked they convey'd
To caves the sleeping maid.

Smelling to his prey,
But their fears allay.
When he licks their hands:
And silent by them stands.

They look upon his eyes
Fill'd with deep surprise:
And wondring behold,
A spirit arm'd in gold.

On his head a crown
On his shoulders down,
Flow'd his golden hair,
Gone was all their care.

Follow me he said,
Weep not for the maid;
In my palace deep.
Lyca lies asleep.

Then they followed,
Where the vision led;
And saw their sleeping child,
Among tygers wild.

To this day they dwell
In a lonely dell
Nor fear the wolvish howl,
Nor the lions growl.

In the deliberate juxtaposing of 'contraries' in *The Songs of Innocence and Experience*, the desert poses alternatively an opportunity for the little girl lost, Lyca, and a threat for her parents. The contrasting attitudes (and experiences) of the desert are brought out in the two poems. Blake persists in spelling 'desert' in the form of 'desart' suggesting that the experience is like the experience of art. The life of the imagination is a wakening, a time of real spiritual renewal and worship. While for Lyca it is a means of discovery and embrace, something which is brought out very clearly in the marginal illuminations and decorations to the versions, where a young woman and a young man embrace. For Lyca's parents, however, there is only a fear that their daughter will be devastated by the encounter with the wilderness. Indeed, as they set out into the 'desart', it is fear and apprehensiveness which determine their journey, and it is only when, in the light of experience, they meet what Lyca herself had enjoyed that, far from going on their journey of rescue, they themselves are rescued (as indeed was Lyca) and end up staying in that situation.[1]

1.   For other references to the desert see *Four Zoas*, 1.89, and 417; *Jerusalem*, 54, 83, 86. See *The Complete Writings of William Blake* (ed. Geoffrey Keynes; Oxford: Oxford University Press, 1972).

So, the place of John's vision in Revelation 17 is primarily a place of insight, which enabled him to glimpse the power of empire and reinforce the spiritual resistance that was needed. It did enable him to have deeper insight into the nature of the beast and its rider. That the desert could be a place of insight and renewal is evident in Hosea 2.14. In this passage God lures Israel back to the wilderness in order for a nation to learn again what makes for its true peace: 'Therefore, I will now allure her, and bring her into the wilderness, and speak tenderly to her. From there I will give her her vineyards, and make the Valley of Achor a door of hope. There shall she respond as in the days of her youth, as at the time when she came out of the land of Egypt.' It was the place whence movements of renewal arose as we know from Josephus' accounts of prophetic renewal movements in the first century CE (Josephus, *Jewish War* 6.281ff, 301ff; *Ant.* 20.97ff, 167ff; cf. Acts 21.38). Similarly, John the Baptist appears on the scene, not in the palaces of kings and princes but in the desert. John preaches a disturbing message, dressed in the garb of the prophet (cf. Zech. 13.3). This message continued to strike a chord with others who went out into the desert, whether literally or metaphorically, to learn afresh the call of God and the way to the New Jerusalem.

Bibliography

Bindman D.
  1991–5   *William Blake's Illuminated Books* (6 vols.; London: Tate Gallery Publications/William Blake Trust).
Bradstock, A., and C. Rowland,
  2002   *Radical Christian Writings: A Reader* (Oxford: Basil Blackwell).
Capp, B. S.
  1972   *The Fifth Monarchy Men: A Study in Seventeenth-Century English Millenarianism* (London: Faber).
Hill, C.
  1972   *The World Turned Upside Down* (London: Penguin).
  1975   *The Experience of Defeat* (London: Faber).
  1993   *The English Bible and the Seventeenth Century Revolution* (London: Penguin).
Hinds, H.
  1996   *God's Englishwomen: Seventeenth-Century Radical Sectarian Writing and Feminist Criticism* (Manchester: Manchester University Press).
Hobby, E.
  1988   *Virtue of Necessity: English Women's Writing 1649–88* (London: Virago).
Mack, P.
  1992   *Visionary Women: Ecstatic Prophecy in Seventeenth Century England* (Berkeley: University of California).
Rowland, C., and J. Kovacs
  2004   *The Apocalypse of Jesus Christ* (Blackwell's Bible Commentaries; Oxford: Basil Blackwell).
Rowland, C.
  1998   *The Book of Revelation* (New Interpreter's Bible, 12; Nashville: Abingdon Press).

2004 'Blake and the Bible: Biblical Exegesis in the Work of William Blake', in J. M. Court (ed.), *Biblical Interpretation: The meanings of Scripture – Past and Present* (London: T&T Clark), 168–84.

Ruether, R. R., and E. McLaughlin
1979 *Women of Spirit in the Jewish and Christian Traditions* (New York: Book World Promotions).

Sabine, G. H. (ed.)
1941 *The Works of Gerrard Winstanley* (New York: Cornell).
www.wwp. brown.edu/texts/wwoentry.html (writings of Mary Cary).

FROM EVIL THOUGHTS TO DEADLY SINS: EVAGRIUS OF PONTUS'S PSYCHOLOGY OF SIN

Angela Tilby

In the course of her distinguished career Professor Frances Young has managed to combine a serious attention to early Christianity with a concern for the mission of the contemporary Church. The pattern of my own career has been very different but we have two things in common. The first is that we both owe a significant part of our interest in theology to study at Cambridge University at a time when it was unusual for women to take this subject. The second is that we both came into pastoral ministry relatively late and after many years of reflection on religious and theological issues.

The Problem of Sin

The needs of the contemporary Church can sometimes be met by revisiting tradition, particularly those parts of the tradition which have been recovered after being lost or distorted by being misunderstood. As an Anglican priest working mostly among candidates for the Church's ministry, I find a troubling conflict between the view of sin presented by conventional spiritual writing and the lived experience of the people for whom am I responsible. In most spiritual writing sin is deliberate trespass, disobedience to God and God's laws through the vicious pursuit of self-interest. Yet in the experience of individuals this language seems over-dramatic and even self-centred. They do not *feel* that they are that wicked. They look for a model of spiritual growth in which sin (which they find easier to see in terms of mistakes and misjudgments rather than deliberate trespass) can provide opportunities for learning.

It is this conflict I hope to engage with in this essay, by exploring an early example of what might be called a psychological account of sin. This comes, appropriately for this Festschrift, direct from the 'wilderness'. It is a fruit of the ascetic movement which emerged after the conversion of Constantine and saw thousands of men and women adopt lives of extreme asceticism in the deserts of Egypt, Syria and Palestine. The Western Christian spiritual tradition would eventually codify its teachings on sin in the notion of the seven capital or deadly sins, with pride at the root and the other six (usually envy, anger, avarice, sloth, gluttony and lust) following on as consequences.

The Seven Deadly Sins

The notion of a collection of especially dangerous sins became familiar to monks of the Western Christian world through the writings of John Cassian and Pope Gregory the Great (Cassian, *Conferences*, Bks 5–12; Gregory the Great, *Moralia* 31.45). But they came into more general prominence in the West after the Fourth Lateran Council in 1214, which established the practice of annual confession for all in preparation for the reception of the sacrament at Easter. This new emphasis on universal confession meant that there was a need to teach the laity about the deadly sins to ensure that they were taken seriously and not indulged in out of ignorance. In the century following the Council, teaching about the deadly, or capital, sins began to be included in mediaeval catechisms and syllabuses of material for the clergy to impart to the laity.

The codification of such sins and their connection to confession and the eucharist represented an elevation of priestly power over the imagination and conscience of the laity. Whereas lesser (venial) sins could be forgiven without priestly mediation, capital sins could not be forgiven apart from the sacrament of confession. The seven principal sins were treated as spiritual sicknesses which, if left unexposed, would have a fatal effect on the individual's spiritual health. Education was important as individuals were justly condemned to hell if they failed to repent of such sins.

In the mediaeval wall paintings and manuscripts which illustrate them we see how fascinating the notion of deadly sins became. They are often shown as a tree of vice, sometimes decorated with horrific caricatures. The paintings frequently depict pride as the root of the tree and show new branches growing from the six main ones, making the point that sin is like an organic growth; once it has taken root, it generates further varieties of sin. Wall paintings preserved or recently discovered in Britain particularly emphasize the link between deadly sin and eternal punishment. Sometimes the sins are contrasted with the specific virtues which, after forgiveness, could be their cure. The seven corporal works of mercy were the antidote to the seven deadly sins, and both together were part of a whole catalogue of mediaeval 'sevens', like the seven canonical hours, the seven joys and seven sorrows of Mary and the seven petitions of the Lord's Prayer.

By the end of the Middle Ages the seven deadly sins were successfully embedded into the didactic and moral programme of the Church. Priests were advised to use the opportunity of confession to teach about the deadly sins and to encourage the practice of virtue. The assumption was that it was the clergy and not the laity who made spiritual judgments, and that these were based on instruction which could be handed down in words and texts rather than communicated person to person. Preparation for confession and communion was based on a response to set questions which are usually accusatory in tone. Have you sinned in this particular way? How? Against whom? And how often? This moralistic, forensic approach survived the Reformation and, though the Reformers dropped the notion of deadly and venial sins, similar methods of questioning, now in the form of *self*-examination, based, say, on the ten commandments or the beatitudes, have continued to play a part in the spiritual lives of millions. I well remember using such methods of self-examination before holy communion when I was a teenager in the 1960s, always nervous that I might have some sinful thought between the absolution and the act of reception, and thus receive unworthily.

Evagrius of Pontus as a Spiritual Teacher

We take the anxious, moralizing tone so much for granted that it comes as a surprise to meet the rather different way of understanding sin and temptation that comes to us from the writings of a figure virtually unknown in the West, Evagrius of Pontus. Evagrius was a disciple of Origen's and the teacher of John Cassian. The reason that he is largely unknown is that his work was condemned at the Fifth Ecumenical Council in 553 along with that of Origen. What we have received of Evagrius' thought has come down to us through John Cassian, but Cassian represses as much as he transmits, editing Evagrius' insights to suit his very different monastic context. The consequence is that what is particular to Evagrian spirituality has not really been absorbed or understood in the West. He has often been portrayed as an extreme Origenist, more Hellenistic than biblically Christian. This portrayal is not without justification, but it is only half the story. Among those who treasured Evagrius' teaching and preserved it (his *Chapters on Prayer* were preserved in some communities by being attributed to Nilus of Sinai), what was most valued was his practical teaching on prayer, his understanding of the workings of the passions and his ability to discern spirits. In other words it was his lived experience that counted more than his metaphysics. Those trying to live the religious life recognized one of their own.

The Life of Evagrius

Evagrius' personal history is known to us principally through the *Lausiac History* of Palladius, though there are also interesting details from Egyptian and Syrian sources. (1961, ed. Festugière; 1904, tr. Budge). Palladius' work is a series of brief biographical sketches of sixty or so holy men and women. It was dedicated to Lausus, the royal chamberlain at the court of Theodosius II. According to Palladius, Evagrius came from Ibora in Cappadocia, a town not far from the monastery of Basil, bishop of Caesarea. Evagrius was himself the son of an itinerant local bishop. It was Basil who made him a lector; he was later ordained to the diaconate by Gregory of Nazianzus. He accompanied Gregory to the Synod of Constantinople, where his keen mind and love of good argument made him a useful assistant. When the Council was over Gregory left him with Bishop Nectarius as his archdeacon. Evagrius flourished in the cosmopolitan hubbub of the imperial city and won a reputation for nosing out heresies and refuting them. But the Egyptian sources (1961: 123) also suggest that the city had a corrupting influence in him – he became obsessed with his appearance and employed a retinue of slaves to support what had become a self-indulgent lifestyle.

He also became passionately involved with a married woman who returned his feelings. She was an aristocrat and her husband appears to have had some influence within the justice system. Exposure would have meant ruin at best and possibly punishment on false charges brought by the woman's jealous husband. Evagrius could not find the strength to break off the relationship, and his mistress became frantic, possibly aware of his inner ambivalence. Eventually he turned to prayer and experienced an angelic vision which was an expression of his worst fears. He saw himself being arrested, led off into custody and subsequently brought to trial in the company of criminals. The angel who had brought the vision warned him that he was not safe to stay on in the city. Evagrius hesitated at the advice, challenging God either to free him from the predicament, or to let him stay on and take his punishment. The angel, though, was not satisfied and made a further appeal to his vocation, insisting that Evagrius take care for his soul and leave the city at once. In the vision the angel even brought the book of the Gospels so that Evagrius could swear on it. So Evagrius made his oath, and even though he did so in a vision, he stuck to it and the next day packed up his belongings and took a sea passage to Palestine.

Arriving in Jerusalem he was welcomed by the formidable and gifted Melania, who had set up a convent and a pilgrim hostel on the Mount of Olives. Evagrius settled down to a new life in Jerusalem, and before long he had abandoned his programme of self-reformation and was once more enjoying the distractions of city life. Palladius interprets this lapse as the result of demonic intervention: his heart had been hardened, like Pharaoh's. But he also suggests that there was a psychological aspect. Evagrius, after all, was still a young man, and prone to personal uncertainties. These were the reason why, in Palladius' judgment, the young Evagrius was tempted by vainglory, one of those temptations Evagrius would later attribute to the virtuous, especially to those with ambitions for the priesthood. Palladius is suggesting that Evagrius had not resolved his inner conflicts and that the result of this was that he fell ill with a wasting fever which went on for six months. Medical intervention failed to find a cure, and eventually Melania, judging that the sickness had a spiritual cause, pressed him into confessing his whole story. When he had done so she asked him to promise to aim at monastic life. This time he agreed and he was well again in a matter of days. Having received a form of monastic habit at Melania's hands he then departed to Nitria in Egypt, where he lived for several years among monks who had been influenced by the teachings of Origen. He later went deeper into the desert, where he stayed, according to Palladius, for 14 years, living on a pound of bread a day and a pint of oil every three months. 'After fifteen years he had so purified his mind that he was deemed worthy of the gift of knowledge and wisdom and the discernment of spirits' (Palladius, *Lausiac History* 113). These gifts were the basis of the books he wrote for the guidance of monks.

The importance of this biographical material is that it reveals the linkage between spirituality and self-awareness in the life of Evagrius. His exposure to the life of the city brought out tendencies we might consider narcissistic, which then found their focus in a secret affair. The angelic vision does not reveal the future so much as his incipient paranoia, and confronts him with the conflict between his desire and his vocation. His second lapse in Jerusalem represents a second attempt to avoid an honest confrontation with himself, hence the significance of his sickness and subsequent final confession to Melania. Here, then, is a person who knows about the attractions of seeking to live through the mirror of admiration, who has fallen into self-deception, has tried to deny it, and only as a last resort adopts a life of prayer and solitude. He has every motive to seek peace and freedom in God by learning to understand his own driving passions.

The Conflict with Demons

For Evagrius, as for most of the desert ascetics, the major spiritual issue was expressed in terms of a conflict with demons. For the desert fathers and mothers the wilderness was permanently infested with evil spirits. The demons were the source of temptation for the monk. This is important, because, whatever the difficulties we may have with the notion of demons, what such a notion represents is the assumption that evil is located outside the human person. Evagrius, like the pioneer of desert spirituality, St Antony of Egypt, is essentially optimistic about human nature. Our problem is not our essential nature, but our passions; those driving instincts, emotions and appetites which respond to demonic provocation, always threatening our equilibrum and distancing us from God. For Evagrius, holiness and integration are found in the state of *apatheia*, a serenity and tranquillity which results when the passions are subdued. The demons play on the passions, but they are outside us, they do not really know or understand the human heart. Their influence, though, is real and is experienced in the form of 'thoughts', the evil thoughts or *logismoi* which are likely to occur to a monk in solitude. Evagrius did not invent the notion of *logismoi*, but he is the first to attempt to codify and analyse them. He is at pains to stress that we have no way of preventing these thoughts occurring, and no way of not being disturbed by them. They are in the air we breathe. What we do have some choice in is whether we let the thoughts stir up our senses, inflame our memories and deprive us of peace and freedom.

Eight Evil Thoughts

There are eight principal *logismoi* in Evagrius' scheme (*Praktikos* 6–14). These are gluttony, lust, avarice, sadness, anger, *acedia* (sloth), vainglory and pride. Evagrius' treatment of the eight thoughts, although clearly intended primarily for monks, reveals a penetrating insight into human nature, which is as fresh as it is unexpected. Evagrius speaks with a voice which is observational, experiential and non-judgmental. He does not moralize, nor does he sound like the spokesman either for an infallible Bible or for an authoritarian Church. He knows that the spiritual life has to be lived rather than taught and that those who seek to come close to God must get to know themselves as well as accepting and learning from the judgment of others.

Gluttony, for example, is nothing to do with the gross demonic caricatures of the compulsively overfed that are familiar from mediaeval Catholicism. It begins rather in a demonic assault on the monk's attempt to live a disciplined life, in which fasting and abstinence have a part to play. It takes the form of a terror of illness, the fear of being left vulnerable in the desert without medical help because of inadequate nutrition. The demon of gluttony goes to work on the memory, reminding the monk of others who may have fallen ill through ascetic practice. It ensures that among the monk's visitors are those who have stomach complaints which they attribute to an ascetic lifestyle. In short, the thought of gluttony tempts the monk to think that religious life is fundamentally unhealthy and dangerous and should be abandoned.

Lust is the consequence of the demon of impurity. This demon targets those who try to be chaste and attempts to persuade them that it is futile. It arouses erotic fantasies which are so vivid as to be almost real and 'bows the soul down' in such a way that the sufferer feels almost as though they have already sinned merely by encountering the thought.

For Evagrius, avarice is not about misers greedily hoarding wealth while living with spectacular meanness towards others. It is about the very obvious fear of poverty and old age, and the particular dread which can so easily afflict the middle-aged of becoming dependent on others. Seen in this light it is an almost unavoidable temptation in our contemporary world.

Sadness does not appear in the later lists, perhaps because the Christian spiritual tradition came to see sadness as a virtue in the context of a spiritual life marked by penitence. Sadness for Evagrius is linked to the real losses involved in the ascetic life. The demon of sadness stirs memories of home, of family and of the normal comforts of life. It drenches the individual in nostalgia, which then turns to grief when the unavailability of what is being remembered is recognized.

Evagrius describes anger as the greatest of the passions. Anger affects the monk at prayer, constantly irritating him with the thought of wrongs done by others and by mental pictures of those who have offended. If the thought of anger is not checked it becomes obsessive, affecting sleep and eventually giving rise to weakness, pallor and terrifying fantasies of being attacked by venomous animals. Evagrius' description is not far from what we would recognize as paranoia.

Acedia comes next and, according to Evagrius, causes the most serious trouble of all. This thought is produced by 'the noonday demon', who times attacks precisely between the fourth and the eighth hour of the day, when, in the desert, the sun would be climbing to, and be at, its zenith. (The usual time for the daily meal was at the ninth hour.) Evagrius describes *acedia* in terms that we might recognize as extreme boredom, a sense that time has slowed down so intolerably that even the hour of the midday meal will never come. The demon of *acedia* then stirs a sense of hatred and distaste towards the place the monk is living in, and towards any manual, repetitive work that the monk might be engaged with. It also rouses resentment of others. The monk becomes touchy and irritable. Thoughts arise of other places that would be more conducive to the spiritual life, and this is followed by the thought that the choice of place does not really matter, since God can be adored anywhere. *Acedia* undermines the ascetic life by cultivating an indifference (which can sometimes look like pious indifference) to the specific demands of the monk's particular life. Eventually this thought, if entertained, drives the monk to the point where he or she really has given up altogether.

For Evagrius vainglory is the most subtle of the thoughts to afflict the monk because it flourishes particularly in those who try to live good lives. Vainglory resonates with the nagging sense that virtue ought to be rewarded. It seeks publicity and praise. The demon of vainglory even brings to the monk's imagination the sound of admiring crowds as the sick and hysterical receive healing through his ministry. Presumably Evagrius is thinking only of male monks at this point as the demon predicts elevation to the priesthood, and plays on the monk's vanity by producing the fantasy of a delegation coming to his cell and insisting on his ordination, and even taking him away bound if he resists. There is a delicious humour here which suggests that Evagrius saw through his own vainglorious tendencies and achieved a good measure of detachment from his own temptations to vainglory. This likelihood is strengthened by the story from the church historian Socrates (Socrates, *Historia Ecclesiastica* 4.23) that he resisted a request from the Patriarch of Egypt that he become bishop of Thmuis. As Evagrius sees it the indulgence of vainglory will inevitably lead to disappointment and bitterness. But though Evagrius treats it with a certain sense of humour he also recognizes its persistence. Even when it is unmasked it tends to appear in some other form. Even among other demons it keeps its smug self-satisfaction:

> I have observed the demon of vainglory being chased by nearly all the other demons, and when his pursuers fell, shamelessly he drew near and unfolded a long list of his virtues. (*Praktikos* 31)

Vainglory, like sadness, disappears from later lists, and is subsumed into pride. Perhaps this is not surprising, as it is, at least for Evagrius and his disciple Cassian, the sin of the religious in general and the clergy in particular!

Last of all, in Evagrius' list, comes pride, the demon which causes most damage to the human soul. Pride causes the monk to abandon any sense of real dependence on God and to ascribe virtues to the self and the self's own efforts. This leads to arrogance and the despising of others. Pride is such a denial of God that it leads to a virtual disintegration of the self. Anger and sadness flood in and make way for a complete collapse of the integrity of the person. This is a victory for the demonic – and an object lesson for monks about the seriousness of giving way to prideful thoughts.

After sketching the main characteristics of the eight evil thoughts Evagrius commends the virtuous practices which enable individuals to resist them. This is not the end of his analysis, the subsequent chapters of the *Praktikos* have more to say on the characteristics of the different thoughts, the relationship between them and the practical ways in which they can be resisted. These are full of sound common sense. For example, Evagrius suggests that it is useless to pray after having been angry. Before attempting to pray it is advisable to get anger out of the system by speaking some angry words. Evagrius, in this way, made room for a positive use of the passion of anger, which would be taken up by other spiritual writers of both East and West.

Temptations and Sin

From this brief introduction to Evagrius' treatment of evil thoughts it is clear that he thinks of them not as sins as much as temptations. This distinction is important but often lost. The origin of evil is in the demonic realm. The demons exploit all the weaknesses they can find in the praying self, but the self is not perverse in its essential nature. The heart of Evagrius' anthropology is that the human soul mirrors the divine image. The state of calm that arises once a monk has resisted the demons and overcome the passions is, for Evagrius, perfect charity, the realization of the image of God. The *logismoi* are unsettling not necessarily because they are dramatic (though they can provoke dramatic responses) but because they mimic rationality, they display a kind of false logic which can be extremely persuasive. Essentially all demonic attacks are designed to persuade the struggling ascetic that the goal of *apatheia* is impossible and the attempt should be abandoned.

There is a contrast here with the later Western tradition, which, having inherited the more depressed Augustinian view of the Fall, assumes that the faults or flaws are already lodged in us, as a result of Adam's sin. We see this assumption beginning with Evagrius' disciple John Cassian, who writes of the passions, 'we are all overcome by them, and they exist in every one' (Cassian, *Conferences* 5, ch. 2). Cassian has much less to say about the demonic source of evil; he assumes that the principal vices are embedded in our nature. The consequence is that the Western spiritual tradition is not always very clear about the distinction between temptation and sin. To have a wicked thought reveals a wicked heart. The evil idea does not come from without but is already lodged within. Growth in understanding is then curtailed because there is no encouragement to the careful analysis and self-observation which Evagrius commends. (If my thoughts are wicked it is better not to think rather than to risk bringing the whole slimy lot into consciousness.) Yet for Evagrius dispassionate observation of evil thoughts is a crucial part of that process of detachment by which the self reaches serenity:

> Let him [the monk] observe their intensity, their periods of decline, and follow them as they rise and fall. Let him note well the complexity of his thoughts, their periodicity, the demons which cause them, with the order of their succession and the nature of their associations. Then let him ask from Christ the explanations of these data which he has observed. (*Praktikos* 50)

The point is that Evagrius expects *logismoi* to occur, but because he puts their origin outside the self he enables his followers to resist them without necessarily identifying with them or indulging them. The point of reference for the struggling ascetic is Christ, who has real knowledge of the monk's heart and has already overcome all evil and demonic assault. When the origin of evil thoughts is solely in our own passions and instincts, this detachment and reliance on Christ is much more difficult, because Christ and the heart are fundamentally at war. Spirituality then becomes a constant attempt to keep vigilance against an internal enemy, a permanent and damaging assault on one's own inner life.

Sin as Self-Dramatization

In the tradition most of us have inherited, sin goes too easily hand in hand with guilt, and this connection often seems to be exploited in such a way as to actively *prevent* spiritual growth and integration. The failure to distinguish between temptation, sin and guilt is expressed in the West in a number of ways. One obvious way is our tendency to over-dramatize sin and evil in a way which makes them secretly attractive rather than repellent. The character of Satan in Milton's *Paradise Lost* is a case in point; he is far more compelling and fascinating than any of the other characters. To prevent the secret attractiveness taking us over we become over-rigorous and moralistic. Gregory the Great made pride the principal sin. If human pride really is at the root of sin, then sin will always been construed as a kind of selfishness to which self-hatred and self-diminishment is the only reasonable response. Paradoxically sin becomes interesting in itself, a subtle focus of self-interest.

The Western view of sin has undoubtedly contributed to the moral and creative energy of the West. Guilt and anxiety always have been powerful motivators. But the downside is obvious. Western Christianity, as its detractors often point out, presents an agonized, compulsive and judgmental face to the world which is neither attractive nor charitable. Evagrius might with justification have interpreted the Western emphasis on guilt and its depressed view of the self as a demonic victory, persuading us that the life of prayer is unrealizable. In the West the primacy of pride as the deadliest of sins dramatizes and even romanticizes our alienation from God. Evagrius, on the other hand, offers us a model of sin which sees it as giving in to the demonic niggling away at our call to spiritual freedom. The demons undermine the self, the true self, and thus keep us from Christ. In reflecting on the Holocaust, the philosopher Hannah Arendt, for all her fascination with St Augustine, expressed an Evagrian view of evil when she described it in terms of banality. Little boring Adolf Eichmann sitting through his trial was no one's idea of what a demonic figure should be. But perhaps Evagrius is right and it is indeed our little, tedious sins which keep us from God, the repeated giving in to shoddy thinking, lack of imagination and false logic which, if unrecognized and unchecked, accumulates into the monstrous inhumanity that destroys the self and other selves.

In the West the language of demonic assault is preserved only in the crudest forms which are repellent and unpersuasive to many. And yet, if we are to do justice to the insights of Evagrius, we may need to find a way of speaking of evil which involves us personally while being more than personal in its scope. As Western societies become more distanced from Christianity, the contemporary Church seems at a loss as to how to deal with this problem. In order not to stir too much personal guilt we have produced liturgical forms of confession that are simply bland and unmemorable. At the same time there has been an attempt to present the notion of sin less as a personal issue than as a social or political one. This may be helpful, in that it shifts the source of evil outside the self, but it leaves us *as* personal selves empty and unsure of whether our disturbances are of a kind which should be taken to a therapist rather than to a minister of the gospel. Ministers of the gospel, at least in the Church of England, are expected to 'guide [the flock] through the wilderness of this world so that they might be saved in Christ for ever' (Church of England rite for the Ordination of Priests). That guidance requires discernment, the kind of understanding of human motivation which comes from having wrestled with one's own demons.

This is something most of us have never been taught to do. The consequence is that while the Church moralizes about everything from sex to ecology, individuals, including clergy, go elsewhere to seek discernment and therapy for their personal problems. In wider society the deadly sins themselves are now seen as something rather comic. On the continent of Europe they are on sale as varieties of ice-cream. You can hardly get more trivial than that.

Sources

John Cassian
        Conferences: Books 5–12 (NPNF, Second Series, 11).
Gregory the Great
    1847   *Morals on the Book of Job (Moralia)* (A Library of the Fathers of the Holy Catholic Church, Oxford: John Henry Parker etc.).
Evagrius Ponticus
    1981   *The Praktikos and Chapters on Prayer* (tr. John Eudes Bamberger, OCSO; Cistercian Studies, 4; Kalamazoo, Mich.: Cistercian Publications).
Palladius
    1954   *The Lausiac History* (tr. R. T. Meyer; Ancient Christian Writers, 34; Washington).
    1961   *Historia Monachorum in Aegypto* (ed. A. J. Festugière; Brussels).
    1904   *The Book of Paradise: Being the Histories and Sayings of the Monks and Ascetics of the Egyptian Desert* (tr. E. A. W. Budge; London).
Socrates
        Historica Ecclesiastica Church History from AD 305–439 (NPNF, Second Series, 11).

Further Bibliography

Louth, Andrew
    1981   *The Origins of the Christian Mystical Tradition: From Plato to Denys* (Oxford: Oxford University Press).

WILDERNESS WISDOM FOR THE TWENTY-FIRST CENTURY
ARTHUR, L'ARCHE AND THE CULMINATION OF CHRISTIAN HISTORY

David F. Ford

Very occasionally one has the privilege of witnessing an 'event in thinking'.[1] I had that sense in December 2002 at Trosly-Breuil in north-west France. The event centred on a simple, daring statement. As so often, that simplicity leads immediately into all sorts of complexities once it is examined in detail. I will only attempt to describe some elements in the immediate context in order to make sense of it. The statement was made by Jean Vanier, founder of the L'Arche residential communities for those with mental disabilities and the assistants who share their lives together.[2] The mother community is in Trosly-Breuil, and that December there was a gathering of around fifty theologians and community leaders who spent some days thinking together about the theology of L'Arche. Among the sessions had been one led by Jean Vanier on the Gospel of John and one by Frances Young on the contribution of L'Arche to theology. There was a great deal of plenary and small-group discussion, we went to different foyers of the community to share meals, and we worshipped together, especially through the L'Arche liturgy of footwashing. The larger consultation was followed by a group of five[3] meeting for 24 hours of intensive conversation. This took themes of the consultation further and also considered the theology and principles of the three-year 'Identity and Mission' programme of discussion throughout the L'Arche communities which was to begin in January 2003. It was a group of friends who could think freely with each other, and the conversation ranged widely.

Frances Young had woken in the early hours of the morning thinking about the possibility of a new edition of her book *Face to Face: A Narrative Essay in*

---

1. The phrase is from Paul Ricoeur in Andre LaCocque and Paul Ricoeur *Thinking Biblically: Exegetical and Hermeneutical Studies* (Chicago and London: University of Chicago Press, 1998), 331. He is referring to the Septuagint translation *ego eimi ho on* in Exod. 3.14, and traces the subsequent history of this event in the interpretation of Exod. 3.14 in Greek-speaking and Latin-speaking traditions (the latter translating it as *sum qui sum*). Some of his reflections on this engagement between, on the one hand, the Hebraic and, on the other, the Hellenic and Latin, will be referred to below.

2. He is the author of a chapter in the present volume. There are now over a hundred L'Arche communities around the world, in all five continents.

3. Jean Vanier, Frances Young, Christine McGrievy (International Coordinator of L'Arche), Colin Maloney (President of L'Arche) and myself. One regular member of the group, Jean-Christophe Pascal, (the other International Coordinator of L'Arche) was unable to attend.

the Theology of Suffering,[4] which centres on her son Arthur who is severely handicapped,[5] both mentally and physically. But what had come to her was another possibility, one that might explore the theological significance of Arthur very differently.[6] This sparked off Jean Vanier's statement:

> I wonder whether that is anything close to a dream I have – the whole of the history of Christianity is culminated in Arthur.

This essay is an experiment in thinking through that statement. I will reflect a little on its terms; explore who Arthur is and what his significance might be; link his significance to L'Arche; and finally take up the hyperbole of Vanier's statement as a prophetic wisdom on which the present century really could turn.

1. *'Nothings' and 'Somethings' in the Culmination of History*

The statement's second half is an extraordinarily strong affirmation, but it is worth pausing over the first half.

'I wonder whether...' frames the whole statement as a personal exploration of possibility. It does not necessarily weaken the affirmation of the second half, yet it allows for questioning, for different possibilities, for reception by others who might contribute to testing, confirming or enriching it. It might be taken as an invitation to do what the present essay is attempting, not least in being addressed primarily to Frances Young. The 'I' is modest – no claim is being made for wider support – but also a definite 'owning' of what is said, linking it to whatever authority Jean Vanier has. This comes from someone who has perhaps unrivalled experience of and involvement with disability and responses to it around the world, and encourages us below to link Arthur with L'Arche and Vanier's own thinking.

'...that is anything close to a dream I have...' invites us to consider what follows as – what? Fantasy? Stimulus to our own capacity to dream? Utopian speculation? Prophetic insight? There is also a biblical association of dreams with divine communication and wisdom – it was in a dream that King Solomon was invited by God to ask for what he wanted, and chose 'an understanding mind' (1 Kgs 3.9); Joseph and Daniel were also wise dreamers.

So the first half of the sentence allows us to take the second half seriously as something important and requiring our own active enquiry and imaginative interpretation, while at the same time we are gently steered away from literalism, dogmatism or overconfident agreement or disagreement.

Trying to follow these indications, what is to be made of the whole of the history of Christianity culminating in Arthur? There is no reason why there

---

4.   Frances M. Young, *Face to Face: A Narrative Essay in the Theology of Suffering* (Edinburgh: T&T Clark, 1990). This was itself an updating and expansion of an earlier version published in 1985.

5.   The issue of terminology, such as 'handicap', 'disability', 'learning difficulty', etc. is one that she deals with in the book.

6.   She was more explicit than this, but any further elaboration is best left to her if and when she wishes to do so.

should not be several complementary meanings approaching it from different angles, using various scriptures, diverse readings of Christian history, and alternative conceptualities. Mine will be through the idea of the wisdom of God embodied in history and opening up God's future for the world. The crucified Jesus Christ as 'the wisdom of God' (1 Cor. 1.24) is a radical challenge to any conception of the meaning of history and its culmination. Paul in 1 Corinthians immediately applies this idea to turn upside-down the usual evaluations of who and what are important:

> Consider your own call, brothers and sisters: not many of you were wise by human standards, not many were powerful, not many were of noble birth. But God chose what is foolish in the world to shame the wise; God chose what is weak in the world to shame the strong; God chose what is low and despised in the world, things that are not, to reduce to nothing things that are, so that no one might boast in the presence of God. He is the source of your life in Christ Jesus, who became for us wisdom from God, and righteousness and sanctification and redemption, in order that, as it is written, 'Let the one who boasts, boast in the Lord.' (1 Cor. 1.26–31)

If Arthur is seen as an embodiment of weakness, foolishness, what is low and despised and counted as of no value by many in our world, then this encourages us to think about him as chosen by God, with a role in God's purposes, helping to learn more of what Paul later calls 'God's wisdom, secret and hidden, which God decreed before the ages for our glory' (1 Cor. 2.7). As the culmination of the history of Christianity Arthur might act as a touchstone for discerning where that history has been in harmony with God's wisdom; who and what, in the light of this, are most significant in the contemporary world; and what the purposes of God might be for the twenty-first century. He is not a culmination in the sense of being an effective integration of our world into a super-church or into a super-state or into a super-network of civil societies or around a super-wisdom – though, as will be suggested below, he has implications for all those spheres. He might be the culmination in the sense of embodying the call of God today in a way that is analogous to the message of the crucified Jesus in the first century: a message that seems foolish according to dominant wisdoms, but that yet shows a power to grip whole lives and communities and lead them into ways of love, joy and peace that fulfil the deepest yearnings of human hearts.

But how can this message be received? It has been around long enough, but does not take easily to translation into doctrines, methods, principles, ways of biblical interpretation or communication or prayer, courses in discipleship, ladders of ascent, rules of life, spiritualities, and so on. All those have of course played roles in its reception, but from Jesus and Paul onwards the heart of its transmission has been through lives that embody it 'in the Spirit' and somehow reveal the wisdom of the cross in the Spirit. Paul in 1 Corinthians 2 goes on to remind the Corinthians both of his own way of embodying his message and of the vital role of the Spirit of God in teaching this wisdom. The reception of the wisdom of God is inseparable both from Paul communicating it in his words and life and from the Spirit of God working in him and in the Corinthian community. There is a mystery of reception and also of rejection, and this mystery is bound up with the scandalous choice of the 'nothings' of the world.

Yet this is no ideology privileging the 'nothings' to the exclusion of the 'somethings'. The 'not many' 'wise by human standards' (or powerful or of noble
birth) is not 'none', and Paul himself is 'something' in education and other ways.
But Paul and the others have recognized and been grasped by a mystery that they
acknowledge as embodied in Jesus Christ crucified who is at the heart of God's
purposes and of the working of God's Spirit in the world now. This is about
'somethings' and 'nothings' together, with Paul as crucial for the articulation and
thinking through of this strange wisdom. I see something similar happening in
Jean Vanier and Frances Young. The Canadian Governor General's son, naval
officer and interpreter of Aristotle becomes a witness to the preciousness and
importance of those with disabilities; the headmaster's daughter, professor of
theology and Pro-Vice-Chancellor of Birmingham University is also the mother
of Arthur.

The golden thread through Christian history is of constantly renewed, embodied testimony to the crucified and risen Jesus Christ. This is no mere repetition of
a message: it is marked by the qualities of prophetic wisdom as the Spirit of God
draws on the past in fresh ways, plumbs the depths of how the world is going
wrong now, and helps to realize the Kingdom of God. It is a wisdom immersed in
the particularities of history, and especially of specific people and relationships,
and cannot be grasped apart from them. Jean Vanier's witness is full of stories of
particular people, friendships and communities. Frances Young's book on Arthur
has a specific 'face to face' at the heart of its 'narrative essay in the theology of
suffering'. To understand further what sense there might be in seeing Arthur as
the culmination of Christian history we have to engage with that narrative and the
wisdom Arthur's mother distils from it.

2. *Face to Face with Arthur*

Frances Young concludes the Introduction to *Face to Face*[7] with an autobiographical psalm of praise, thanks and testimony based on Psalms 30 and 116. But
whereas in those psalms the word 'wilderness' does not occur, in hers it appears
three times:

> O Lord my God, I cried out in my emptiness,
>   and you have made me whole.
> You brought me back from the wilderness places...
>
> But the Lord drove me into the wilderness
>   and hid his face from me...
>
> For this I prepared you from birth,
>   for this I led you through the wilderness,
>   for this I am setting you on your feet
>   and putting my joy and love within your heart.

Central to the wilderness experience is Arthur: 'My first-born was handicapped.' Closely connected with this in her psalm and in the book is her vocation

---

7.   Frances Young, *Face to Face*, 4–7.

to ordination as a Methodist minister: 'Go, teach and preach, be my minister.' In between the birth of Arthur and the call to ordination is a revelation of God:

> In the inner depths of my mind,
> I heard a voice:
> I am the Lord,
> believe in me or not –
> it makes no difference to *me*.

2.1. *Love in the Ordinary*

Her discussion of that insight, and of the ways in which God may and may not be spoken of as unchanging, impassible, and transcending emotions and suffering, is the theological culmination of the book in the final chapter, and it will be discussed briefly at the end of this chapter. It is inseparable from the radical involvement of God with history and suffering, and paradox is never far away. But in the narrative of Arthur what is most striking is the ordinariness. It rings true as a story of family life with multiple pressures and worries. The details of handling a disabled child and coping with the rest of the family as well as with doctors, schools, social workers, bureaucracies, demanding job, reactions to Arthur in public and other places, and all sorts of joys and difficulties, resist the sense of paradox. It is somewhat like the place of the Gospel narratives in telling who Jesus is: their ordinary realism, rooted in a world of stables, families, farming and commercial life, weddings, synagogues, debt, taxation, injustice, illness, bickerings, footwashing, and religion in many forms, is always primary, appropriate though it was that the further questions they gave rise to should lead to the apparent paradoxes about the relation of Jesus to God and of divinity and humanity in Jesus.

So the first thing to be said about this account of Arthur in relation to Jean Vanier's dream of him as the culmination of Christian history is that it is a twentieth-century variation on something essential in the formation of Christianity's identity. There is a realistic narrative of one person, deeply involved in ordinary life, who is testified to as a profound challenge and gift both to those close to him and to society more widely, whose message is centred on love, and who provokes fundamental questioning about God, humanity, life, death, salvation and the Kingdom of God. There is no question of Arthur being salvific or in competition with Jesus, but as his mother unfolds his story woven into her own he emerges as a sign of salvation. There are of course less ordinary dimensions, which will be discussed shortly. But the centrality of daily face-to-face life needs to be appreciated first. Arthur's nappies still need changing every day. This is the setting where, in solidarity with all the rest of human historical existence, love needs to happen.

It is of the greatest importance that Paul, in the middle of a discussion of things quite out of the ordinary, such as speaking in tongues, apostleship, prophecy, miracles, and healing, emphasizes the 'still more excellent way' of love (1 Cor. 12.31). In contrast to matters that might seem 'really' to have historical impact, such as powerful prophecy, comprehensive knowledge, moving mountains, and dramatic self-sacrifice, Paul describes long-term, ordinary loving:

> Love is patient; love is kind; love is not envious or boastful or arrogant or rude. It does not insist on its own way; it is not irritable or resentful; it does not rejoice in wrong-doing, but rejoices in the truth. It bears all things, believes all things, hopes all things, endures all things.

This is the wisdom of love, and it is also striking that the immediate context is building up a community in which 'the members of the body that seem to be weaker are indispensable, and those members of the body that we think less honourable we clothe with greater honour, and our less respectable members are treated with greater respect... If one member suffers, all suffer together with it; if one member rejoices, all rejoice together with it' (1 Cor. 1.22–6). *That is Paul's criterion for historical significance in God's sight.* Frances Young's account of Arthur is a variation on that theme, and the nappy-changing, with all the other aspects of relating to Arthur, earth the theology, politics, ethics and vocational issues that arise. It is as if there is an implicit maxim: *for all the need to be concerned with those big questions, it is even more necessary always to be immersed in the loving of ordinary life, and to try to answer the big questions 'standing before the face of Arthur'.* This is very much the experience of Jean Vanier and the L'Arche communities too.

2.2. *Out of the Ordinary: Probably the First Time in Christian History ...*
Yet the extraordinary is also essential: the God of the ordinary is also the God of events that hit the headlines and lives that change the ways large numbers of people live, imagine and think. Christianity's history is about these too, and perhaps the most problematic matter is how the extraordinary relates to the ordinary. So many of the leading events and big names in Christian history raise awkward questions about their earthing in love, in honouring the weak and poor, and in the wisdom of the cross. Jean Vanier's dream is that here those the world labels 'nothings' and 'somethings' come together in a way that lets us see what that history is about at its best.

So what about the historical significance of the less ordinary side of the story of Arthur? The first thing to be said here is about Frances Young as an out-of-the-ordinary mother. Comparisons are, of course, invidious: is there, in the eyes of her children, any such person as an ordinary mother? But in a loose, common-sense way it is possible to distinguish some mothers with an unusual range of influence and significance beyond their own families. This is true of Frances, and it is worth examining.

2.2.1. *Mary.*
Perhaps the most sensitive yet fruitful question is about her relationship with Mary the mother of Jesus. One phenomenon of the years as Arthur's mother is her growing identification with Mary. She has this in common with a great many of the world's Christians (and some Muslims), though it is not quite so usual among Methodists. In Frances' case one special element is her articulation of her relation to Arthur and to God in vigorous poetry. This is the Mary of the Magnificat, and Frances has poems with a similar combination of praise and

prophecy. However, it is a more lyrical, intimate poem that perhaps best distils the relationship:

> Mary, my child's lovely.
> Is yours lovely too?
> Little hands, little feet.
> Curly hair, smiles sweet.
>
> Mary, my child's broken.
> Is yours broken too?
> Crushed by affliction,
> Hurt by rejection,
> Disfigured, stricken,
> Silent submission.
>
> Mary, my heart's bursting.
> Is yours bursting too?
> Bursting with labour, travail and pain.
> Bursting with agony, ecstasy, gain.
> Bursting with sympathy, anger, compassion.
> Bursting with praising Love's transfiguration.
>
> Mary, my heart's joyful.
> Is yours joyful too?

2.2.2. A Theology for the Twenty-first Century. The dialogue with Mary has been carried on at Lourdes, in conversations with Orthodox theologians, in sermons, and in scholarly work on the early centuries of Christian literature and history. The twentieth century is probably the first time in Christian history in which a mother could also be a professor of theology, a Christian minister and Pro-Vice-Chancellor of a major university. This opens another angle on the meaning of 'culmination'. She interprets Arthur with resources, and from locations in society, available to few mothers before her, and that possibility is itself the outcome of a history in which Christian and other strands have played complex roles.

Besides being a biblical and patristics scholar, steeped in the early Christian centuries, her first degree was in classics. This study of Greek and Roman civilizations through their history, culture, religion, poetry, drama, rhetoric and art has made her alert to the interplay between those civilizations, on the one hand, and Judaism and Christianity on the other. It was a paradigmatic encounter, deeply formative for Christianity, and repeated with variations down the centuries in other contexts. To understand it well is a great advantage in trying to discern how analogous encounters today might contribute to the flourishing of the Church and the world. Those first Christian centuries can offer a wisdom of special significance in the aftermath of Christendom, as Christianity relates to powerful secular forces in our world. Many scholars and thinkers seek this, but her time in the wilderness into which Arthur's birth drove her has inspired in her a prophetic wisdom whose full dimensions are, I suspect, yet to be revealed.

This is in the first place a form of theology that is most influenced by Scripture and patristic literature, but it is by no means an attempt to repeat the past. It has taken account of later centuries and especially the challenges of modern Western thought and the traumas of twentieth-century history. Among her teachers was one of the most profound and rigorous British philosophers of religion, Donald MacKinnon, who drew his students into his own wrestling with Kant, contemporary British philosophy, theologians such as Barth and von Balthasar, and above all the problem of evil exemplified by Auschwitz. Her theology is therefore rooted in the early classics of Christian thought but has been through modernity without being contained by it.

One might call it a form of postmodernity, if that term had any clear meaning – what I would mean here is three things: first, her refusal to be intimidated by demands to conform her theology to the more reductive modern rational criteria, while yet insisting on the importance of reasoning vigorously (especially in matters of history and philosophy); second, her freedom in learning from and criticizing both the premodern and the modern without being stuck in either, and in taking into account the 'hermeneutics of suspicion' as well as the 'hermeneutics of retrieval'; and third, the constant interrelating of the intellectual with the practical or ethical or political. This form of theology might be seen as a culmination of the history of Christian thought, attempting to be true to its origins and its best traditions over the centuries while also doing justice to critical and constructive contributions from other sources.

I would see this as a form of 'wisdom theology' that is better suited than most modern or postmodern approaches to the special circumstances of the twenty-first century. One might see modernity as something of a wilderness experience for Christianity, especially in the West, during which it has been radically tested and tempted. Frances' intellectual journey has taken her through this desert, and has been marked by anguished wrestling with doubt and meaninglessness. Trying to make sense of Arthur and of human suffering has intensified this and interconnected the more intellectual aspects of modernity and its terrible sufferings (in a way graphically exemplified by Donald MacKinnon). Her husband Bob, a scientist and non-Christian, has also been a constant check on her intellectual integrity in relation to the sciences, the aspect of modernity that has perhaps more than any other been responsible for problematizing Christian understanding of reality. The combination of all these does not lead to a theological system or comprehensive set of answers to the big questions. Rather it has generated a tested wisdom that can at the same time make strong theological judgments and also remain vulnerably incomplete at many points.

2.2.3. *Universities in a Religious and Secular World.* It is not, however, just a theological wisdom in the terms I have been using. There is simultaneously a secular wisdom that has been seen in her work as a professor and especially as Pro-Vice-Chancellor in Birmingham University. It is often hard to see how this comes together with her theology, especially where it has involved tough managerial decisions and controversial policies dictated by political and economic forces according to questionable values. Yet this may be recognized as a culmination of Christian history in the West. She is embodying something of the contemporary situation. British society, and indeed the wider world, is not simply secular, and nor is it religious. Recent centuries have seen a variety of secular forces play an increasing role in shaping our world; yet at the same time in most regions religions have also thrived, and even where they have not there is often a complex interplay of different types of religion and different types of secularity. This has led to massive tensions in many areas, and most of the major points of conflict in the world have religious dimensions. For those committed within a specific religious tradition one of the prime challenges of our time is how to negotiate relationships both between different religious traditions and between the religious and the secular. Universities are key sites for both sets of negotiations. They contain those with allegiance to the whole range of religions and to none, and in a 'knowledge economy' and 'learning society' they relate to most spheres of life. Frances Young's university responsibilities have given her an unusual role in this.

In relation to the denominations of Christianity she has been a strong advocate of ecumenism in theological education (especially through her leading role in the ecumenical Queen's Theological College) and in helping all the denominations to have appropriate academic relations with universities. As regards the religions she helped develop the Department of Theology in Birmingham University into a thriving centre for the study of Judaism, Christianity and Islam together, with close relations to many religious communities in Birmingham and elsewhere. In this setting the religions can both relate to each other and also to the range of disciplines, many of which are closely tied into formative forces in society – the professions, technologies, the economy, aspects of culture. Frances Young has not just engaged in this from the Theology Department; she has also played a leading role in the university as a whole. Her immersion in the inevitably ambivalent world of university administration and management has been costly, and the 'inside story' has understandably not been told. But in relation to the theme of this chapter it is important that she has sustained, for the good of the churches, the religions and society as a whole, a demanding simultaneous involvement with ecumenism, interreligious engagement, and a leading secular institution.[8] The peace of the world in the twenty-first century may especially require a wisdom of negotiation in these spheres, leading to the formation of places of community and collegiality between traditions and the sort of global civil society that can recognize the importance of both the religious and the secular.

2.2.4. *Institutions: From the Family to L'Arche.* What about Arthur in relation to all this? It is clear in *Face to Face* that Frances' work in the university has been a vital factor in enabling her to cope with the problems and pressures of coping with his disability. But there is another aspect which links into Jean Vanier's statement and into L'Arche. This is to do with the significance of institutions.

---

8.   The University of Birmingham is an explicitly secular foundation, but it is interesting to see how, partly through the influence of leading members of the Department of Theology such as Frances Young and her predecessor as Head of Department, J. G. Davies, it has been generally hospitable to theology and the study of religions. In 2000 on the occasion of its centenary it even held a service in Birmingham Cathedral. In my terms, whatever the constitutional position, it has in practice recognized that it is part of a 'religious and secular' world.

Again and again in *Face to Face* the demands of disability show up the fragility of the nuclear family. Arthur has in fact been part of an extended family for most of his life, with grandparents in residence or close by. Friends and other voluntary helpers have also been important, but none of this diminishes the need for the sort of support that can only be provided by institutions, whether voluntary or statutory. Hospitals, medical practices, schools, holiday homes, social services, advocacy groups, churches and other religious organizations have all been part of Arthur's life. But disability only sharpens a more general lesson about the vital part that various communities, organizations and institutions play in human flourishing. Frances' story of Arthur constantly emphasizes this, and her dedication to the Church and university (and Bob her husband's to the discipline of physics in the university and later to Mencap) is therefore deeply in line with her commitment to Arthur (and of course to her and Bob's other two children). Any imagined culmination of Christian history needs to do justice to this dimension of life, and in fact *Face to Face* includes a passionate vision of the potential transformation of society's institutions in the light of being Arthur's mother.

The family is the primary institution of society in coping with disability as well as in many other respects, and it may be fitting that Jean Vanier's dream should be about Arthur rather than about one of the many members of L'Arche communities about whom he has often spoken and written. L'Arche has over a hundred residential communities in about 26 countries; Faith and Light, the sister organization dedicated to people with mental disabilities, their families and friends, has over 1300 non-residential communities in about seventy countries. The natural family remains statistically primary.

Yet in the years since the publication of *Face to Face* Frances and Jean have become close friends and Frances has given a considerable amount of time and energy to L'Arche. It is a natural extension of *Face to Face*, but it also adds a new dimension to it. It is no accident that the statement by Jean Vanier discussed in this chapter was made in L'Arche at a meeting dedicated to learning for it and from it. The lens through which Jean Vanier perceives Arthur has been formed mainly through L'Arche. There we find a new institution that complements the family as a place where those with disabilities can find community, and which also complements and enriches the dream of Christian history culminating in Arthur. How might the wisdom of L'Arche be part of that culmination?

3. *The Wisdom of L'Arche*

L'Arche lives out on a global stage many of the themes and insights discussed so far. At the time of writing it is in the middle of the 'Identity and Mission' consultation to help orient it during the first part of the twenty-first century, and Jean Vanier's statement about Arthur was made during discussion of that consultation. An earlier meeting of the same[9] small group at Trosly-Breuil in September 2001

---

9.   See n. 3 above. There was one change in September 2001: Jean-Christophe Pascal was present but Colin Maloney was not.

had also considered its identity and mission, and this led to a statement express-ing something of what is at the heart of L'Arche. It reads:

> God
> through the wisdom of the Gospel,
> meets the brokenness, anguish,
> and deepest desires of human bodies and hearts
> in a long-term community
> of mutual presence,
> service,
> and friendship.
> This is a sign of hope for all people.

Unfolding that dense statement adequately would take many books. I will just make two preliminary points and then comment briefly on three of its lines before a concluding section on its last line. The first point is that the terms were in fact distilled from the experience of L'Arche but are phrased so as to have far wider applicability – for example, they could be referred to the 'long-term com-munity' of the family. The second point is that, just as the sections above have taken Frances Young's writings as their primary point of reference, so this sec-tion assumes the writings of Jean Vanier as background.[10]

The statement opens by referring to God. What if this is connected with Frances Young's key theological insight quoted in her autobiographical psalm above?

> In the inner depths of my mind,
> I heard a voice:
> I am the Lord,
> believe in me or not –
> it makes no difference to *me*.

The positive side of this, that God is primarily to be believed in and loved for God's own sake, is a core affirmation of the Christian tradition, as well as some others. The strong Jewish tradition of hallowing the name of God, which was practised even in Auschwitz, is taken up by Jesus in the first petition of the Lord's Prayer. Frances' retrieval of the classical Christian teaching on the impassibility of God and God's aseity as a liberating wisdom for our century rings true with what is found in L'Arche.

This is about the contemplative moment, adoring God for who God is, 'for his name's sake'. L'Arche has had a close affinity with contemplative traditions and communities, and many former assistants have joined contemplative religious orders. Others live their life in L'Arche as a form of contemplative vocation. I see this as deeply connected with the pivotal recognition in L'Arche of the rightness and wisdom of *loving the other for the other's own sake*. When the above September 2001 statement was circulated around L'Arche the response by

---

10. Of his recent writings I especially have in mind two that are condensations of his wisdom about being and becoming human: Jean Vanier, *Our Journey Home: Rediscovering a Common Humanity Beyond our Differences* (Sydney and Auckland: Hodder & Stoughton, 1997) and Jean Vanier, *Becoming Human* (Toronto: Anansi, 1998).

the communities in India included a beautiful meditation on loving people not because of what they do or what they have but for themselves, for who they are. Jean Vanier's writings play many variations on this theme. Our deep desire is to be loved like this, for our own sake. This is the mystery of the best friendships, including those that many in L'Arche have testified to. Yet this is a mystery embraced in an even greater mystery: *God loves each of us for our own sake*. Each is created beautiful, precious, and in God's image, and each is affirmed, judged and transformed through God's wise loving. But beyond that is this further possibility: *we may love God for God's sake*. That was the other side of Frances Young's key revelation, liberating her for a new relationship with Arthur as well as with God, and it seems to me to go to the theological heart of L'Arche too.

The second line, 'through the wisdom of the Gospel', connects to the discussion above of Jesus Christ as the wisdom of God in 1 Corinthians, a text that is frequently referred to in Vanier's and other L'Arche writings. My comment on L'Arche and the gospel aims to connect the two with what is called for in the twenty-first century in line with the second petition of the Lord's Prayer: 'Your kingdom come'. Dietrich Bonhoeffer in his *Ethics*,[11] written as he struggled against the Nazis before he was imprisoned and executed, summed up the gospel as God coming together with the world in Jesus Christ for the sake of its affirmation, judgment and transformation. In his incarnation Jesus Christ fully affirms the goodness of the world, he radically judges it by his crucifixion, and he transforms it through his resurrection. L'Arche too, in its own way, embodies an affirmation of the goodness of creation and of every person, a judgment on the values and ways of the world, and a glimpse of the transformation in God's new creation. There is something about the way the three dimensions are held together that signifies the sort of maturity that Jean Vanier is so concerned to teach.

The eighth line is simply about 'friendship'. In gospel terms, if Frances and Arthur are seen as types of Mary and Jesus, the L'Arche communities are more analogous to Jesus with his disciples. At the culmination of the Gospel of John (the interpretation of which has been a core concern of Jean Vanier for many years) Jesus calls the disciples friends. The friendships that happen in L'Arche are perhaps the most amazing signs of the Kingdom of God to be found there. Many stories testify to deep, transforming friendships between people with disabilities and assistants, and Jean Vanier himself constantly refers to them. Such friendships add new dimensions to the meaning of friendship itself. *If their stories were gathered with those of natural families such as the Youngs under Jean Vanier's favourite heading of 'communion of the heart' we would perhaps have a fair portrayal of what a culmination of Christian history might be like.*

4. *A Sign of Hope for All People*

The last line sees L'Arche as 'a sign of hope for all people'. Here we finally face Jean Vanier's use of the phrase 'history of *Christianity*'. Is that a modest limi-

---

11. Dietrich Bonhoeffer, *Ethics* (London: SCM Press, 1964).

tation to one Christian strand of history as distinct from, for example, Muslim or Hindu or secular? Or is it a Christian imperialism, subsuming all history into Christian history? There is no space to argue in detail why I think neither of those is correct, but I will try in conclusion to state briefly one alternative interpretation.

In the forty years of L'Arche history one of the most striking things is the way it has maintained its core identity while changing the nature of its boundaries. Most obviously this has meant the expansion of its geographical boundaries beyond France to embrace all five continents. After beginning as all-male and celibate, there were further shifts to mixed households and to include married couples as members.

But it is coping with and transforming religious boundaries that goes to the heart of L'Arche's identity. Beginning as Catholic, the first shift was to become ecumenical with other Christian churches. Now, there are also communities with largely Hindu and largely Muslim identities, there are members of other faith traditions, and there have always been members with no faith allegiance. These and other boundary issues have especially challenged L'Arche to develop beyond any precedents. The result is an institution which has step by step taken on the responsibility of facing, in its own sphere, many of the key problems, divisions and differences of our world, and therefore needs ever-richer wisdom to cope with them. There are, of course, many strands to this emerging wisdom, and the current 'Identity and Mission' process is helping to weave them together, but Jean Vanier's own recent thinking is perhaps the best way to see the way that is being followed.

It has a double thrust: going deeper into the Christian gospel and at the same time deeper into what it means to be human. The first is exemplified by his preoccupation for some years with the Gospel of John, which has fed into his television broadcasts, videos, addresses and writings. The second is summed up in the subtitle of his recent book mentioned already: 'rediscovering a common humanity beyond our differences'. The two converge in the centrality of the communion of hearts, and the forgiveness that is essential to communion. So when he refers to the history of Christianity finding a culmination he cannot mean a separate Christian strand of history: the oneness of God and the oneness of humanity rule out that sort of pluralism. There is a bad future for the world if each tradition aims at separate development.

But nor can he mean a Christian imperialism. The move towards universality is made patiently person by person, tradition by tradition, with utter respect for the other in his or her difference. Otherness is honoured to the point of mystery: each person is a mystery who is to be loved for their own sake. Those with disabilities enable deeper appreciation of the mystery and beauty of our common humanity. Around them and in communion with them there are possibilities for interrelating religious traditions in friendship that have hardly begun to be explored. It is a way neither of imperialism nor of assimilation to each other, but one of affirmative, critical and transformative communion, whose consequences are unforeseeable.

So for the religions and for all aspects of life L'Arche represents a prophetic wisdom. This is best expressed in the testimonies to life and death in L'Arche.

These give vivid stories of suffering, crises, love, growth, bereavement, and ordinary life in community. Their distinctiveness is perhaps not only that for the first time in history people with disabilities are at the centre of communities and are being given unprecedented attention by doctors, psychiatrists, social workers, assistants and members of religious traditions, but also that this is being fruitful in so many ways – in friendships, spiritual awakening and growth, and effects rippling out through professions, religious communities and societies. The testimonies are also realistic about the tensions and conflicts that L'Arche has brought. In societies (including some religious groups) that want to ignore or even eliminate those with severe disabilities, and whose dominant values are being challenged, there is often resistance, revulsion and hostility to L'Arche.

This points to a more general prophetic dimension. Our habitual understandings, values and practices are called into question by L'Arche. None of our previous answers is left unchanged. How do we understand the human worth, dignity and fulfilment of ourselves and others? How do we cope with vulnerability, suffering or death? What about the nature and role in our lives of recognition, success, education, health, wealth? How are power and weakness related? Whom do we value most, and why? What happens to our hearts and souls when we are opened up to friendships such as those in L'Arche? What might happen to Christianity, to other religions, to secular groups, or to social services if they were to learn and practise some of the wisdom being learned in L'Arche?

This prophetic wisdom can be improvised upon in any sphere of life. But doing so calls into a similar path that members of L'Arche have followed. It involves service and friendship, distillation of wisdom in particular situations and relationships, and coping with suffering and anguish; but before all that *it is about recognizing that we are being offered something so precious that it is worth immeasurably more than whatever it costs us*. That is the good news Jean Vanier discovers through L'Arche and through Arthur and Frances Young and their family. It is a sign of hope that – once we have allowed our very ideas of 'history', 'Christianity' and 'culmination' to be transformed through considering their stories and testimonies in the light of the gospel – might allow us to see the whole history of Christianity as indeed culminating in Arthur, and being a sign of peace and friendship in the religious and in other spheres.

FROM WILDERNESS TOWARDS HOME

Jean Vanier

Some years ago, a small boy with severe disabilities was found by the police on the streets of Harare in Zimbabwe. They took him to the local hospital where nurses took care of him; bathing, clothing and feeding him. However, he remained sullen and withdrawn, hiding his face behind his arms. They named him 'Moses'. Later he became the first person welcomed into a newly created L'Arche community in Harare.

Six months after his arrival in L'Arche, I visited the community. I had been told about Moses and knew a little of his story. I tried to imagine his inner pain and was expecting to find him prostrate on the ground, enveloped in sadness. I found just the opposite: a small boy beginning to open up and live, his eyes and face beaming as he was held in the arms of the community leader. It was clear to me that Moses was moving from wilderness towards home.

Home is a place of warmth and security; a place where we belong, are loved, cherished and made to feel important. Wilderness on the other hand is a hostile place where we feel lost and confused. We do not know where to go. It is a place where we feel unwanted and we are increasingly submerged in fear and loneliness, unsure of our identity. Wilderness is a place of chaos, empty of affection and peace.

Since 1964, my fundamental preoccupation has been with healing and transformation, helping people who, because of a mental disability, have felt unwanted, lost in the wilderness, to find their way home. I have tried to help them move from inner pain to inner peace, from depression to wholeness, from withdrawal to openness to others.

My aim here, based on the experience of healing and change, is to try to reveal what human beings need in order to come home and find inner peace and maturity.

What Is This Wilderness?

Children are so vulnerable and weak at birth; they have no defence mechanisms. They are totally dependent on others and can do nothing by themselves. Children need a mother who will nourish them. But even more than food, they need to feel wanted and loved. If they are seen only as a nuisance, they will feel that they are a nuisance. If they are seen as a source of joy, they will begin to realize that they give joy; that they are someone important in the eyes of others.

Old people live a similar experience when they too are seen only as a nuisance. If they feel put aside, they too withdraw in loneliness and depression. But if an older person feels loved, cherished and listened to, they continue to discover new life. This touches the mystery of the human being, who is born in weakness, who grows old and dies in weakness. What is the meaning of this weakness? Is it only a part of infancy and old age that becomes a negative element during our productive years that we have to hide by cultivating our strength and competence, our capacity to be autonomous and to control others? Or does it have a meaning in love, friendship, cooperation, community and simply being human? We are not made of steel. Our bodies are constituted mainly of liquid. The weakness of our bodies reveals our mortality and one day our flesh will corrupt. Our hearts are also vulnerable. Our deepest hurts come when the heart is wounded, when we feel ignored, rejected and put aside. We then fall into depression and neurosis and hide behind interior barriers that protect us; we refuse to live in reality. If our weakness is seen only as a nuisance or a handicap, it turns us into a wilderness of fear and loneliness and confusion. On the other hand, weakness can lead us to sharing and friendship and compassion.

Michael Ignatieff in his book *The Needs of Strangers*[1] reminds us of the different needs of a human being in order to live fully. There are what are called the basic needs: food, shelter, education, medical help, etc. These needs can be regulated by law. A government can decide that every citizen should have enough money for food and lodging and should have education and medical insurance. But there are other fundamental needs for human beings: We need to be recognized fully as a person, having an intrinsic value and special gifts. We need to be loved and to be admired. If these last needs are not fulfilled, human beings cannot attain full maturity and a real, human plenitude. They fall into discouragement and depression; they enter into an interior wilderness. But no government laws, no rules or regulations can oblige people to love.

In his book *I and Thou*, Martin Buber recognizes that if we are taken up more and more by things – things to do, things to buy, things to sell, things to possess, things to clean or to discard – we risk forgetting the treasure of humanity which is being in relationship and friendship. Obsessed by things, we lose our capacity to love, to be open and welcoming to others.

No human being can survive in isolation. We need others in order to live and to develop fully. We need them so that our various physical and psychological needs are met. We need them as friends, to be loved and appreciated and they in turn need our love and appreciation. Together we build a place of unity and peace, a place of belonging.

What Does It Mean To Love?

To love is to find joy in the presence of another, to see the other person as important and precious. Love is not just to do things for another, but to reveal to

---

1.   Michael Ignatieff, *The Needs of Strangers* (London: Vintage/Ebury Press, 1994).

them their value. It is trusting another and finding rest in their presence. It is being attentive to them, listening to them, understanding their needs. Love is revealed through our whole way of being, through the expression of our face, especially through the eyes. Love involves our emotions but is not just a question of emotion or sentimentality, it means being in a relationship that helps the other to become more fully human, developing confidence and self-esteem. To love is to leave our own self-centred reality in order to perceive the needs of another. Love involves commitment.

This capacity to relate and be open to others which Martin Buber and Michael Ignatieff speak about is not as simple as it sounds. We fear and reject some people just as we try to hold on to and possess others. Our affectivity and our capacity to love are deeply influenced by all that we have lived during our childhood and in fact throughout our life. Sometimes, we idealize people and then, when they react in an unexpected, aggressive or defensive way, the love or attraction we had for them fades and gives way to disappointment and perhaps, rejection; barriers rise up which make relationship difficult. We come to realize that we are not in full control of our emotions or the responses that they trigger within us. Some people attract us; others create indifference; others evoke fear, anguish and even hatred.

We are all aware of how certain actions or relationships that appear loving can prevent human growth. I remember a young helper in L'Arche who came to see me because she was wondering whether she should stay in L'Arche or not. I asked her to tell me her story. She told me that she had studied music at university. I asked her why she had chosen to study music. 'Mummy wanted me to do music.' As we shared it came out more and more 'Mummy wanted this…mummy wants that.' Finally I asked her 'What do you want?' The admiration she had for her mother had prevented her from discovering her own self and had even cut her off from her own desires.

Such fusional love comes when the frontiers between two people are not clear. The fear of conflict or of losing the other holds them psychologically and physically stuck together. There is no freedom. Parents easily fall into the trap of fusional love for their children. During the nine months of pregnancy hadn't the child been one with the mother? The mother and father talk about their children, as if they belong to them. Of course they do, but only so that they can bring them up to make their own choices and grow towards greater inner freedom. Parents have to learn to let go so that their children may be.

All forms of violence prevent children from discovering who they are and what they want, and from growing towards inner freedom. Shouting, physical or sexual abuse create terrible anguish and loneliness. Children are too vulnerable to bear rejection or feeling unloved. The precise nature of each individual child and the many ways they can be made to feel unwanted, even for a short time, obviously means that the anguish they live will be vastly different. To protect their hearts, children hide behind more or less strong interior barriers, but these same barriers cut them off from reality and relationships.

Being in relationships with others is not easy. We have difficulty bearing the pain and anguish of relationship. Beginning a relationship can be exhilarating: the two people feel understood and take pleasure in each other's company; they have fun together and discover they have the same interests and values. Each one is able to come out from the pit of loneliness. The bright sun of one enlightens and fulfils the other. As time goes by, however, each person evolves, and not always in the same way, and the shadow area in each one begins to appear. The relationship becomes difficult. The two begin to feel estranged from each another. This causes inner pain and anguish. The journey from loneliness to togetherness, which had begun so well, ends. Each one retreats back into painful loneliness, accusing the other of all sorts of things; perhaps even more accusing themselves, as they become aware of their own difficulties in relationship.

The evolution of the marital state in France since the 1950s tells us something about the difficulties in relationships. Civil and religious marriages used to be the usual way of couples living together as man and wife; divorce was acceptable but rare. Since then it has become easier and more frequent for couples to separate, divorce and remarry. Living together without any religious or legal contract has become more or less the way lived by many. People no longer want to be bound by a legal contract but only to be held by love. They want to be free to choose to live with a partner or not, or to live on their own. They are unable to go through difficult moments in a relationship which would lead them to greater depth and maturity.

We see this same movement in community life in L'Arche. Assistants often tell me that it is easy to be in relationship with people with disabilities but they have difficulty living with the other assistants in the house. We expect and accept that people with disabilities have particular needs and difficulties. We are here to help them. We have a certain authority over them. At the same time, we do not expect nor accept that assistants will have limits or personality problems; it is as if we expect them to be perfect. So when difficulties arise, when anger, jealousy and fear rise up in us, not only do we judge, condemn or express our dislikes of other assistants, but we also judge, condemn and express our dislikes of ourselves. It is the chaos within us that renders love, friendship and acceptance of others so difficult.

The Chaos Within

Children with disabilities are often seen by their parents as a disappointment. All parents expect and hope for a healthy child. Their disappointment, which is so understandable, can however be difficult for the child to bear and in some cases is extremely painful. The mother of a Down syndrome boy once told me in a loud voice (which I am sure he could hear) that the father was so shocked when he saw his son's handicap that he had a heart attack and died. At that time the son was having great difficulty living in reality. He would slip away into a world of the imagination. He could not face the chaos within him caused by the fact that he 'had killed' his father.

There are many less extreme situations. One day while we were eating with John and his father, one of the helpers sitting between them remarked: 'You have the same eyes.' The father reacted immediately and forcefully: 'No, he has the eyes of his mother.' He spoke with such force and anger that all of us interpreted him as saying: 'He has nothing of me in him.' His son, John, felt the pain of the situation and after a few minutes left the table and went into the garden. His father turned to me and said 'Where has he gone?' He was obviously unaware of how much he had hurt his son. When a child is young he cannot bear the pain of feeling rejected and unwanted. It pushes him into the wilderness of isolation and loneliness.

The joy of a child is to be the object of the joy of his parents. As he laughs and smiles and his parents laugh and smile with him, he is aware that he is a source of joy. The opposite is also true. So it is that our self-confidence grows or shrinks. A young woman I know lacks so much self-confidence that she is unable to make any clear decisions or to take on any responsibility in her home. 'My parents kept telling me that I was worthless and stupid in school.'

The inner chaos of some people is so powerful that they are obliged to hide it behind strong walls around their heart, like the man I met in a Montreal prison who had been condemned to death for murder. I do not remember what we talked about together. All I remember is the terrible unease I felt in his presence. I have never met anyone so devoid of any emotion in his eyes and body. He was like a huge block of ice, totally closed off from the reality around him and the reality of his own heart or emotions; he was hermetically sealed off. He was obviously a very dangerous man who had to be in prison. Yet, I could imagine how he had arrived at that point. Perhaps he had been unwanted from the start of his life in the womb of his mother. He had probably been hurt, physically and maybe even sexually, as a child, treated more like a thing than as a person. Gradually, he also began treating others as things. If he had to hide and defend himself from the violence and hatred of his parents, how could he begin to trust adults? His deepest self and his capacity to love and respect others had been buried under all the pain and chaos that he had lived. To survive, he had to develop his own force in order to beat down anyone who might threaten him. And the chaos that developed within him eventually made him a source of chaos around him.

Light and darkness, life and death, trust and chaos appear to be in conflict with each other within us. What are those forces within us which seem chaotic and which prevent us from being open to others? The forces that keep us isolated from each other, in the wilderness?

The Birth of Chaos In Us

Children are terribly vulnerable. They need unconditional love. When they feel that for one reason or another they are not wanted, they live in extreme inner pain, a pain they cannot understand and which plunges them into confusion. Their anguish is experienced by feelings of confusion and death, of loneliness, of being no good. But children react to the unjust, aggressive attitude of their parents; either anger and hatred rise up within them or they withdraw in sullenness. Then they fall into a world of contradictions. How can children hate the ones who gave them life? To hate in that way means death. Then children begin to feel guilty. They are aware of the wolf inside them and sense their capacity to hurt someone. Feeling even more guilty, sensing that they are totally bad, they become even more aggressive until they fall into depression, hiding all the chaos within them behind strong walls, trying to forget all the mess. They have reached the heart of wilderness.

In all of us there is a shadow side that we cannot control but that can control us, as long as we remain unaware of it. This shadow side is hidden in the unconscious or subconscious self and is formed by all the impossible situations we lived as a child: things we were unable to express and that we had to hide away behind inner walls. In the shadow area we cannot know our true identity. It is the place of our loneliness.

The Road Out of Chaos to Freedom

Are we all condemned to live from this chaos within us, to build barriers around our hearts and to remain locked behind them? These barriers stop our true, deepest self from emerging and prevent us from making positive choices. Children who have been mistreated or abused will obviously have to create stronger barriers than children who have been listened to and treated well. If children have experienced love and acceptance, there will be less chaos inside their heart and their defence mechanisms will not need to be so strong.

Freedom comes in relationships that heal and transform our hearts. In such relationships children become more aware of who they truly are and what they are called to be. They open up to others. If they have been treated as people and not as things, they will perceive others as persons and will want to respect and be kind to them. They will also recognize their inner struggle with regard to some people who appear to be rivals or who threaten their growth. They become more conscious of their inner chaos. If their education, their family life, their models and their religious faith have all grown in the same direction of respect for others and belief in their personhood, they will learn to harness the chaos within them and not be governed by it. Within the heart of each person, no matter how wounded they may be, there is light. Even that man condemned to death may one day find a road out of his chaos. If he finds someone who trusts him, he will begin to trust that person and his own self.

If a family or a group can hurt people and close them up through a lack of love and respect, healthy families and groups are places where each one discovers that they are valued and important. A family, a group, a network of friends can then become a place of growth and healing for each one; a place where we begin the struggle to grow in love, to accept those who are different, to learn how to forgive and to live in trust. We can use people or we can serve them. We can think and act as if we are the centre of everything or we can realize that we are part of something much bigger than ourselves. Our vulnerability can become a place of pain and chaos causing us to withdraw from the world, or it can become the place where we welcome others into ourselves.

As we grow in maturity, with family, friends and community, this opening up is called to increase and develop further. If we remain closed up behind the walls of our group, thinking our group is the only good one, our group becomes a wilderness. Real human growth calls for a constant opening up to others, to all people, accepting them as they are, seeing the value and potential of each and every person. We become aware that we are all part of the wider human family, bonded together in our common humanity, and that every person whatever their race, religion, ethnic group, abilities or disabilities is important.

Shared life in community means that each member is making the transition from 'community for me' to 'me for the community'. Just as each person has to make this passage, the community as a whole is called to make the transition towards openness to other people and other groups, from the community for itself to community for others and for society.

Being for others means not imposing, manipulating or coercing others into our way of thinking and living. It is seeing the value and beauty in others, giving ourselves to them and receiving from them. Being there for others of course implies a growth and development of our affectivity, our capacity for cooperation, an attentiveness to and affirmation of others. To be for others also means that we ourselves have discovered our own beauty and fundamental value. We realize that we are called to develop our talents and competence and use them for others, to serve them and help them to become who they are called to be.

Loneliness or Solitude

Loneliness and subsequent anguish are so painful that they can cause us to fight our way into success and admiration. They push us constantly to go up the ladder of success, until we reach the 'top', becoming a star. But sooner or later the pain of loneliness causes us to question our life. Admiration and success do not nourish our hearts. One day we know we will no longer be able to shine. Sooner or later we will all know weakness. We are all mortal beings. We cannot avoid growing older and weaker.

Loneliness is wilderness. It is the absence of being in communion with others. Solitude is different. Solitude is when we know and accept who we are and can rest in peace where we are. We are at home in our bodies and in our whole being, with our gifts and our limits. We have good friends who we know are there for us, but we are not totally dependent on them and we do not have to run after them. We are able to trust them, their friendship and their presence.

Being a friend is not the same as being generous. Friendship is something unique which implies vulnerability and openness. Generosity means that we have something that we can give to another or others; but it also means that we are in some way superior. When we can give of our gifts, knowledge and competence we know we are someone. Friendship however is based on reciprocity; we give and receive from one another. We need each other for our mutual growth and coming into being. We recognize the bonding between us and give thanks.

We rejoice when we are together. But we are able to rejoice as well when we are separated, each one living their call in life, knowing that the bonds of friendship are there. Each one can be alone and at peace. We have discovered the joy and peace and silence of solitude.

Friendship, Community and Family

As we live together and accept and forgive each other, we recognize the growing bonds between us. We learn to be patient with one another. We learn a lot about who we are, our anguish, our fears, the violence within our own hearts. We learn not only to tame the chaos but to let the light of truth come through it. We will never be totally in control of it but we can learn to live with it and not let it govern our lives.

I was told a wonderful story about an eleven-year-old boy with learning disabilities who made his first communion in a church in Paris. After the church service, his uncle, who was also his godfather, remarked to the boy's mother. 'Wasn't the service beautiful! The only thing that is sad is that he did not understand anything.' The small boy had heard his uncle's remarks and said to his mother with tears in his eyes: 'Don't worry Mummy, Jesus loves me just as I am.'

This small boy, like Moses in Harare, had made the journey from wilderness and loneliness to being at home in himself. He was not lost or confused about his value or identity. He had discovered perhaps that his love for his mother was also important for her growth in love and her feeling at home. He had discovered even more, through his own inner, mysterious experience, that he was loved by God. When we discover that we are held in God's hands, then we are truly safe and deeply at home.

WILDERNESS WANDERERS AND THEIR THEOLOGICAL SIGNIFICANCE IN J. R. R. TOLKIEN'S *THE LORD OF THE RINGS*

Emily Hunt

It is an honour to contribute to Professor Young's Festschrift. During my time as a student at Birmingham University, she supported me both academically and personally. She has taught and inspired so many fledgling scholars from a large number of fields, and it seems entirely appropriate that this volume should celebrate her wide range of teaching interests. I studied Tolkien's *The Lord of the Rings* with Frances during my final undergraduate year. I would therefore like to present an essay on wilderness wanderers in *The Lord of the Rings*.

In discussing *The Lord of the Rings* (*LoR*), I will assume some knowledge of the book itself. Otherwise, this article will become a plot outline with little space to explore the underlying theology. For those who haven't read the book yet, I hope that this article will whet your appetite. Beyond all the current hype, *LoR* remains a very interesting piece of literature with many layers of meaning.

The Wildernesses of Middle-Earth

Wandering in the wilderness is a central theme in *LoR*. The quest to dispose of the Ring is essentially a journey through varying degrees of wilderness. Tolkien uses the term 'wilderness' repeatedly, and also uses 'wild', 'Wilds', 'Wilderland', 'ruins', 'wastes' and 'desert'. His description of the landscape of Middle-earth depicts vast stretches of land that have been destroyed or abandoned.

The lands travelled by the Ring-bearer and his companions become progressively less habitable. The lands between the Shire and Moria are wild because they are now sparsely populated and evil things have crept in. The same is even truer of the icy wilderness of Caradhras and the darkness of Moria. As they travel further south on the river Anduin, the 'brown lands' lie on the east bank, a reminder of the last war against Sauron. From this point on the lands become increasingly bleak, and Tolkien's language becomes stronger. Passing through the barren hills of the Emyn Muil, the Ring-bearer crosses the Dead Marshes and is confronted by the 'desolation' that lies before Mordor. Mordor itself is depicted as a choked, volcanic region.

The story is told almost exclusively from a hobbit's perspective, and this is significant in considering the wildernesses of Middle-earth. By nature, Tolkien's hobbits are home bodies. Even to leave one's own hole to travel to a different part of the Shire becomes an adventure. Any hobbit travelling beyond the boundaries of the Shire is considered a bit 'queer'. To a certain extent, then, simply by leaving the Shire, Frodo and his companions are wilderness wanderers. Upon their return to the Shire, our four hobbits become known as 'the Travellers' (Tolkien 1993b: 1060).

However, there is something more here than merely leaving the comfort of home. Hobbits are tied to the earth. They live in a pre-industrial society, with a preference for farming. Thus they are part of a natural order that tends and nurtures the land; a crucial symbiosis. A key indication of this is the fact that Tolkien portrays his hobbits with large, bare feet; hobbits are grounded in the earth. As a gardener, Sam is the archetype of this aspect of hobbitness, and it is no accident that he accompanies the Ring-bearer. Without Sam's earthy common sense, his intuition for where he and others belong, there are several places where the quest would have failed.[1]

From this hobbit perspective, many of the lands of Middle-earth (e.g. Hollin and Ithilien) have lost the folk that cared for them and the wilderness is encroaching. The least hospitable areas of Middle-earth (e.g. Mordor) are places where nurture of the land has become a desecration, and the masters of these realms have no respect for land or people.

Tolkien's Wilderness Wanderers

Having established Tolkien's wildernesses, let us turn now to consider his wanderers. Although Tolkien intended no inner message when writing *LoR* (Tolkien 1993b: 10), he was a Catholic, and this influenced him deeply. When writing to a family friend, Tolkien called *LoR* a 'fundamentally religious and Catholic work; unconsciously so at first, but consciously in the revision' (Carpenter 1981: 172). This influence comes across quite clearly in his presentation of three key wilderness wanderers.

As the Ring-bearer, Frodo suffers physical and mental torment, and does so selflessly with the end-goal of protecting Middle-earth from the domination of Sauron. In this he is a reflection of Christ-as-servant. In the prophecies and epiphanies that lead to Aragorn's coronation, there are strong parallels with Christ's messiahship, and Aragorn therefore represents the aspect of Christ-as-king. In Gandalf's death and 'return', meanwhile, there are links with the power and majesty of the post-resurrection Christ, and Gandalf can be seen as Christ-as-victor. Let us consider each in turn.

Frodo: Christ-as-Servant

Jane Chance has suggested that Frodo represents 'Christian-king-as-servant' (Chance 2001b: 179). His position as servant can be seen in his acceptance of the burden of the Ring, and his sense of responsibility towards others. I believe that

---

1.   e.g. when Sam rejects the temptation of the Ring (Tolkien 1993b: 935). When 'the Travellers' return to the Shire, they discover that 'ruffians' have tried to make their homeland into a 'desert' (Tolkien 1993b: 1051). Sam in his role as gardener is crucial in the process of restoring balance to the land. Jane Chance (2001b: 137) sees Sam as an alter ego Adam.

we can take this designation one step further and see Frodo as a portrayal of Christ-as-servant. Frodo suffers greatly because of the Ring, and his responsibility towards others is expressed as a desire to 'save' them, without expectation of praise or reward. This could be seen as a parallel to the suffering and humility of Christ. As we shall see, there are several more specific parallels with passages in the Gospels. It is also possible to see a gleam of divinity in Frodo's relationship with the elves.

In *The Silmarillion*, Tolkien relates the tale of the creation of Middle-earth as a musical composition, and its unfolding in time and reality. Creation is orchestrated by the Creator Ilúvatar ('Father of all') and performed by celestial beings. A number of these beings (known as the Valar) choose to descend to Middle-earth and act as guardians. The Valar seem to be equivalent to the pantheon of Norse gods, or to the angelic hierarchy of Christianity. The firstborn are the elves, and when they appear on Middle-earth, the Valar extend an invitation to this race to live with them in 'the Blessed Realm'. A number of clans accept, but for reasons too complicated to explain here, they later choose to exile themselves to Middle-earth. Because they have lived in the Blessed Realm, however, this group of elves (the Eldar) possess enormous powers. They exist simultaneously in the corporeal and the incorporeal; and in the realm of the Ring (e.g. when the Ring-bearer wears the Ring), the Eldar appear as white light.[2] In this I suspect that the Eldar possess a portion of the power or divinity of the Valar.

If this connection between the Eldar and divinity is valid, then there are some significant ties between Frodo and the elves. Almost from the outset, Frodo is called 'Elf-friend' (Tolkien 1993b: 94, 98, 139, 151),[3] and twice he dreams of the sea (Tolkien 1993b: 123, 383). This is significant because the elves are drawn to return to the sea and the Blessed Realm.[4] As the quest progresses and Frodo's identity becomes increasingly tied to the Ring, he begins to take on elvish qualities: at Rivendell, Gandalf notices that Frodo (especially his injured arm) is becoming transparent, and speculates that he may become like 'a glass filled with clear light' (Tolkien 1993b: 239); as they travel in Ithilien, Sam notices a light shining from within Frodo (Tolkien 1993b: 678); a little later, Faramir discerns an 'elvish air' to Frodo (Tolkien 1993b: 694), and in Mordor Sam sees an 'elvish beauty' in him (Tolkien 1993b: 760). Towards the very end of the quest, Frodo's appearance changes for a moment to one of light and power, a white robed figure with a wheel of fire at his chest – the Ring (Tolkien 1993b: 979). At the end of the book, Frodo joins the last of the elves as they sail towards the Blessed Realm (Tolkien 1993b: 1067–9).

As we shall see, there are also strong connections between Aragorn and the elves, and I suspect that there is also a more direct link between Gandalf and the Valar. The relationship between the Valar, elves and our wilderness wanderers

2.   At the Ford of Bruinen, where Frodo is almost overcome by the Morgul-wound, Glorfindel becomes a figure of shining white light (Tolkien 1993b: 231).

3.   Tom Bombadil calls Frodo 'friend Frodo' (Tolkien 1993b: 158). Could this be a shortened form of 'Elf-friend'?

4.   Cf. Legolas' experience on hearing seagulls cry (Tolkien 1993b: 907).

highlights the existence of a quality, or even power, that could be interpreted as an element of divinity. If such an element of divinity can be traced in Frodo, it would certainly take him beyond Chance's Christian-king-as-servant to Christ-as-king. Let us now consider Frodo's place in the story.

Frodo expresses reluctance about bearing the Ring from the outset. 'Why me?' is a question that he throws at Gandalf on learning that his heirloom is the One Ring (Tolkien 1993b: 74). Yet he recognizes that he must take responsibility for the Ring, and accepts that to protect the Shire and its folk, he must leave his homeland (Tolkien 1993b: 75–6). Frodo's initial journey through the Wilds between the Shire and Rivendell (his first experience of wilderness wandering) is a preparation for the next part of his quest.[5]

This is a significant point. Throughout *LoR* the experience of travelling through the wilds changes the travellers and prepares them for the next stage of their involvement in the quest to overthrow the enemy, Sauron. For Frodo, the journey to Rivendell is a maturation, a process that provides him with the knowledge and wisdom to stand up to the challenge of destroying the Ring, and the experience to deal with surviving in the wilderness. Christ's 40 days in the wilderness could likewise be seen as a preparation for his ministry.

Frodo's knowledge is gathered in several ways; firstly through the hints of the elves that the hobbits meet as they flee the Shire; in the example of Aragorn – a seasoned traveller; and also by Frodo's own encounter with the Black Riders and the wound that he takes. Together with possession of the Ring, all these elements change Frodo and prepare him for his decision at the Council of Elrond.

At the Council of Elrond, again we find a reluctant acceptance of his role in the quest to destroy the Ring. He perceives it as a long-foreseen doom (Tolkien 1993b: 288). For Frodo, this is a significant turning-point. Now matured and fully aware of the risk and danger involved, he freely agrees to take on the quest of destroying Sauron's ring. In this there is a parallel to Christ's reluctant acceptance of the cup in the garden of Gethsemane.[6] Frodo knows that he will be exposing himself to danger and suffering, that even if he succeeds he is unlikely to return from it. Yet Frodo still accepts this 'doom' because the alternative, the loss of the Shire and everything he has ever cherished, is simply unthinkable.

So, in a sense, at Rivendell, Frodo becomes a type of Christ-as-servant, bearing the cross with all the suffering that entails. The journey on from Rivendell changes him again, as too do his wounds (a possible parallel to Christ's suffering on the cross) and his possession of the Ring. This is most clearly seen in the journey through the wastes of Mordor.

As Frodo and Sam enter Mordor, Frodo is attacked by Shelob and Sam believes him to have died (although in fact Shelob has merely administered an incapacitating venom, as spiders do when stocking their larders). It is possible to see Frodo's 'death' and journey through Mordor as a parallel to Christ's victory over death and the devil at his resurrection, a journey to defeat death. The

5. See Chance (2001a: 47–8), where she highlights the significance of Frodo's travels in preparing him for the quest.
6. Mt. 26.36–46; Mk 14.32–42; Lk. 22.40–6.

analogies of Sauron as the devil and Mordor as the devil's realm are not hard to find.

Throughout Frodo's travels in the wilderness, there is a further struggle that he is subject to; the temptation of the Ring itself. The devil's third temptation to Christ after His wilderness experience is domination of all the kingdoms of the world.[7] This mirrors the temptation offered by the Ring; the power to rule Middle-earth. This desire for power corrupts Saruman. Gandalf, Aragorn and Galadriel all have the wisdom to recognize the Ring's lure and have the strength to reject it. Ultimately the Ring would corrupt the wearer, and a wearer with strength and power would become a substitute for Sauron. During his brief spell as a Ring-bearer, Sam is offered the power to create a garden from the wastes of Mordor. His love for Frodo and his 'plain hobbit-sense' help Sam to overcome the Ring's temptation (Tolkien 1993b: 935).

Being the true Ring-bearer, Frodo's urge to use the Ring is even stronger, and increases as they near Mount Doom. On the brink of throwing the Ring into the fire, Frodo's resolve wavers, and he gives in to the Ring's temptation (Tolkien 1993b: 981). In this he fails his quest. Yet throughout *LoR*, Tolkien introduces an element of divine grace; men (and hobbits) are not left entirely alone. There are hints throughout the book that Gollum has a significant role left to play. Gollum represents the element of grace that absolves Frodo's failure; Gollum bites the Ring and its finger from Frodo's hand and accidentally topples into the volcano, destroying the Ring. Could Frodo have destroyed the Ring himself? I think not; the power of the Ring was too strong. There is another parallel here with the story of Christ's betrayal; Jesus knew that he was to die. Would he have surrendered himself to the Jewish authorities? It was through Judas' betrayal that Jesus' arrest and death was achieved.

One final note on Frodo's theological significance. I have mentioned several times how wilderness wandering changes him; his journey to Rivendell prepares him for the next stage of the quest, and his journey on towards Mordor likewise prepares him for Mordor itself. His experience in Mordor alters him almost beyond recognition, and ultimately the suffering he goes through to complete the quest affects him so deeply that he loses what one might term his 'hobbit wholeness'. There is no 'happily ever after' ending to Frodo's story. He has sacrificed too much of himself:

> I have been too deeply hurt, Sam. I tried to save the Shire, and it has been saved, but not for me. It must often be so, Sam, when things are in danger: some one has to give them up, lose them, so that others may keep them. (Tolkien 1993b: 1067)[8]

Frodo leaves Middle-earth and sails with the last of the elves into the West. Thus in Frodo's final sacrifice, there is a further parallel with Christ's suffering and death on the cross to save mankind.

To summarize, there are several connections between Frodo's portrayal and Christ. As a type of Christ-as-servant, Frodo experiences a suffering and self-

---

7. Mt. 4.8–9.
8. Cf. Tolkien 1993b: 1026.

sacrifice similar to that of Christ in the Gospels. More specific parallels include wilderness as a preparation, the temptation of world domination, the reluctant acceptance of his task, his betrayal and his 'death' and journey through Mordor. Overlying all of this is a selfless desire to save the Shire and Middle-earth from Sauron.

Aragorn: Christ-as-King

Aragorn is our second wilderness wanderer. Like Frodo, Aragorn has close ties with the elves. The Numenorean kings, from whom Aragorn is descended, have elf blood in their line as their first king was of mixed race. Aragorn himself is called 'child of Lúthien' (Tolkien 1993b: 910), and 'Elf-friend' (Tolkien 1993b: 361), and as we shall see assumes the title 'Elessar', meaning 'elfstone'. Aragorn also refreshes the Numenorean connection with the elves through his relationship with Arwen. It is significant that in order to win Arwen's hand, Aragorn must first defeat Sauron and ascend to the throne of Gondor.

Aragorn represents the messiahship of Christ-as-king. There is a verse that encapsulates Aragorn's position in the story:

> All that is gold does not glitter,
> Not all those who wander are lost;
> The old that is strong does not wither,
> Deep roots are not reached by the frost.
> From the ashes a fire shall be woken,
> A light from the shadows shall spring;
> Renewed shall be blade that was broken,
> The crownless again shall be king.
> (Tolkien 1993b: 186)

This verse highlights Aragorn's status as heir of Isildur and foretells his ascendance to the throne of Gondor. The element of prophecy is crucial in presenting Aragorn as future king.

There is a real sense of destiny surrounding Aragorn. Even before we meet him in Bree, he is introduced in a vision of the Kings of the North (Tolkien 1993b: 161).[9] The elfstone in the vision is given to Aragorn during the story and becomes one of his titles; Elessar (elfstone). The use of this imagery is particularly significant because it is also part of a prophecy. At birth, the name 'Elessar' is foretold for Aragorn. Galadriel reminds him of this prophecy when she gives him the elfstone, and in Minas Tirith the people call him 'Elfstone' because of the green stone he wears. This is presented as a fulfilment of prophecy.

Another prophecy related to Aragorn concerns the Paths of the Dead. I shall discuss this in more detail shortly. What is significant is that in treading the Paths of the Dead and binding the Oathbreakers in the cause against Sauron, Aragorn is fulfilling a prophecy uttered some 1,000 years earlier (Tolkien 1993b: 812).

---

9. Although this son of forgotten kings is not named, we can identify him by the depiction of a star on his brow. This foreshadows a later depiction of Aragorn with an elfstone (probably a green beryl) on his brow as he leads his company into battle (Tolkien 1993b: 881).

Aragorn also displays the ability to prophesy. He warns Gandalf of passing into Moria (Tolkien 1993b: 314), and recalls his words after Gandalf's fall at the bridge of Khazad-dûm (Tolkien 1993b: 351). Likewise, before setting out on the Paths of the Dead Aragorn tells Éomer that they will meet even though Sauron's army lies between them (Tolkien 1993b: 810). This happens during the battle of the Pelennor Fields (Tolkien 1993b: 881).

In Tolkien's use of prophecy there is a strong parallel with Christ's messiahship. There are many Old Testament texts that have been interpreted as foretelling the coming of Christ. His position as Messiah is intimately connected with those texts, and I believe that we find an echo of this in the prophecies relating to Aragorn in *LoR*. Christ also prophesied,[10] providing a further link with Tolkien's presentation of Aragorn.

Connected with Aragorn's 'messiahship' is the use of titles, and lists are presented for him.[11] There may be a reflection of 'Emmanuel' ('God with Us')[12] in Aragorn's title 'Elessar' ('elfstone'). This is particularly poignant given my suggested link between elves and divinity.

To return to the verse quoted above, perhaps the most significant line in the context of this essay is; 'Not all those who wander are lost.' The Rangers (of whom Aragorn is the chieftain) are a race of men, descended from the Numenoreans who live and labour in the wilds of the North. Once, the lands that they patrol were filled with their own people, but their numbers dwindled following Isildur's death, perhaps perceived as a punishment for Isildur's failure to destroy the Ring. They were further lessened following the division of the land, dissension between later kings, and the attack of the witch-king of Angmar. There is a sense that somehow the Rangers must atone for the failures of their ancestors, and they therefore labour to protect the other peoples (like the hobbits) that live in the North.

Aragorn feels this responsibility especially keenly. As the heir of Isildur, he seems to feel that Isilidur's error is his personal failure, and he must work to atone for it. In recounting his search to capture Gollum, Aragorn states:

> It seemed fit that Isildur's heir should labour to repair Isildur's fault. (Tolkien 1993b: 269)

As a boy Aragorn was raised in Rivendell, ignorant of his roots. When his ancestry is revealed, Aragorn leaves to spend 30 years in the wilderness, labouring against Sauron and his allies (Tolkien 1993b: 1097). This is almost an apprenticeship for Aragorn; while he is coming to terms with his destiny during this time, he is also earning his right to kingship, and partly this is a process of atoning for ancestral wrongs.

Like Frodo, Aragorn's experience in the wilderness changes him, both physically and mentally; again this can be seen as a preparation for his assumption of the kingship and his confrontation with Sauron. Tolkien expressly links the changes in Aragorn and his kingship with his journeys in the wilderness (Tolkien 1993b: 1097).

---

10. e.g. Christ's words to Peter in Mt. 26.34, and Peter's denial of Christ in Mt. 26.69–75.

11. Tolkien 1993b: 454, 881, 897, 1003.

12. Mt. 1.23.

As Urang has pointed out, Aragorn's rise to kingship is marked by a series of epiphanies (Urang 1971: 117). Aragorn is initially introduced to the hobbits as Strider the Ranger (Tolkien 1993b: 172), then, in proving himself trustworthy, he gives his true name; Aragorn son of Arathorn (Tolkien 1993b: 187). At Rivendell he is revealed as the heir of Isildur, and the significance of his involvement in the Ring quest becomes clear (Tolkien 1993b: 263). His commitment to the people of Gondor is stressed as his relationship with Boromir develops, and following Boromir's death and Aragorn's promise to go to Minas Tirith (Tolkien 1993b: 434), there is a distinct flavour of a king returning from exile.

At the battle of Helm's Deep, Aragorn shows strong kingly qualities; leadership, battle courage and wisdom (Tolkien 1993b: 563). When he takes possession of the palantír (a 'seeing stone') of Orthanc (Tolkien 1993b: 617), in a sense he is acknowledging and accepting his inheritance, and preparing for the confrontation with Sauron.

Particularly important for our concerns here in tracing Aragorn's theological significance are the 'Paths of the Dead'. The 'Dead' are a race of men cursed for not holding faith with the Numenoreans in the last war against Sauron. They roam the land as ghosts. As king, Aragorn has the power to summon them to fulfil the oath that they broke (Tolkien 1993b: 821). In this, Aragorn becomes king of the dead, and although the overtones don't go quite as far as resurrection, Aragorn provides peace for the oathbreakers.

Likewise, Aragorn's ability to heal the injured has strong messianic overtones. To cure the 'black breath' that affects Faramir, Éowyn and Merry, he asks for the herb 'athelas', otherwise known as 'kingsfoil'(Tolkien 1993b: 898–9). The notion that the hands of the king are the hands of a healer is one that grows in significance as the time draws nearer for Gondor to acknowledge Aragorn's claim to the throne, and of course there are clear parallels to Christ's healing work in the Gospels.

Aragorn is strongly presented as the aspect of Christ-as-king. He survives his testing in the wilderness (including the lure of the Ring), moves actively against the powers of Sauron, and atones for the wrongs of his ancestors. Perhaps in this he could be seen as an alter ego Adam, correcting the fall. Aragorn also demonstrates the kingly power of healing, and his ability to command the dead. His foretold title of 'Elessar' may also parallel titles given to Christ, such as 'Emmanuel'.

Before I turn to consider the role of Gandalf in *LoR*, there is one last issue in Aragorn's role as King that must be addressed. We have seen how the wilderness has changed and prepared Aragorn to fulfil his destiny. Tolkien also turns this around; as King, Aragorn has the power to change the wilderness by reclaiming and repopulating the Northern Kingdom (Tolkien 1993b: 1030).

Gandalf: Christ-as-Victor

Tolkien leaves Gandalf's identity unclear in *LoR*; he is a wizard and is neither man nor elf. In a conversation with Edmund Fuller in 1962, Tolkien revealed that

Gandalf is an angel, and after his battle with the Balrog, the wizard returns as an angel 'in the incorruptible body of resurrection' (Isaacs 1968: 35). If we see the Valar as representing angels in *LoR*, then it seems likely either that Gandalf is one of the Valar himself, or that he is a lower order of angel, sent by the Valar.

Gandalf's wilderness wandering is quite different to that of Frodo and Aragorn in that it is partly spiritualized. It takes place during and following his battle with the Balrog in the mines of Moria. Tolkien's Balrog is a spirit of fire, and in *The Silmarillion*, Tolkien calls the Balrogs 'demons' (Tolkien 1994: 54).

Gandalf's battle with the Balrog is presented as his greatest challenge, and as his time of testing. He is taken through fire, deep water and darkness in pursuit of the Balrog. Eventually he corners his adversary on a mountain peak,[13] and the Balrog is destroyed. Gandalf describes what happened afterwards as a wandering:

> Then darkness took me, and I strayed out of thought and time, and I wandered far on roads that I will not tell. (Tolkien 1993b: 524)

Gandalf is here relating his experience of death, as he later claims to have returned from death (Tolkien 1993b: 606). It is frustrating that Tolkien does not tell us more of these roads, and Gandalf's experience of wandering them. This is a spiritual journey away from the body, as Gandalf was 'sent back':

> Naked I was sent back – for a brief time, until my task is done. (Tolkien 1993b: 524)[14]

On his return, Gandalf is far more powerful and becomes Gandalf the White. He is changed by his experience of fighting the Balrog (itself a form of wilderness wandering) and the spiritual journey that follows. He represents the aspect of Christ-as-victor,[15] and can be seen as the post-resurrection Christ returning in power and glory. Gandalf is repeatedly described using imagery of post-resurrection divine manifestation; Gwaihir the eagle says that the sun shines through him (Tolkien 1993b: 524); the hobbits speak of Gandalf as having 'grown' (Tolkien 1993b: 613); and he is described as radiating light (Tolkien 1993b: 521–2). This last point is particularly significant. Gandalf the White carries the power and majesty of Christ-as-victor.

Conclusion: Tolkien's Term 'Eucatastrophe'

In his essay 'On Fairy Stories', Tolkien coins the term 'eucatastrophe' to describe the point at which climactic events turn to produce a happy ending; 'a sudden and miraculous grace: never to be counted on to recur' (Tolkien 1947: 81). The 'joyous turn', then, is the unexpected resolution of events that would otherwise turn to catastrophe, and it is important to Tolkien that it stimulates an emotional

---

13. Perhaps a reflection of the devil's temptation of Christ 'on a very high mountain' in Mt. 4.8–9?

14. Who sent Gandalf back? I suspect it was the Valar, although it may have been Ilúvatar, Tolkien's 'father of all' and the ultimate creator of Middle-earth.

15. Urang (1971: 119) terms this Christus Victor.

response in the reader, and in that moment provides the reader with a glimpse of 'truth'. Gandalf's resurrection, his return 'for a brief time' to complete his task, presents us with just such a eucatastrophe. A force beyond Middle-earth has stepped in to change Gandalf's end. The same is true in Gollum's final role in destroying the Ring.

Tolkien took a very wide view of what a 'fairy story' should be. He saw the storyteller as sub-Creator (a mirror of God as Creator), essentially creating a consistent world with a life and essence of its own. He speaks of the Christian story as the greatest fairy story, the birth of Christ as the eucatastrophe of Man's history, and the Resurrection as the eucatastrophe of the Incarnation story (Tolkien 1947: 83). The Incarnation of Christ is an act of divine grace, which facilitates a resolution to mankind's downwards spiral, and the Resurrection is the ultimate resolution to death. He expresses the deep Christian joy he experiences at the realization of this 'primary truth':

> The joy would have exactly the same quality, if not the same degree, as the joy which the 'turn' in a fairy-story gives: such joy has the very taste of primary truth... It looks forward... to the Great Eucatastrophe. The Christian joy, the 'Gloria', is of the same kind; but it is pre-eminently (infinitely, if our capacity were not finite) high and joyous. Because this story is supreme; and it is true. Art has been verified. (Tolkien 1947: 84)[16]

If Tolkien relates the key elements of the Christian faith to the happy ending essential (in his view) to 'fairy stories', it is hardly surprising that we find reflections of Christ in his most elaborate fairy story, *LoR*. As sub-Creator he still works from within his own frame of reference and imbues his creation with those ideologies that move him most. It is also possible that Tolkien was not entirely aware of his influences when writing – his Catholic roots seem to have run deep.

Tolkien's presentation of the three key wilderness wanderers Frodo, Aragorn and Gandalf is thus enriched by his belief in the nature of Christ. Frodo's self-sacrifice strikes a chord in the reader, which is an echo of the feeling that Christians experience when contemplating Christ's death on the cross. The reader's hope and belief in Aragorn's destiny is a reflection of the Christian belief in Christ as Messiah. Gandalf's return inspires the same kind of joy in the reader that Tolkien connects with the Great Eucatastrophe; the birth, death and resurrection of Christ. Had his interests not lain in Scandinavian and Anglo-Saxon languages and mythology, I suspect that Tolkien would have made an engaging theologian.

Bibliography

Carpenter, H.
    1981   *The Letters of J. R. R. Tolkien* (London: George Allen & Unwin).
Chance, J.
    2001a   *The Lord of the Rings: The Mythology of Power* (Lexington, Ky.: University Press of Kentucky).

16. Cf. Carpenter 1981: 100–1.

2001b   *Tolkien's Art: A Mythology for England* (Lexington, Ky.: The University Press of Kentucky, rev. edn).

Isaacs, N. D., and R. A. Zimbardo (eds.)

1968   *Tolkien and the Critics: Essays on J. R. R. Tolkien's 'The Lord of the Rings'* (Notre Dame, Ind.: University of Notre Dame).

Tolkien, J. R. R.

1947   'On Fairy Stories', in *Essays Presented to Charles Williams* (London: Oxford University Press).

1993a   *The Hobbit* (London: HarperCollins, [1937]).

1993b   *The Lord of the Rings* (London: HarperCollins, [1968]).

1994   *The Silmarillion* (London: HarperCollins, [1977]).

Urang, G.

1971   *Shadows of Heaven: Religion and Fantasy in the Writing of C. S. Lewis, Charles Williams and J. R. R. Tolkien* (London: SCM Press).

JESUS IN THE QUR'AN, THE HISTORICAL JESUS
AND THE MYTH OF GOD INCARNATE[1]

Neal Robinson

It is now more than a quarter of a century since the publication of *The Myth of God Incarnate* took Christians in the United Kingdom by storm.[2] On many issues, including the nature of myth, and the origins and early development of belief in Jesus' divinity, the seven scholars who contributed to that volume were far from unanimous. They were, however, united in their desire to affirm the paramount importance of Jesus for Christian faith and practice without endorsing the traditional metaphysical claims about his person. Although most of them were aware that abandoning a literal belief in the incarnation might have implications for inter-faith relations, none of them, apart possibly from John Hick, seems to have realized that their theological enterprise was especially pertinent to Christian dialogue with Muslims. At one point, Hick acknowledges that

> understood literally the Son of God, God the Son, God-incarnate language implies that God can be adequately known and responded to *only* through Jesus; and the whole religious life of mankind, beyond the stream of Judaic-Christian faith is thus by implication excluded as lying outside the sphere of salvation.

In his opinion, this

> did little positive harm so long as Christendom was a largely autonomous civilization with only relatively marginal interaction with the rest of mankind. But with the clash between the Christian and Muslim worlds, and then on an ever broadening front with European colonization throughout the earth, the literal understanding of the mythological language of Christian discipleship has had a divisive effect...[3]

1.   I wish to thank Professor Mohammad Shaker, Head of Quranic Sciences in the University of Qom, and Greg Barker, one of my research students, both of whom read this essay in an earlier form and made valuable suggestions. I am also indebted to Oxford University Islamic Society for inviting me to deliver the essay as a public lecture on 20 February 2004, and to the audience for making many perceptive comments. Needless to say, I accept sole responsibility for this final version published here.
2.   J. Hick (ed.), *The Myth of God Incarnate* (London: SCM Press, 1977). This book, to which Frances made a substantial contribution, was published not long after she finished supervising my doctoral research on Luke's Gospel. She is an exemplary teacher, whose high standards have been an inspiration to me throughout my career. She will perhaps be surprised to learn that the book, and the controversy that it caused, had an enormous influence on my intellectual and spiritual development.
3.   Hick, *Myth of God Incarnate*, 179f.

It is strange that Hick does not mention the harm inflicted on Jews and so-called heretics even before the rise of Islam. Here, however, I am more concerned with another apparent oversight. Despite drawing attention to the clash between the Christian and Muslim worlds, he seems not to have realized that his criticisms of incarnational theology, far from being avant-garde, are very similar to those made in the Qur'an.[4] The Qur'an devotes considerable space to Jesus (Arabic *'Īsā*), acknowledging that he was a prophet and repeatedly referring to him as 'the Messiah'. But it castigates Christians for regarding him as divine and alleging that because of him they enjoy an exclusive relationship with God.[5]

One possible explanation for Hick's omission is that the quranic Jesus is in other respects very different from the historical Jesus as envisaged by radical theologians and biblical scholars. Indeed, many Christians are still inclined to dismiss the quranic Jesus material as a confused mishmash of apocryphal legends and naive anti-Christian polemic. In this article, I shall seek to remedy that state of affairs. I shall argue that, unlike their modern Western counterparts, the Christians of seventh-century Arabia would have found the quranic account of Jesus coherent because the Qur'an deliberately drew on stories that they had heard, and used exegetical methods with which they were familiar. Its primary concern was not with history but theology – not with the events themselves but with their religious significance. As the stories on which the Qur'an drew had taken root in the collective imagination, it only questioned their historical accuracy when serious theological issues were at stake. Instead, it sought to transform the consciousness of Muhammad's audience, by accepting their understanding of what happened more or less at face value but giving the alleged events a consistently theocentric interpretation.

1. *The Coherence of the Qur'anic Jesus Material*

Nowadays, when Christians read about Jesus in the Qur'an they are usually puzzled. In the first place, this is because of the presence of details that are not mentioned in any of the four Gospels now in use. They include the miraculous appearance of ripe dates and a refreshing stream after Mary gave birth (*Q*19.24–6); Jesus' speaking from the cradle (*Q*19.29–33); his creating birds from clay (*Q*3.49; 5.110); and his disciples' asking him whether his Lord could send them down a table spread with food (*Q*5.112–15). A second puzzling feature is the apparent confusion of Mary and Jesus with Old Testament characters that bore

4. From the Muslim standpoint, the Qur'an is the Word of God revealed to Muhammad. Non-Muslims, on the other hand, generally regard Muhammad as in some sense its author. To avoid prejudging the issue, I shall attempt to employ expressions that neither presume the Qur'an's divine origin nor preclude it.

5. For a fully referenced summary of the quranic Jesus material, see N. Robinson, *Christ in Islam and Christianity: The Representation of Jesus in the Qur'an and the Classical Muslim Commentaries* (Albany: SUNY, 1991), 3–7. And for non-Muslim assessments of this material see Robinson, *Christ in Islam and Christianity*, 8–40. References to the Qur'an in this essay, as there, are to the standard Egyptian edition of the Arabic text; quotations have been rendered into English by the author.

names similar to theirs. Thus Mary (Arabic *Maryam*) is addressed as 'Sister of Aaron' (*Q*19.28) as if she were Miriam, and Jesus asks for helpers 'in God's cause' (*Q*3.52; 61.14) as if he were Joshua. A third ground for bewilderment is that some of the Qur'an's criticisms of Christian beliefs appear wide of the mark. Christians do not consciously claim that God is the third of three (*Q*5.73); that God is the Messiah Son of Mary (*Q*5.72); or that Jesus and his mother are two deities in addition to God (*Q*5.116). The upshot of all this is that they are inclined to dismiss the quranic image of Jesus as the product of the Prophet's limited and somewhat confused knowledge of Christianity.

The details that modern Christians find puzzling would not have perturbed the Prophet's contemporaries. Their knowledge of Jesus was probably derived mainly from storytellers and preachers. As I suggested earlier, the Qur'an therefore alluded to the versions of the stories with which they were familiar. Some of the details including the appearance of ripe dates and a refreshing stream, Jesus' speaking in the cradle, and the miracle of the birds, are attested in apocryphal gospels.[6] Others are explicable in the light of the typological approach to the Old Testament that was prevalent before the rise of modern critical study. In this method of interpretation, incidents in the Old Testament were not viewed merely, or even primarily, as literal narratives but as 'types' that foreshadowed the life of Jesus.[7] For example, Abraham's intended sacrifice of Isaac was held to foreshadow God's sending Jesus to expiate for human sins, because Isaac and Jesus were both only sons and Isaac carried the wood on which he was subsequently bound just as Jesus later carried his own cross.[8] For people with this mindset, there would be nothing odd in the Qur'an's assimilating Mary to Miriam. After all, Mary preserved the infant Jesus from Herod's slaughter of the innocents much as Miriam saved Moses from an earlier massacre instigated by Pharaoh.[9] Moreover the stigma that she bore, as an unmarried mother, was comparable to Miriam's shame when God temporarily inflicted her with leprosy so that her flesh became like that of a still-born child.[10] Christian exegetes had long regarded Joshua's mission as foreshadowing that of Jesus. In Hebrew and Greek their

---

6.   The miracle of the birds is mentioned in the *Infancy Story of Thomas*, of which a Syriac translation existed in pre-Islamic times. The ripe dates and the stream are mentioned in the Latin *Gospel of Pseudo-Matthew*, and Jesus' speaking from the cradle features in the *Arabic Infancy Gospel*. In their present form, these two works are both later than the Qur'an but their compilers probably drew on earlier Syriac sources that are no longer extant.

7.   See e.g. G. W. H. Lampe and K. J. Woolcombe, *Essays on Typology* (London: SCM Press, 1957).

8.   See Chrysostom, *Homilies* 85.1 and compare Gen. 22.1–19 and Jn 1.29; 3.16; 19.17. Gen. 22.2 refers to Isaac as Abraham's only son despite the fact that Gen. 16.2 mentions that Abraham's wife's maidservant earlier bore him Ishmael. Muslims hold that the intended sacrifice was of Ishmael not Isaac.

9.   Compare Exod. 1.8–2.10 with Mt. 2.13–18.

10.   Compare *Q*19.28 with Num. 12.10–16. Miriam was punished for challenging Moses' unique authority on the grounds that God had also spoken through her and Aaron. In connection with this, note that in the Bible the expression 'Sister of Aaron' occurs only in Exod. 15.20, where she is also called a 'prophetess'.

names are identical; they both chose twelve men for a special task;[11] and whereas Joshua brought victory over the Canaanites, Jesus had vanquished Satan and the demonic forces.[12] Typological interpretation of the Old Testament also throws light on the quranic episode of the table: the Psalmist states that the Israelites were given manna in response to their question, 'Can God spread a table in the wilderness?' (Ps. 78.19) and Paul, who describes participating in the Eucharist as sharing in the Lord's 'table' (1 Cor. 10.21), implies that the manna foreshadowed the Eucharistic bread (1 Cor. 10.3; 11.23–7). Finally, for a plausible explanation of the odd-sounding theological statements anathematized in the Qur'an we need look no further than the intra-Christian disputes between Nestorians and Ortho-dox. From a Nestorian perspective, by honouring Mary with the title 'Mother of God', the Orthodox laid themselves open to ridicule. For they appeared to have relegated God the Father to third position after Jesus and Mary, to have identified God with Jesus, or to have made Mary and her son into two additional deities. The Qur'an reiterates Nestorian anti-Orthodox polemic but develops it to its logi-cal conclusion, denying that Christ was in any sense divine.[13]

For ease of presentation, one important element of the quranic Jesus material has been left until now, namely the numerous references to 'the gospel'. To Chris-tians, this term denotes the good news of salvation through the death and resur-rection of Jesus. When, on the other hand, they speak of 'the Gospels' in the plural they usually mean the four New Testament lives of Jesus. The quranic usage is strikingly different: the word occurs only in the singular and denotes the revelations that God vouchsafed to Jesus and, by extension, a book possessed by the Christians which incorporates those revelations. Some non-Muslim scholars see in this further evidence that Muhammad's knowledge of Christianity was superficial. They surmise that he had come into contact with members of a sect that drew exclusively on one of the apocryphal gospels. Alternatively, having learned from the Jews that God had revealed the Torah to Moses, and believing that God was in the process of revealing the Qur'an to him, he simply assumed that Jesus had likewise received a divine revelation. A closer look at the quranic data will show that these hypotheses are unnecessary.

According to the Qur'an, God bestowed the gospel on Jesus and taught it to him (*Q*3.48; 5.110; 57.26). It confirms the Torah and contains guidance, light and admonition (*Q*5.46). It prophesies the advent of Muhammad (*Q*7.157; cf. 61.6) and his followers (*Q*48.29). It contains God's binding promise to the believers that they will be admitted to Paradise in return for surrendering their lives and property (*Q*9.111). The People of the gospel should judge by what God has re-vealed in it (*Q*5.47). If only the People of the Scripture (the Jews and Christians) would establish the gospel along with the Torah and what has been revealed to

11. Compare Josh. 4.2 with Mk 3.13.

12. See L. W. Barnard, *Justin Martyr: His Life and Thought* (Cambridge: Cambridge University Press, 1967), 159.

13. For a detailed discussion along these lines see C. Schedl, *Muhammad und Jesus* (Vienna: Herder, 1978), 523–7.

them from their Lord, they would receive bountiful provision, but they will get nowhere until they do establish it (*Q*5.66ff).

For the ultimate source of most of these statements we need look no further than the utterances of Jesus as they have come down to us in the four canonical Gospels. According to Luke, before Jesus gave his programmatic address at Nazareth, he read the following passage from Isaiah:

> The Spirit of the Lord is upon me, for he has anointed me. He has sent me to preach good news to the poor, to proclaim release for prisoners and sight for the blind, to send the downtrodden away in relief, and to proclaim the Lord's year of favour. (Lk. 4.18)[14]

Then, after handing the scroll back to the synagogue attendant, he said to the congregation, 'Today this passage of scripture is fulfilled in your hearing' (Lk. 4.19). I shall return to this later. For the moment, suffice it to note that the reference to being anointed with the Spirit and sent to preach good news could be taken as implying that Jesus thought that his utterances constituted a divinely inspired 'gospel'.[15] In Matthew's 'Sermon on the Mount', Jesus confirmed the Torah and proffered guidance, light and admonition.[16] And, in his teaching on renunciation, Jesus assured believers of a heavenly reward for sacrificing their lives and property.[17] It is only the alleged predictions of the rise of Muhammad and his adherents that require further explanation. The Qur'an says that in the Gospel the latter

> are represented as sown seed that sends forth its shoot and strengthens it and rises firm on its stalk delighting the sowers … (*Q*48.29)

This is surely an allusion to the parable of the sower.[18] From the quranic perspective, with the rise of Islam, Jesus' monotheistic teaching, long obscured by the Church, at last bore fruit like the seed sown on good soil. If one concedes the legitimacy of this interpretation, there is no real problem about the further claim that Muhammad is

> the unlettered Prophet whom [the Jews and Christians] will find written about in the Torah and the Gospel that are in their possession… (*Q*7.157)

and that Jesus foretold the coming of a Messenger 'whose name is Ahmad' (*Q*61.6). As the promised Paraclete, Muhammad led the believers 'into all truth'. Being unable to read or write he did 'not speak as from himself' but uttered what he heard (compare Jn 16.13), as and when it was revealed to him. Muhammad means 'praised'; Ahmad 'highly praised'. Both are approximate equivalents of the Greek *periklutos*, a word with the same consonantal skeleton (and hence, to native speakers of Semitic languages, the same essence) as *paraklētos*, 'Paraclete'.[19]

14. Rendered into English by the author from the Greek text in *H ΚΑΙΝΗ ΔΙΑΘΗΚΗ* (London: British and Foreign Bible Society, 2nd edn, 1958).

15. Luke has the verb *euangelisasthai*. For the substantive, *to euangelion*, see the redactional comment in Mk 1.14.

16. See e.g. Mt. 5.14–19; 6.22f; 7.13f; 24–7.

17. See e.g. Mt. 16.25f; 19.21, 29.

18. The closest parallel is Mk 4.8.

19. On this reckoning, there is no need to suppose, as many Muslim scholars do, that Christians

From a modern critical perspective, the way in which the Qur'an interprets Jesus' words might seem highly selective and somewhat forced. However, it accords with Jesus' own approach to the Jewish scriptures. Although the prophecy that he quoted at Nazareth was an autobiographical oracle of Trito-Isaiah, he apparently had no compunction about applying it to himself.[20] Moreover, he made a number of changes to the text. For instance, he omitted the phrase 'the day of vengeance of our God', presumably because the negative element in the prophecy did not suit his purpose. This is not as cavalier as it may sound. Most of the congregation would have been unable to understand the original Hebrew and so Jesus probably followed the standard practice of giving a rather free Aramaic paraphrase of the passage, and it is probably this that lies behind Luke's Greek. We may surmise that the situation in seventh-century Medina was very similar. Jewish preachers would have made ad hoc Arabic renderings of the set readings from the Hebrew Bible. Christian preachers would have done the same with their scriptures, although the readings were probably from a Syriac version of the *Diatessaron*, a Gospel harmony based on the four Gospels, rather than from the Greek text of the Gospels themselves.[21] This would explain why the Qur'an refers to 'the Gospel' possessed by the Christians, rather than 'the Gospels'.

2. The Qur'an's Theo-centric Interpretation of Jesus' Mission

The fourth-century Nicene-Constantinopolitan Creed, which is still frequently recited in Christian services, affirms that Jesus Christ is

> the only-begotten Son of God,
> begotten of the Father before all worlds.[22]

Probably as a deliberate counterblast to this, the Qur'an asserts that God is One and self-subsistent, and that 'He neither begets nor is begotten' (*Q*112.3). Consequently, it repeatedly styles Jesus 'Son of Mary', never Son of God, for 'it is far removed from His transcendent majesty that He should have a son' (*Q*4.171). However, the Qur'an's response to other Christian beliefs is on the whole more measured. As we have seen, it draws on the stock of stories about Jesus and Mary that were known to Muhammad's contemporaries and resorts to traditional Christian methods of biblical exegesis. Nevertheless, the interpretation that it gives to this material is radically theocentric, as I wish now to demonstrate.

The creed asserts that the Son

> became incarnate of the Virgin Mary
> and was made man.

---

deliberately tampered with the Gospel text, substituting *paraklētos* for *periklutos* in order to eliminate the prophecy.

20. Lk. 4.18; compare Isa. 61.1.

21. Some, however, doubtless knew at least a little Greek – enough to engage in discussions about the identity of the Paraclete.

22. This and all subsequent quotations from the creed are translated from the Greek text printed in T. H. Bindley, *The Oecumenical Documents of the Faith* (London: Methuen, 4th edn, 1950), 64.

Christian theologians arrived at this full-blown doctrine of incarnation by somewhat artificially interpreting the virginal conception, which is attested by Matthew and Luke, in the light of John's statement that 'the Word became flesh'.[23] Moreover, by the time that the creed was promulgated, Christians had begun to venerate Mary as Mother of God, and before long some were claiming that she miraculously remained a virgin despite giving birth.[24] The Qur'an mentions the virginal conception (*Q*3.47; 19.18–21; etc.) and even calls Jesus God's 'Word' (*Q*3.45; 4.171). But from the quranic perspective, this title, far from implying his pre-existence or divinity, points rather to God's creative power, for it is a reminder that Jesus came into being in his mother's womb as a direct result of God's spoken command, 'Be!' (*Q*3.47, 59). Thus Jesus and his mother together constitute a divinely appointed sign (*Q*23.50). Although, in choosing Mary to conceive Jesus, God honoured her above all other women (*Q*3.42), she nevertheless experienced labour pains – a hint that there was nothing miraculous about the birth itself (*Q*19.23).[25] Moreover, if God had wished to destroy her and Jesus along with everyone else on earth none could have prevented him (*Q*5.17) for they were both mortals (*Q*5.75) and, when questioned by God, Jesus will emphatically deny that he told people to regard them as divine (*Q*5.116).

Unlike the alleged virgin birth and incarnation, Jesus' miracles are not mentioned in the creed. They do, however, feature in the canonical and apocryphal gospels. The *Arabic Infancy Gospel* begins with an account of how Jesus spoke from the cradle. Although in its present form this work post-dates the rise of Islam by several centuries, the episode must surely have been familiar to the Prophet's contemporaries. Rather than denying the occurrence of the miracle, the Qur'an merely seeks to put the record straight about Jesus' utterance. Far from asserting that he was the Son of God who had been sent into the world for its salvation, he would have acknowledged that he was God's servant and prophet on whom God had enjoined life-long prayer, almsgiving, and filial piety towards his mother.[26]

According to Ibn Ishaq, the Prophet's biographer, an embassy of Christians from Najran claimed that Jesus' healings, his knowledge of the unseen, and his creation of birds from clay, were proof that he was divine.[27] This should be borne in mind when reading the two passages in the Qur'an that list some of Jesus' other miracles. The first narrates that the angels of the annunciation foretold that Jesus would be God's messenger to the Children of Israel and would say to them

> I have come to you with a sign from your Lord. Behold! I fashion clay in the form of
> birds and I breathe into it so that it becomes birds with God's permission. And I heal

23. Mt. 1.18–25; Lk. 1.26–38; Jn 1.14.

24. Mary was first called *Theotokos* in Alexandria *c*.324 – J. Pelikan, *The Christian Tradition* (vol. 1; Chicago: University of Chicago Press, 1971), 241. For her perpetual virginity, see for example *The Protoevangelium of James* 19.2 and Ambrose *The Consecration of a Virgin and the Perpetual Virginity of Mary* 8.52, both of which imply that her hymen remained intact.

25. Contrast *Ascension of Isaiah* 11 and *Odes of Solomon* 19.

26. Contrast *Q*19.29–33 with *The Arabic Infancy Gospel* 1.2.

27. A. Guillaume, *The Life of Muhammad: A Translation of Ibn Ishaq's Sirat Rasul Allah* (Oxford: Oxford University Press, 1945), 271.

the blind from birth and the leper and bring the dead to life with God's permission. And I declare to you what you eat and what you store up in your houses. Surely in all that there is a sign for you if you are believers. (*Q*3.49)

The second indicates that, on the Day of Resurrection, God will remind Jesus of how he showed favour to him and his mother, including

when with my permission you fashioned clay in the form of birds and when you blew into it and it became birds with my permission, and you healed the blind from birth and the leper with my permission, and brought forth the dead with my permission… (*Q*5.110)

From the quranic perspective, the real issue is not the historicity of miracles but their significance. Rather than being proofs of Jesus' divinity, they constituted a sign for the Children of Israel that he was an authentic messenger sent by God; they were evidence of God's favour towards him, and he performed them with God's permission rather than by some innate supernatural power.

The New Testament relates that on two occasions Jesus miraculously fed crowds of people who followed him.[28] The various accounts of these feeding miracles all highlight how he took bread and gave thanks, thereby foreshadowing the Last Supper at which he instituted the Eucharist with a similar action.[29] The Qur'an does not refer to these feeding miracles. However, as we saw earlier, it mentions God's provision of a table spread with food, apparently at this point assimilating the Last Supper to the story of the gift of manna in the wilderness[30] – the archetypal Old Testament feeding miracle. The quranic narrative runs as follows

Remember when the disciples said, 'O Jesus Son of Mary, is your Lord able to send us down a table from heaven?' Jesus said, 'Fear God if you are believers!' They said, 'We want to eat from it and for our hearts to be calm, and to know that you have told us the truth and that we may be among those who witness it.' Jesus Son of Mary said, 'O God Our Lord, send us down a table from heaven to be a festival for us now and for those who come after us, and to be a sign from you. And provide for us, you are the best of providers.' God said, 'I am sending you it down, and whoever of you disbelieves afterwards I shall punish with a punishment that I have never inflicted on any creature.' (*Q*5.112–15)

Several details are reminiscent of the Last Supper. The latter was a festival for the disciples because it was their Passover meal (Mk 14.12). It was also a festival for those who came after them, insofar as Christians regularly re-enacted it in their celebration of the Eucharist. At the Last Supper, Jesus urged the disciples not to let their hearts be troubled (Jn 14.1). Finally Paul, who as we have seen described participating in the Eucharist as sharing in the Lord's table (1 Cor. 10.22), also held that God severely punished Christians who did not participate

28. The feeding of 5,000 in Mt. 14.13–21; Mk 6.30–4; Lk. 9.12–17; Jn 6.1–15; the feeding of 4,000 in Mt. 15.32–9; Mk 8.1–10.

29. Mt. 26.17–29; Mk 14.12–25; Lk. 22.14–20; 1 Cor. 11.23–7. John's account of the Last Supper, Jn 13.1–17.26, does not mention the blessing of the bread.

30. It does not, however, confuse the two incidents, because elsewhere (*Q*2.57; 20.80) it correctly situates the gift of manna in the time of Moses.

with due reverence (1 Cor. 11.28–32). However, in other respects, the quranic version differs markedly from traditional Christian accounts. This is because it offers a deliberate corrective to Christian teaching, as can be seen if it is read in context. It occurs at the climax of a long sura that deals at length with community boundaries, sin and forgiveness.[31] The sura mentions the failure of the Jews and Christians to keep God's covenants (*Q*5.12–14). It stresses that God loves those who do good and does not love those who merely claim that they are his children and loved ones, as some of the Jews and Christians of Arabia apparently did (*Q*5.13, 18). It refers to crucifixion as a punishment for brigands (*Q*5.33), rather than as a redemptive act. It states that if the unbelievers were to offer everything in the earth twice over it would not be accepted to redeem them from the punishment of the Day of Resurrection (*Q*5.36). And it holds that those who make extravagant claims about Jesus and Mary are unbelievers (*Q*5.72–3). In keeping with this, the quranic account of the Last Supper is consistently theocentric rather than christocentric. Jesus does not instruct his disciples to 'Do this in remembrance of me' (contrast Lk. 22.19; 1 Cor. 11.24) for it is God who at the Judgment will charge him, 'Remember my favour unto you' (*Q*5.110). He makes no reference to his blood poured out for the forgiveness of sins (contrast Mt. 26.28) because God has forbidden the consumption of blood (*Q*5.3) and because God forgives whom he wishes and punishes whom he wishes (*Q*5.18; cf. 5.118). Nor does he share a cup, because wine causes strife and has idolatrous associations and is therefore to be avoided (*Q*5.90–1). Finally, Jesus does not promise to confer a kingdom on his disciples (contrast Lk. 21.29), because sovereignty over everything belongs solely to God (*Q*5.120).

According to the Creed, Jesus' mission culminated in his death, resurrection and ascension

> He was crucified also for us under Pontius Pilate.
> He suffered and was buried.
> On the third day he rose again according to the scriptures.
> He ascended into heaven and sits on the right hand of the Father.

Christians generally believe that his death by crucifixion atoned for human sin and that his resurrection furnishes them with grounds for hope that they too will be raised at the general resurrection.[32] The Qur'an does not mention Jesus' resurrection on the third day.[33] From the quranic perspective, it is not this but the manifestation of God's power in creation that provides proof of his ability to raise the dead to face judgment.[34] It does, however, mention the crucifixion and ascension, but in the course of a polemic against the Jews

31. Sura 5 is widely held to be a ragbag of largely unrelated revelations. However, I have demonstrated that it has an intricate chiastic structure and that it can be read as a single coherent discourse. See Neal Robinson, 'Hands Outstretched: Towards a Re-reading of Surat al-Ma'ida', *Journal of Quranic Studies* 3/1 (2001), 1–19; and 'Covenant, Community Boundaries, Sin and Forgiveness: A Re-reading of Surat al-Ma'ida', *Journal of Quranic Studies* (forthcoming).

32. See e.g. 1 Pet. 1.3.

33. In *Q*19.33 the reference is almost certainly to his participation in the general resurrection. Compare the similar statement about John the Baptist in *Q*19.15.

34. See e.g. *Q*75.36–40.

And because of their saying, 'We killed the Messiah Jesus son of Mary, God's messenger'. They did not kill him or crucify him, but it so appeared to them. Behold those who disagree about it are in doubt about it. They have no knowledge about it except pursuit of a conjecture. They did not kill him for certain, but God raised him into his presence. God is Mighty, Wise. (*Q*4.157–8)

The majority of the classical commentators interpret this as meaning that God projected Jesus' likeness onto someone else, whom the Jews duly crucified by mistake, whereas God had already caused Jesus to ascend bodily to heaven. However, the Qur'an is here primarily concerned with refuting the Jews' boastful claim that *they* crucified Jesus. It says nothing about the crucifixion of a substitute and does not necessarily indicate Jesus' *bodily* ascent.[35] It nonetheless indicates that God did not abandon Jesus on the cross, contrary to what Christians have frequently imagined because of his alleged cry of dereliction.[36] Nor does the Qur'an leave grounds for the Christian claim that Jesus was 'crucified for us', because elsewhere it asserts that God holds human beings responsible for their own wrongdoing, and that no one can bear another's burden. It should also be clear from what was said earlier that from the quranic perspective there can be no question of Jesus' sharing in God's power and glory after his ascension; on the contrary, he is depicted as behaving with humility and deference when summoned into God's presence (*Q*5.116–18).

Finally, the quranic view of the gospel as a revelation that Jesus received from God, rather than the Church's proclamation of the saving power of his death and resurrection, is of course entirely in keeping with the Qur'an's theocentric perspective.

3. *Some Further Reflections*

The Qur'an repeatedly asserts that, far from being the invention of a mere mortal, it is a revelation from the Lord of the Worlds.[37] The issues discussed in this essay have a bearing on that claim. If, as many non-Muslims allege, the quranic image of Jesus is confused, the claim is, to say the least, highly questionable. If, on the other hand, as I have tried to demonstrate, the quranic image of Jesus is perfectly coherent, that particular objection can be overruled. Nevertheless, by suggesting that certain features of the Jesus material are only intelligible when viewed in their historical context, I have implied that in some respects the Qur'an is timebound. On this reckoning, those who wish to maintain that the Qur'an is divine revelation must needs distinguish its abiding core message from peripheral elements that are historically contingent.

35. For a full discussion of how the classical commentators interpreted this passage see Robinson, *Christ in Islam and Christianity*, 1991, 127–41. The chains of guarantors supporting the traditions about the projection of Jesus' likeness onto someone else all contain the name of the Kufan traditionist A'mash. The idea probably originated in Kufa, where there were similar theories regarding the Shiite imams. The belief that Jesus ascended bodily is an inference from hadiths that assert that he will descend to earth again to kill the Antichrist.

36. 'My God, My God, why have you forsaken me' (Mt. 27.46; Mk 15.34).

37. For example *Q*53.1–5.

It may help to put this problem into perspective if we focus on the numerous *ayas* of the Qur'an that refer to the created order. The Arab pagans worshipped other divinities in addition to Allah, and they denied that there was an afterlife. The Qur'an therefore urged them to reflect on the world around them and to recognize that it is full of signs of the generosity of the one God, the sole Creator, and of his power to recreate them on the Day of Resurrection.[38] Most of the phenomena that it mentions in this context are familiar to people the world over. They include the alternation of day and night; the orderly motion of the sun and moon; the gravity-defying flight of birds; food and clothing obtained from animals; rainfall that causes plants to grow; and the role of seminal emission in human reproduction. However, from time to time it mentions other phenomena that were familiar to the Arabs but which are not encountered everywhere – for instance date palms, camels and pearls. In addition, very occasionally, it alludes to less tangible things that the Arabs nonetheless took for granted because they were part of their world-view – for instance the existence of seven heavens.[39] If, for the sake of argument, the Qur'an had been revealed in early-sixteenth-century Mexico instead of seventh-century Mecca and Medina, it might well have mentioned maize plants, llamas and jade rather than date palms, camels and pearls, and have contained allusions to thirteen heavens rather than seven.[40] If, on the other hand, it had been revealed in twentieth-century Britain, it would perhaps have mentioned wheat, automobiles and diamonds, and have stressed the vastness of intergalactic space.[41] However, although these 'signs passages' make concessions to the geographical and historical context of the Qur'an's original auditors, this does not detract from the abiding validity of their message: the summons to worship God alone, to whose generosity and power the whole creation bears witness. I maintain that this is equally true *mutatis mutandis* of the quranic Jesus material. The historically contingent details that many Christian readers now find puzzling are in themselves relatively unimportant. What matters is the challenge to Christians to accept the consistently theo-centric interpretation of Jesus' mission. This entails recognizing that Jesus was a humble servant of the one God, not his Son, and that the crucifixion has no bearing on God's willingness and ability to forgive human wrongdoing.

Dialogue between conservative Christians, who hold to the literal truth of the incarnation, and Muslim traditionalists, who insist on the complete historical accuracy of the quranic Jesus material, has reached an impasse. However, for Christians who are broadly in agreement with the views expressed in *The Myth of*

38. See for example the following signs passages: *Q*16.10–18; 22.5f; 67.19; 75.36–40.
39. *Q*67.3 etc.
40. See M. D. Coe and R. Koontz, *Mexico: From the Olmecs to the Aztecs* (London: Thames & Hudson, 5th edn, 2002); R. Townsend, *The Aztecs* (London: Thames & Hudson, 2nd edn, 2000); M. Miller and K. Taube, *An Illustrated Dictionary of the Gods and Symbols of Ancient Mexico and the Maya* (London: Thames & Hudson, 1993).
41. *Pace* Maurice Bucaille and other advocates of so-called 'scientific exegesis' there are no sound reasons for thinking that the Qur'an accords with modern cosmology. See Neal Robinson, 'Sectarian and Ideological Bias in Muslim Translations of the Qur'an', *Islam and Christian–Muslim Relations* 8/3 (1997), 261–78, esp. 269–74.

God Incarnate, and Muslims who are sympathetic to the approach to Jesus in the Qur'an advocated in this article, there are at least four avenues that merit further exploration:

First, despite wishing to dispense with the doctrine of the incarnation, one of the essayists described it as 'an interpretation of Jesus appropriate to the age in which it arose'.[42] Might this not be said with more justice of the Qur'an's denial of Jesus' divinity and rejection of Christian teaching on atonement?

Second, if due allowance is made for details in the Qur'an that echo popular stories or employ traditional methods of biblical exegesis, do the findings of modern historical-critical investigation of Christian origins corroborate the Qur'an's assessment of Jesus and his mission?

Third, if Jesus' teaching, as recorded in the four Gospels, enshrines what the Qur'an refers to as 'the gospel' that God bestowed on him, which contains guidance, light and admonition, what is the enduring significance of this teaching?

Fourth, to what extent can Muslims empathize with Christians who have abandoned belief in the incarnation as an objective metaphysical fact, but who nevertheless hold that the Bible stories about Jesus, and the figure of Jesus himself, are 'a personal focus of the transforming power of God in the world'?[43]

42. Maurice Wiles, in Hick, *Myth of God Incarnate*, 4.
43. Wiles in Hick (ed.), *Myth of God Incarnate*, 9.

LIST OF PUBLICATIONS

1969

'Christological Ideas in the Greek Commentaries on the Epistle to the Hebrews', *JTS* (NS) 20: 150–62.

1971

'A Reconsideration of Alexandrian Christology', *JEH* 24: 103–14.

1972

'The Idea of Sacrifice in Neoplatonic and Patristic Texts', *Studia Patristica* 11: 278–81.

1973

'Temple, Cult and Law in Early Christianity: A Study in the Relations between Jews and Christians in the Early Centuries', *NTS* 19: 325–38.

'Insight or Incoherence? The Greek Fathers on God and Evil', *JEH* 24: 113–26.

1975

Sacrifice and the Death of Christ, London and Philadelphia: SPCK and Westminster Press.

'Atonement and Theodicy', *Studia Patristica* 13: 330–3.
'New Wine in Old Wineskins: XIV Sacrifice', *ET* 86: 305–9.

1976

'Not by Bread Alone: Notes on Deuteronomy 8', in J. H. Eaton (ed.), *Readings in Biblical Hebrew*, vol. 1, Birmingham: University of Birmingham.

1977

'A Cloud of Witnesses', and 'Two Roots or a Tangled Mass?', in John Hick (ed.), *The Myth of God Incarnate*, London: SCM Press, chs. 2, 5.

'Redemption: The Starting-point of Christian Theology I', and 'Redemption: the Starting-point of Christian Theology II', in *ET* 88: 360–4; 89: 9–13.

'Christian Attitudes to Finance in the First Four Centuries', *Epworth Review* 4/3: 78–86.

1978

'Reflections in *The Myth of God Incarnate*', *Epworth Review* 5/2: 79–83.

1979

'The Finality of Christ', in Michael Goulder (ed.), *Incarnation and Myth: The Debate Continued*, London: SCM Press.

Sacrificial Ideas in Greek Christian Writers, Patristic Monograph Series, 5; Cambridge, Mass.: Philadelphia Patristic Foundation.

'God and Religious Language', in W. R. Schoedel and Robert Wilken (eds.), *Early Christian Literature and the Greek Intellectual Tradition*, Festschrift for R. M. Grant; Theologie Historique, 53; Paris: Editions Beauchesne.

'Syriac: A Tool for the Student of Early Christian Doctrine', in J. H. Eaton (ed.), *Horizons in Semitic Studies*, Birmingham: University of Birmingham.

1981
'God: An Essay in Patristic Theology', *The Modern Churchman* 29: 149–65.

1982
Can These Dry Bones Live? London: SCM Press.
First Studies in New Testament Greek, Birmingham: University of Birmingham.

'Notes on the Corinthian Correspondence', *Studia Evangelica* 7: 563–6.

'Did Epiphanius Know What He Meant by Heresy?', *SP* 18: 199–205.

1983
Sacrifice and the Death of Christ, republished London: SCM Press.

From Nicaea to Chalcedon, London and Philadelphia: SCM Press and Fortress Press.
Sixteen articles in Alan Richardson and John Bowden (eds.), *A New Dictionary of Christian Theology*, London: SCM Press.

'Adam, the Soul and Immortality: A Study of the Interaction of "Science" and the Bible in some Anthropological Treatises of the Fourth Century', *VC* 37: 110–40.

'Salvation Proclaimed: Some Concluding Reflections', *ET* 94: 100–4.

1984
'Early Fathers', in John Sutcliffe (ed.), *A Dictionary of Religious Education*, London: SCM Press.

'Traditional Religious Cultures and the Christian Response I', and 'Traditional Religious Cultures and the Christian Response II', in *ET* 95: 235–9, 265–9.

1985
Face to Face, London: Epworth Press.

1986
With Kenneth Wilson, *Focus on God*, London: Epworth Press.

'John Chrysostom on I & II Corinthians', *Studia Patristica* 18/1: 349–52.

'Note on II Cor.1.17b', *JTS* (NS) 37: 404–15.

'Suffering and Belief', *The Franciscan* 28: 140–5.

1987
With David Ford, *Meaning and Truth in 2 Corinthians*, London: SPCK.

'Salvation and Pastoral Care', in Alastair Campbell (ed.), *A Dictionary of Pastoral Care*, London: SPCK.

'Allegory and Atonement', *Australian Biblical Review* 35 (Festschrift vol. for E. F. Osborn): 107–14.

'The Crooked Timber of Humanity: The Challenge of the Handicapped', the Keswick Hall Lecture, University of East Anglia.

'The Critic and the Visionary', Inaugural Lecture, University of Birmingham.
'Educating for Excellence', in *Report of the Annual Meeting*, Headmasters Conference, 32–41.

1988
'The Critic and the Visionary', *SJT* 41: 297–312.

'Educating for Excellence', *British Journal of Educational Studies* 22/2: 100–10.

Meaning and Truth in 2 Corinthians, republished Grand Rapids, Mich.: Eerdmans.

'The Significance of John Wesley's Conversion Experience', in Frank Baker (ed.), *John Wesley: Contemporary Perspectives*, London: Epworth Press.

1989
'Mission in the Corinthian Correspondence', *Epworth Review* 16: 76–84.

'The Early Church: Military Service, War and Peace', *Theology* 92: 491–503.

'The Rhetorical Schools and their Influence on Patristic Exegesis', in Rowan Williams (ed.), *The Making of Orthodoxy: Essays in honour of Henry Chadwick*, Cambridge: Cambridge University Press, 182–99.

'Exegetical Method and Scriptural Proof: The Bible in Doctrinal Debate', *SP* 24: 291–304.

1990
The Art of Performance: Towards a Theology of Holy Scripture, London: Darton, Longman & Todd.

Face to Face , revised and enlarged, Edinburgh: T&T Clark.

'Atonement', in Everett Ferguson, Michael P. McHugh and Frederick W. Norris (eds.), *Encyclopedia of Early Christianity*, New York: Garland.

Ten articles in Leslie Houlden and Richard Coggins (eds.), *A Dictionary of Biblical Interpretation*, London: SCM Press.

'Understanding Romans in the Light of 2 Corinthians', *SJT* 43: 433–46.

1991
'*Creatio ex nihilo*: A Context for the Emergence of the Christian Doctrine of Creation', *SJT* 44: 139–51.

'The Work and Writings of the Greek Fathers', in Ian Hazlett (ed.), *Early Christianity: Origins and Evolution to AD 600: In Honour of W. H. C. Frend*, London: SPCK.

'Creative Tensions in a Penultimate World: Lessons from the Christian Past', in *A Christian Vision for the New Europe*, Oxford: Farmington Institute for Christian Studies.

'Death', in Julia Neuberger and John A. White (eds.), *A Necessary End: Attitudes to Death*, London: Papermac.

Two brief invited articles for *Epworth Review*, on homosexuality, 18/1: 29–34; on atonement, 18/2: 60–7.

The Making of the Creeds, London: SCM Press.

1992
'The Pastorals and the Ethics of Reading', *JSNT* 45: 105–20.

Can These Dry Bones Live? republished with new preface, London: SCM Press.

1993
'Allegory and the Ethics of Reading', in Francis Watson (ed.), *The Open Text* (London: SPCK), 103–20.

'*Paideia* and the Myth of Static Dogma', in Sarah Coakley and David Pailin (eds.), *The Making and Remaking of Chrisian Doctrine: Essays in Honour of Maurice Wiles*, Oxford: Clarendon Press, 265–83.

Virtuoso Theology: The Bible and Interpretation, first published (as *The Art of Performance,* 1990) Cleveland, Ohio: Pilgrim Press.

Can These Dry Bones Live? An Introduction to Theology (first published 1982, 1992) Cleveland, Ohio: Pilgrim Press.

'Panegyric and the Bible', *SP* 25: 194–208.

1994
'On *Episcopos* and *Presbyteros*', *JTS* (NS) 45: 142–8.

The Theology of the Pastoral Epistles, Cambridge: Cambridge University Press.

'The Mark of the Nails', in Stephen Barton and Graham Stanton (eds.), *Resurrection: Essays in Honour of Leslie Houlden*, London: SPCK, 139–53.

'A Marriage Made in Heaven?', in Susan Durber (ed.), *As Man and Woman Made*: *Theological Reflections on Marriage*, London: United Reformed Church, 99–103.

'The Temple of the Spirit: On Being Embodied', in *Christ and the Cosmos: Being Human in a Cosmic Context*, Plymouth: The Christ and Cosmos Initiative, and Westminster College, Oxford, 107–32.

'Typology', in Stanley E. Porter, Paul Joyce and David E. Orton (eds.), *Crossing the Boundaries: Essays in Biblical Interpretation in Honour of Michael D. Goulder*, Leiden: Brill, 29–48.

'Salvation and the New Testament', in Donald English (ed.), *Windows on Salvation*, London: Darton, Longman & Todd, 28–41.

'Presbyteral Ministry in the Catholic Tradition', or 'Why Shouldn't Women Be Priests?'. Pamphlet published by the Methodist Sacramental Fellowship.

'Nemesius von Emesa', in *Theologische Realenzyklopädie*, xxiv.1/2, Berlin and New York: W. de Gruyter, 256–9.

1995
Editor, *'Dare We Speak of God in Public?'*: *The Edward Cadbury Lectures for 1994*, London: Mowbrays; author in ibid., ' "A Time for Silence". Dare We Mention Prayer?'

'Interpretative Genres and the Inevitability of Pluralism', *JSNT* 59: 93–110.
'Opfer', in *Theologische Realenzyklopädie* xxv.1/2, Berlin and New York: W. de Gruyter, 271–8.

1996
'The Family in the Early Church', in Hugh S. Pyper (ed.), *The Christian Family: A Concept in Crisis*, Norwich: Canterbury Press, 29–45.

'From Analysis to Overlay: A Sacramental Approach to Christology', in David Brown and Ann Loades (eds.), *Christ: The Sacramental Word*: *Incarnation, Sacrament and Poetry*, London: SPCK, 40–56.

'Paideia: What Can We Learn from the First Four Centuries?', in David F. Ford and Dennis L. Stamps (eds.), *Essentials of Christian Community: Essays for Daniel W. Hardy*, Edinburgh, T&T Clark, 229–40.

'Reconciliation in a Theological Dimension', in *Ecumenical Dialogue on Reconciliation*. Conference of European Churches and the Theological Faculty of the Serbian Orthodox Church, Belgrade, 19–22 February 1996. Geneva: Conference of European Churches.

1997
Biblical Exegesis and the Formation of Christian Culture, Cambridge: Cambridge University Press.

'Profile: Gordon Wakefield', *Epworth Review* 24: 28–37.

'Parents of a Child with Mental Disabilities: In Search of Meaning in their Family Life', in Th. A. Boer, R. Seldenrijk and J. Stolk (eds.), *Zinvolle Zorgvelening*, papers from an international congress, 4–5 April 1997, Amsterdam: Vereniging 's Heeren Loo.

'The Pastoral Epistles and the Ethics of Reading', originally published in *JSNT*, republished in Stanley E. Porter and Craig A. Evans (eds.), *New Testament Interpretation and Methods*, Sheffield: Sheffield Academic Press.

'They Speak to Us across the Centuries. 3. John Chrysostom', *Expository Times* 109: 38–41.

'From Suspicion and Sociology to Spirituality: On Method, Hermeneutics and Appropriation with respect to Patristic Material', *Studia Patristica* 29: 421–35.

'The Fourth Century Reaction against Allegory', *Studia Patristica* 30: 120–5.

Editor, *Encounter with Mystery: Reflections on L'Arche and Disability*, London: Darton, Longman & Todd; and authored in ibid., 'The Creative Purpose of God', 167–79, as well as Introduction, ix–xiv.

1998
'The Non-Pauline Letters', in John Barton (ed.), *The Cambridge Companion to Biblical Interpretation*, Cambridge: Cambridge University Press, 290–304.

1999
'*The Confessions* of St. Augustine: What is the Genre of This work?'. The 1998 St Augustine Lecture, *Augustinian Studies* 30/1: 1–16.

'Greek Apologists of the Second Century', in Mark Edwards, Martin Goodman and Simon Price (eds.), in association with Christopher Rowland, *Apologetics in the Roman Empire: Pagans, Jews and Christians*, Oxford: Oxford University Press, 81–104.

'Antiochene School', 'Epistle to the Hebrews', and 'Theodore of Mopsuestia', in John H. Hayes (ed.), *Dictionary of Biblical Interpretation*, Nashville: Abingdon Press.

2000
'Essence and Energies: Classical Trinitarianism and "Enthusiasm" ', in M. Douglas Meeks (ed.), *Trinity, Community and Power: Mapping Trajectories in Wesleyan Theology*, Nashville, Tenn.: Abingdon Press, 127–41.

'Christianity', in Christopher Rowe and Malcolm Schofield *et al.* (eds.), *The Cambridge History of Greek and Roman Political Thought*, Cambridge: Cambridge University Press, 635–60.

'Parents of a Child with Mental Disabilities: In Search of Meaning in their Family Life', in Joop Stolk, Theo A. Boer and Ruth Seldenrijk (eds.), *Meaningful Care: A Multidisciplinary Approach to the Meaning of Care for People with Mental Retardation*, papers from an international congress, 4–5 April 1997; Dordecht, Boston and London: Kluwer Academic, 3–10.

'Christology and Creation: Towards an Hermeneutic of Patristic Christology', in T. Merrigan and J. Haers (eds.), *The Myriad Christ*, Leuven: Leuven University Press, 191–205.

'Suffering', in Adrian Hastings, Alistair Mason and Hugh Pyper (eds.), *The Oxford Companion to Christian Thought*, Oxford: Oxford University Press, 2000.

'The New Testament and Sexuality', in Heather Snidle and Paul Ballard (eds.), *Sexuality and Spirituality*, Cardiff: Cardiff Academic Press, 9–16.

2001
'Sexuality and Devotion: Mystical Readings of the Song of Songs', in *Theology and Sexuality* 14: 80–96.

'The *Apostolic Constitutions*: A Methodological Case-Study', *Studia Patristica* 36: 105–15.

'The Council of Chalcedon 1550 Years Later', *Touchstone* 19/1: 15–27.

'The Great Thanksgiving Prayer', in Stephen Conway (ed.), *Living the Eucharist. Affirming Catholicism and the Liturgy*, Darton, Longman & Todd, 79–94.

2002
'Suffering', in Wesley Carr *et al.* (eds.), *The New Dictionary of Pastoral Studies*, London: SPCK, 360–2.

'Inner Struggle: Some Parallels between the Spirituality of John Wesley and the Greek Fathers', in S. T. Kimbrough, Jr (ed.), *Orthodox and Wesleyan Spirituality*, New York: St. Vladimir's Seminary Press, 157–72.

'*Theotokos*: Mary and the Pattern of Fall and Redemption in the Theology of Cyril of Alexandria', in William McLoughlin and Jill Pinnock (eds.), *Mary for Earth and Heaven: Essays on Mary and Ecumenism*, Leominster: Gracewing, 340–54.

The Making of the Creeds, reissue, London: SCM Press.

'Ministerial Forms and Functions in the Church Communities of the Greek Fathers', in Richard N. Longenecker (ed.), *Community Formation in the early Church and in the Church Today*, Peabody, Mass.; Hendriksen, 157–76.

2003
'*Theotokos*: Mary and the Pattern of Fall and Redemption in the Theology of Cyril of Alexandria', in Thomas G. Weinandy and Daniel A. Keating (eds.), *The Theology of Cyril of Alexandria: A Critical Appreciation*, London and New York: T&T Clark, 55–74.

'Proverbs 8 in Interpretation (2): Wisdom Personified', in David F. Ford and Graham Stanton (eds.), *Reading Texts, Seeking Wisdom*, London: SCM Press, 102–15.

'Alexandrian and Antiochene Exegesis', in Alan J. Hauser and Duane F. Watson (eds.), *A History of Biblical Interpretation*, vol. 1, Grand Rapids, Mich.: Eerdmans, 334–54.

2004
The Cambridge History of Early Christian Literature, Editor, with Lewis Ayres and Andrew Louth, Cambridge: Cambridge University Press.

'Books and Their "Aura": The Functions of Written Texts in Judaism, Paganism and Christianity during the First Centuries CE', in Judith Frishman, Willemien Otten and Gerard Rouwhorst (eds.), *Religious Identity and the Problem of Historical Foundation*, Leiden: Brill, 535–52.

'The Interpretation of Scripture', in G. R. Evans (ed.), *The First Christian Theologians*, Oxford: Basil Blackwell, 24–38.

'Christian Scripture and "the Other" ', in Michael Ipgrave (ed.), *Scriptures in Dialogue. Christians and Muslims studying the Bible and the Qur'an together*, London: Church House Publishing, 102–11.

Forthcoming

'The Gospels and the Development of Doctrine', in Stephen Barton (ed.), *The Cambridge Companion to the Gospels*.

'Wisdom in Augustine's *De Doctrina Christiana*', *Studia Patristica*.

'God's Word Proclaimed: The Homiletics of Grace and Demand in John Chrysostom and John Wesley', in the proceedings of conferences of Orthodox and Methodist theologians to be edited by S. T. Kimbrough, Jr, and published by St Vladimir's Seminary.

'Wisdom in the Apostolic Fathers and the New Testament', to be published among the papers of the Oxford project on the Apostolic Fathers by Oxford University Press.

In Preparation

Editor, with Margaret M. Mitchell, the first volume of *The Cambridge History of Christianity*; and sole author of three chapters.

NEW TESTAMENT

INDEX OF AUTHORS